The Easter Monday Baseball Game

ALSO BY TIM PEELER

Waiting for Godot's First Pitch:
More Poems from Baseball (McFarland, 2001)

Touching All the Bases:
Poems from Baseball (McFarland, 2000)

The Easter Monday Baseball Game

North Carolina State and Wake Forest on the Diamond, 1899–1956

Tim Peeler

McFarland & Company, Inc., Publishers
Jefferson, North Carolina, and London

LIBRARY OF CONGRESS CATALOGUING-IN-PUBLICATION DATA

Peeler, Tim, 1957–
    The Easter Monday baseball game : North Carolina State and Wake Forest on the diamond, 1899–1956 / Tim Peeler.
    p.   cm.

    Includes bibliographical references and index.

    ISBN 978-0-7864-7452-3
    softcover : acid free paper ∞

    1. North Carolina State University — Baseball — History. 2. Wake Forest University — Baseball — History. 3. Baseball — North Carolina — History. 4. Sports rivalries — North Carolina — History. I. Title.
    GV875.N68P44 2013
    796.357'6309756 — dc23   2013009798

BRITISH LIBRARY CATALOGUING DATA ARE AVAILABLE

© 2013 Tim Peeler. All rights reserved

No part of this book may be reproduced or transmitted in any form or by any means, electronic or mechanical, including photocopying or recording, or by any information storage and retrieval system, without permission in writing from the publisher.

On the cover: (left) 1910 North Carolina A&M baseball team (courtesy of R. G. Utley); (right) 1913 Wake Forest College baseball team (courtesy of Wake Forest University)

Manufactured in the United States of America

McFarland & Company, Inc., Publishers
  Box 611, Jefferson, North Carolina 28640
    www.mcfarlandpub.com

Table of Contents

Preface 1
Introduction 3

Early Games 9
Living in the Dead Ball Era
    1900–1910 13
    1911–1920 43
The Roaring Twenties
    1921–1930 81
Depression and War
    1931–1940 113
    1941–1950 145
End Games
    1951–1956 184

Appendix A: Major League Statistics—
    N.C. State Players 197
Appendix B: Major League Statistics—
    Wake Forest Players 204
Bibliography 217
Index 221

Preface

Hank Utley introduced me to the story of the Easter Monday baseball classic six years ago when we were working on the manuscript later published as *Outlaw Ballplayers* (McFarland 2006). He had just donated his research papers on the topic to the library of his alma mater, North Carolina State University. Hank understood my tendency to become obsessed with historical research, especially when it related to regional baseball, and he wanted someone to confirm his belief that it is a compelling story.

I was hesitant to start another baseball book project, having already completed three during that decade, and when I sampled the huge packet of documents, I was admittedly a bit overwhelmed. The research consisted mostly of mimeographed copies of articles from the Raleigh media that tracked the event from 1899 to its conclusion in the mid–1950s. Besides the game articles, there were numerous news articles and pictures that documented and described the event most often associated with the game, the annual PiKA Ball. Yes, the story, a huge rivalry between two college baseball teams that shared a capital city location and a social event that drew young coeds from several states, piqued my interest; but how was I to approach such a mass of information?

In the summer of 2011, at Utley's insistence, I began to look more closely at the research package and quickly realized that the core of the story and what makes this a broad and compelling topic are contained in the local sports articles. The writing there is colorful, full of hyperbole and wit, and so a joy to read in its own right. It is not unusual to find vituperatively critical passages alongside those that exaggerate the level of ballplaying excellence to the point of the fantastic. Anyone who has read much sportswriting from the early decades of the twentieth century

Preface

knows that this is simply the way it was done. But it is remarkable to see how, in addition to the changing style of play in baseball, these articles' prose style of the early part of the century slowly gave way to the more restrained and often sterile prose that is still common in mainstream modern day sports journalism.

The final elements that make this story so compelling are the players themselves and the drama that they create on and off the field. By following the chronological development of the series, one is able to witness the players' improvement as they move through their time of eligibility, the gamesmanship of the coaches during the buildup to the event, and the many shenanigans that took place on the periphery of the contests. As noted in the appendixes, the number of players that participated in the Easter Monday Classic that eventually made their way to the Major Leagues is a testament to the level of play in the series.

What cannot be emphasized enough is the importance of the game, not just to the two institutions but also to the Raleigh area business and civic community. That a sports event could dictate the day for a statewide holiday seems improbable, but for over 50 years, that was the case. The Easter Monday Baseball Classic and PiKA Ball was, as Hank Utley has said, a "cultural double-header" that drew thousands of fans and students to the Raleigh area and touched the lives of many beyond the ballfields and the ballrooms.

Introduction

For nearly two centuries North Carolina citizens celebrated Easter as a holiday that extended through the following Monday. In fact, this holiday was reserved for recreation and celebration. The beginning of spring and the popularity of baseball made it a natural activity for bringing the community together on this holiday. Mill and town teams had long gathered for the occasion, so it didn't take long for the idea to catch on with college ball as well. North Carolina State (then North Carolina A&M) and Wake Forest College offered a cross-county rivalry that immediately drew an enormous amount of interest from the citizens of the state capital.

By the 1930s the game had become so popular that in 1935, the state legislature made Easter Monday an official holiday so that municipal workers could attend without fear of retribution. While there were a few interruptions in the rivalry, the tradition continued for nearly six decades and only ended when Wake Forest moved its campus to Winston-Salem in 1956. This move also coincided with the move from the Southern Conference to the new Atlantic Coast Conference.

The baseball game was not the only popular event of the Easter Monday celebration. The local women's colleges of St. Mary's, Peace, and Meredith maintained a heavy presence at the baseball games, and their beauty and sense of fashion were nearly as important as the action on the field. After the games ended, the evening was highlighted by another tradition that began in 1906, the PiKA Ball. For the students, this double header of activity offered an entire day off from classes and a spring event to balance with Fair Week and Carolina football game in the fall. The pre–PiKA parties extended back into the weekend to Friday and Saturday nights, making it quite the holiday for the State players who were also

Introduction

often PiKA members. A veteran of three games and four of these weekends, Hank Utley, confided to me that the partying is at least partially responsible for State's poor overall record in the series.

During the heyday of the Easter Monday celebration, most of the citizens depended on trains to travel to the games and to the ball. As automobiles became the predominant means of travel, students were more apt to leave for the long weekend or to opt for other entertainment. The popularity of the event began to wane after World War II, and the last Easter Monday Classic was played in 1955 (actually a makeup for a rainout). The last PiKA Ball took place in 1961, and the state finally discontinued the holiday that baseball made in 1987 in order to accommodate the banking industry.

State–Wake Series

Not long after its founding in 1895, North Carolina A&M began fielding a baseball team, and in 1899 played its first Easter Monday baseball game, a contest with the Bingham Institute from Mebane, N.C. The game drew 700 fans and was the first played on A&M's new field. The following year, A&M played the "Baptists" from Wake Forest for the first time. The series continued for three years, and though attendance figures are not available, it was noted that a huge crowd attended as early as 1901 including women from the Raleigh colleges. For the three years that followed A&M played games with Trinity (later Duke) and Carolina. In 1907, the rivalry resumed, and media coverage included mention of a "shoofly" train that brought nearly the entire Wake Forest student body.

The students sat in blocks with the Baptists to the left and the Farmers on the right. The same operation brought fans again the following year, and the attendance was listed at 2,500. The game had gotten so big that it drew front page coverage from the Raleigh paper. By 1910, the appeal had become regional, and fans were arriving by train from other colleges and towns including as far away as Fayetteville. A 1911 article noted that the bleachers were overrun with Easter bonnets and white dresses of the women from Peace, St. Mary's and Meredith, and while

Introduction

the two former might split their allegiance, the Meredith women were solidly with their Baptist brothers at Wake Forest.

The year 1913 saw the return of A&M's star catcher, Frank Thompson, after a brief professional career. His return, however, was to coach the rival school, a not-so-popular situation, which eventually caused a one year skip of the rivalry in 1916. Thompson shortly thereafter entered World War I and was killed in combat. State College named their new gym after him in 1925, a venue that would serve for many years as the site of the PiKA Ball.

In the 1920s the game reached the zenith of its popularity, once drawing over 8,000 fans in 1925 and 1926. The increasing availability of automobiles contributed to the rise, but though preparations and predictions of even bigger crowds were made, the game never reached this level again. During this decade and the one to follow, the level of competition also rose with numerous players from both programs enjoying professional baseball careers. Top shelf pitchers like Rae Scarborough and Vic Sorrell went on to successful Major League careers. Play also included monumental levels of contention between the programs with protests over odd plays, such as a fly ball being dropped because of hovering train smoke or an obvious home run being called a ground rule double. The 1921 game was called for darkness in the 12th inning, and then the makeup game ran 11 innings only to end in a tie.

Although money was scarce during the Great Depression, the game and weekend remained popular, with fans enjoying half-rate ticket prices and attendance remaining at high levels. The Easter Monday Classic even survived World War II with games being played against the local Pre-Flight teams, Wake Forest having suspended its program. After the war, the rivalry was renewed and the game and ball again enjoyed a modicum of success. But with increased competition for entertainment and the ease of automotive travel, the interest began to wane. During the twilight years of the series, Wake Forest built a nationally competitive program and at one stretch held five consecutive victories in the game. During the 1950s, Wake fielded a national runner-up team and its only national championship team.

From 1899 through 1956, N.C. State hosted 58 Easter Monday baseball games. N.C. State won 21 games and lost 33 games; three games ended in a tie and one game was rained out and never replayed. Against Wake Forest, State won 17 games and lost 29; two ended in a tie and one was rained out and never replayed.

PiKA Dance

While the baseball game drew coverage from the local sports pages, the PiKA Ball was a feature of the social calendar and an event that for 50 plus years drew regional and even statewide attention to the campus and the host fraternity, the Alpha Epsilon, a local chapter of the national Phi Kappa Alpha order. Established in 1904, this group drew from a pool of possible activities, the "Easter german" as their spring event. The "german" was a cotillion that had a long history in the southern part of the United States and origins that dated back to Europe.

The first of these dances was held on Easter Monday night in 1906. The 50 invitees included chaperones, who, as tradition would have it, led the first dance. The event was declared a success and over the next several years, "out-of-town" men were included to supplement the low number of fraternity members. By 1911, it was already a tradition for PiKA alums to attend and perform in the opening dance. As the popularity of the event increased, other fraternities were invited, and by the end of World War I, the dance had been moved to a country club to accommodate a larger attendance. When the Frank Thompson Gymnasium opened on State's campus, the ball was moved there and became a huge event. By 1928, two thousand invitations were sent out, and that level held for the remaining years of the PiKA Ball. During the 1920s, social activities on the N.C. State campus flourished, and a second "german" was added to meet the needs of the German Club. This dance at times was held on Easter Monday morning as a sort of warm up for the one in the evening.

During the next several decades, the PiKAs would vacate their house on Hillsborough Street so that their guests could stay there during the festivities. Other activities included banquets at Raleigh hotels and picnics at local parks, depending on the weather. Although the PiKAs were one of the few fraternities to survive the Great Depression, the ball went on a hiatus from 1932 through 1934. After resuming in 1935, the ball attained such great status that three governors served as honorary chaperones, including O. Max Gardner, who had once coached the State baseball team in the early part of the century. In 1937, a regional radio station began broadcasting the performances of the bands engaged by the PiKAs, and the broadcast was then picked up by a CBS station out of Philadelphia, further building the event's reputation.

The ball was again suspended during World War II, but returned and flourished and continued as a tradition for six years after the Easter Monday Classic baseball game had ceased.

Early Games

The last five years of the 19th century were a time of change and growth in North Carolina. The Cone family established the largest textile and denim factories in the U.S., and the state was poised to usurp that industry from the New England states. In New Bern, a young pharmacist developed a new soda drink which would eventually be sold as Pepsi.

On the political stage, George Henry White was elected to two terms in Congress, but would be the last African-American representative of North Carolina for over a quarter of a century; and when a bill championing women's suffrage was introduced to the state legislature, it was quickly tabled by being sent to the Committee on Insane Asylums. In 1898, the Wilmington Race Riot occurred, in which white Democrats overthrew the legally elected black Republican government. A white supremacist government was created, and the black government officials and many business owners fled the city.

It was during this decade, which saw a 10 percent growth in population, that the first female student was enrolled at the University of North Carolina and the first female college, Meredith, was established in Raleigh.

The North Carolina College of Agriculture and Mechanical Arts was founded a few years before by the North Carolina legislature on March 7, 1887 (University's Founder's Day).

On October 3, 1889, North Carolina A&M opened its doors to 72 students who arrived as the first freshman class. Only 19 of these original students were among the graduating class of 1893.

Despite limited enrollment, a news report in the *News and Observer* indicates that an A&M baseball game took place in Greensboro against Guilford College on April 13, 1895, the Saturday before Easter.

The Easter Monday Baseball Game

The first freshman class at North Carolina A&M. On October 3, 1889, North Carolina A&M opened its doors to 72 students who arrived as the first freshman class. Only 19 of these original students were among the graduating class of 1893 (courtesy R.G. Utley).

Bad for the Farmer Boys
Greensboro, N.C. April 13
    The Agricultural and Mechanical College team of Raleigh was butchered by the Guilford College team this afternoon to the tune of 19 to 2. The spectators were disgusted with the game.

The same issue announced a game for the following Monday.

More Baseball Monday
On Monday the Wake Forest baseball team will come up and give our home team another chance at them. Our boys are determined to make a desperate effort to win the game and a lively game may be expected. The Lehigh baseball team went to Chapel Hill today by private conveyance and played the U.N.C. boys there this evening.

Early Games

There is no follow-up report of this first Easter Monday game. It can only be speculated that the game was a rainout, and there are no newspaper reports of Easter weekend baseball games in 1896 or 1897.

The following year, a brief article dated April 12 reported an Easter Monday game in Greensboro:

A&M Defeated
Greensboro, N.C. April 11
The Guilford College baseball team defeated the Agricultural and Mechanical College by a score of 16 to 6 this afternoon.

On Easter Monday, April 3, 1899, North Carolina A& M hosted its first Easter Monday game. The opponent was the Mebane Bingham

The 1899 North Carolina A&M baseball team: Left to right, back row, left to right: W.H. Person, Ed Person, Bill Fenner, Ned Wood (coach), J.W. Shore, Leslie Norman, Colon R. Love. Front row, left to right: Henry G. Dorsette, F.D. Ross, Paul F. Faison, William W. Caserley, F.W. Bonitz, Wallace Riddick (mascot). This team hosted the first Easter Monday game on April 3, 1899, defeating Mebane Bingham Military School 5-4 in 11 innings before 700 fans (courtesy N.C. State Archives and R.G. Utley).

School. This home game garnered increased coverage from the local paper including an enlarged font headline:

A&M DEFEATS BINGHAM
BY A SCORE OF 5 TO 4 IN ELEVEN INNING GAME

A large crowd witnessed the game which was close, clean and well played. Seven hundred people saw the A and M College defeat MEBANE BINGHAM SCHOOL at the ground of the former yesterday afternoon by a score of 5 to 4. But it took eleven innings to do it.

It was the christening game for the new A and M diamond and the ground was a trifle loose and powdery on the surface, but the patch of the surface evened things up as between fielders and batters.

This short article included the first mention of the female presence at the Easter Monday baseball games, a fact that would prove to be a theme for game coverage for the first 40 years of game coverage: "A large number of ladies were present and the attendance, as a whole, was a sufficient answer to the assertion that Raleigh will not support a ball park."

The teams were as follows, in batting order:

A&M — Shore (captain) first base; Person, W. catch; Dorsett, left field; Caserly, center field; Love, third base; Ross, right field; Faison, short stop; Bonitz, second base; Person, E. pitch.

Bingham — Alford and LeGrand, short stop; LeGrand and Alford, catch; Johnson, first base; Calfree, third base; Mangum (captain) left field,; Keith, pitch; Darden, right field; Boone, center field; Cocke, second base.

The article continued: "Highlights of the game were A and M's pitcher, E. Person hitting a triple, Bonitz's 3 hits and Shore's fine catch on first. For Bingham, Cocke's pick up of a dangerous grounder at second was outstanding."

Living in the
Dead Ball Era

1900–1910

By the turn of the century, North Carolina began to experience an increasing shift from an agrarian economy to one based on industry. In 1900, there were 217 textile mills and 101 tobacco factories. The following year industrial leaders met in Charlotte to discuss regulations for their businesses. They agreed to a 66-hour work week and that children under 12 should not be employed during the school year. Unfortunately, many failed to abide by their self-regulation.

On the political front, a constitutional amendment was approved that required a literacy test for voting. It also included a grandfather clause for illiterate white citizens and effectively disenfranchised the African American population in the state. The Democratic Party regained control of the governor's office through a hardcore white supremacist campaign, and would maintain that control for 72 years.

Transportation became increasingly important. The first automobiles began to appear, and a highway commission was formed in order to better maintain the state's roads. This was also, of course, the decade when Wilbur and Orville Wright transformed the world with their flight experiments at Kitty Hawk.

The decade as well saw a new emphasis on education. The state legislators passed the first compulsory public school law, and two new teacher training colleges were established at either end of the state, one in Greenville and the other in Boone.

The following is a reflection from the 1906 *Wake Forest Howler* on the importance of the baseball games at that point in their history:

The Easter Monday Baseball Game

We do not know the wild, almost insane enthusiasm engendered by a victorious football team, because we do not have the game. But we do know the enthusiasm that makes us carry on our shoulders a man who saves a baseball game by a sensational play or wins it by a dexterous stroke with the willow. This is the chief sport in which our enthusiasm and feeling finds vent. Perhaps this is why our college spirit soars so high in the spring time and makes the man on the ball team feel that he has a friend in every man in college. In this lies the secret that makes the men work so hard. They know that the student body is with them when they are trying at their hardest, even if they are losing.

Easter Monday, April 16, 1900, was to see the first of many Easter Monday games between Wake Forest and N.C. A&M. The *News and Observer* continued its colorful reporting with a headline: "The Farmers Win." The game was called "the best of the season, the only run made was in the last inning.

April 17, 1900

The A. and M. College defeated Wake Forest here yesterday by the score of 1 to 0. From start to finish it was one of the prettiest games ever seen in Raleigh. Neither side scored until the ninth inning, when Fenner crossed the plate for the A. and M. team.

Both teams played a good steady game, but the fielding of the "preachers" was the stronger. The Wake Forest boys could not touch "little" Persons, they only made three hits off of him during the entire game. Wake Forest came very near scoring in the sixth inning, when with a man on third and one on second and only one man out. Moore came to the bat and knocked what would have ordinarily been a hit, but Person, H., unassisted, made a beautiful double on it and retired the side.

Fenner, who scored the winning run got first on a hit, stole second and third and came home on a long fly to centre field. Person's pitching for the A. and M. has been pronounced by critics as the finest ever seen in Raleigh. His work in the box yesterday will assure his rank as one of the best pitchers in the state.

The author noted that the Wake Forest players played with much determination, calling their game an excellent one with only "one error to their credit a feat which is not often duplicated." He called it a "fast" game, a description often used in this time to denote a well-played game, but also possibly meaning that the game moved quickly because of the mostly error-free play. Here we see little of the sharp criticism that was often present in the early articles. "It was a fine game. This contest between the boys in old gold and the boys in red, — well played from start to finish, and both sides deserved to win."

Wake Forest	Runs	Hits	Errors
Sams 3 b.	0	0	0
Royster c. (captain)	0	1	0
Tarlham 1 b.	0	1	1
Weaver 2 b.	0	0	0
Moore p.	0	1	0
Rodgers l. f.	0	0	0
Hodgod l. f.	0	0	0
Griffin r. f.	0	0	0
Freeman s. s.	0	0	0
A&M College	Runs	Hits	Errors
Persons, E.P.	0	0	0
Fenner, 1 b.	1	1	0
Person, H. 3 b.	0	0	0
Person, W.C.	0	1	0
Dorsett, l. f.	0	0	0
Morson, c. f.	0	1	0
Ross (captain), r. f.	0	0	0
Caserly, 2 b.	0	0	1
Cochran, s. s.	0	1	1

BATTERIES: Wake Forest — Moore and Royster; A&M — Person, E., and Person, A.
STRUCK-OUT: Moore, 6: Person, E., 13.
STOLEN BASES: Wake Forest, 4; A. and M., 3.

The first Easter Monday game of the twentieth century was played on April 8, 1901, as reported in the *News and Observer* the following day. This article, which lacks a byline, included wonderful descriptive, figurative language.

Again Defeat for the Cadets — April 9, 1901
That was a lively game yesterday afternoon between the ball teams of Wake Forest College and the College of Agriculture and Mechanic Arts, though the score of twelve for Wake Forest against six for the Cadets would indicate otherwise. The wind blew cold, the dust was everywhere, and the knickerbockered ball hitters endeavored to keep warm by running the bases, while the umpire shivered inside of his overcoat.

The Easter Monday Baseball Game

As in the Lehigh game the first inning was the hoodoo one for the boys in red, while the Wake Forest ball sluggers organized an Easter egg hunt around the bases, every man on the team taking a whack at the leather sphere with the stick and six of them landing safe at home. At no time were the cadets in it, though they made a game fight after the disaster of the first inning.

The author notes that the Wake Forest pitcher, Hobgood, was the star of the game. Not only did he strike out eight batters, quite a feat for the era, but he also cleanly fielded numerous balls and in a future box score would have registered an ample number of assists. At the plate, Hobgood completed three inside-the-park home runs, a further sign of his athletic prowess, and impetus for the biggest roars heard from the crowd on this day. The article continued: "Bonitz of the A and M team did some fine work, too. Of the six runs made by the cadets three were his, and twice during the game he made splendid running catches that brought cheers from the spectators. An extremely large crowd was present, in it being many ladies and among those the students from the various female schools (Baptist Female University, Peace Institute and St. Mary's School) in Raleigh."

Lineups (not necessarily batting order):

Wake Forest — Hobgood P, Harris C, Powers 1B, Weaver 2B, Pace 3B, Freeman SS, Caddell LF, Rogers CF, Mull RF

A&M — Miller P, Welch C, Hall 1B, Pate 2B, Asbury 3B, Allen SS, Ross LF, Bonitz CF, Heath and Dalton RF.

The 1902 game was played on March 31 and reported two days later on Wednesday, April 2, in the *News and Observer*. The headlines declared:

Wake Forest Won
Superior Pitching Did the Job. A and M Make a Stout Fight

Once again, the writer begins his discourse on Wake Forest's 4–0 win with a reference to the weather and how it affected the play. This would prove to be a theme over the years in the Easter Monday contests, and anyone who has ever played spring baseball can attest to the fact that this is usually the case. On this early spring day, high winds were responsible for a number of errors. The weather, however, did not stop Mr. Hobgood from completing another superior performance:

> Wake Forest's pitcher, Hobgood, succeeded in striking out fourteen men and allowing only two hits, while Shuford, for the A and M pitched great ball, allowing only four hits but struck out only five men.
> Good ball playing was the order all through the game. At no time did either team lose control.
> A dropped ball by Hall netted Wake Forest two runs in the second inning and a bunching of a two base and two one base hits in the eighth earned out two more.
> Special features of the game were the pitching of Hobgood and the brilliant fielding of Hall for A and M, who made the most phenomenal catch ever seen on the local grounds, easily redeeming himself from the error made in the first part of the game."

Note: Hall, who is credited with both "brilliant fielding" and for committing the key two-run error, is not listed in the A and M lineup. The article concludes: "Two more games will be played with Wake Forest this season, one in Wake Forest and the last in Raleigh sometime in May."
Lineups:

> Wake Forest — Sams 3 B, Royster C (captain), Trarlham 1b, Weaver 2B, Moore CF, Rodgers LF, Hobgood P, Griffin RF, Freeman SS.
> A&M — Persons, E. P, Fenner 1B, Persons, H. 3B, Persons, W. C, Dorsett LF, Morson CF, Ross (captain) RF, Caserly 2B, Cochran SS.

The 1903 A&M team, coached by future governor Max Gardner, produced a record of 10–3, which included three wins over rival Wake Forest. The 1903 Easter Monday contest with Oxford, North Carolina's Horner Military Academy, resulted in a rain-shortened scoreless tie. Despite a small crowd, the *News and Observer*'s coverage on Tuesday, April 14, was extensive. For the first time in the series, the writer gives an inning-by-inning account of the action. His description is lively and includes antiquated spellings and invented words such as the hilarious "rooterines." At this point, the game had not settled into the routine contest between A&M and Wake Forest, so that without the rivalry and as a result of inclement weather, only 200 fans attended.

The Easter Monday Baseball Game

Rain Stops Game
Horner and A&M Were Hard at It When Water Fell

The ball game yesterday between Horner and A and M College promised to be a scorcher, but as luck would have it, the rain stopped the game.

About 200 enthusiastic rooters came out, the majority wearing the red and white of A and M, with an occasional old gold and purple.

The Horner boys were confident of victory for they had at their backs such veterans as David Crockett, Pool, Everitt, Osteen, Turner and Fencer. The A and M boys, though not confident, went into the game with a grim determination to win.

The game started with a snap and ginger with A and M at the bat. Asbury, the little captain of the farmer boys, was first up, but Everett was too much for him and "Diddle" only knocked a fly to left field, which was gobbled up by James. Hadley was not to go this way, however, and on the first ball of Everett's delivery cracked out a pretty hit to centre field. Knox, next up, hit an easy one to shortstop and the ball went from Osteen to Crockett to Turner, making a pretty double and retiring the side.

Pool, the first man up for Horner fell a victim to the invincible Holt and vainly punched the air three times. Crockett followed, hit an easy one to Holt and was thrown out at first. Everett then followed the lead of Pool and hit the air for three.

In the second inning Welch went out from Crocket to Turner. Holt died on a pop to the catcher. Isler was not to go so easily, however, and made a pretty hit in left. Shannonhouse, next up, went out on an easy one to Everett, leaving Isler on base.

Horner's second was a repetition of her first. Osteen, the heavy hitter of the league teams, punched hard, but all in vain, for Holt was too much for him. Woodruf tried hard for a hit and put one over first which might have been a clean hit, but our old reliable Welch held that bag and Woodruf died without seeing it. Turner then came to the bat, but he, too, fell a victim to Holt's delivery.

At this stage of the game a heavy downpour of rain came and the rooters and rooterines had to seek shelter as best they could.

After everyone had waited some time for the rain to stop, the game was called off and the crowd went home disappointed. A rain ticket was given to everyone at the gate and these were good at the next game, Wednesday, with Red Springs.

The writer notes that both teams played well, committing no errors in the brief game, and that A&M's Holt was the star on the mound as he struck out four of the six batters he faced in two innings of pitching.

	Innings					
	1st	*2nd*	*3rd*	*Runs*	*Hits*	*Errors*
A&M	0	0	0	0	2	0
Horner	0	0	-	0	0	0

BATTERIES: A&M — Holt and Brockwell; Horner — Everett and James
SUMMARY: Struck out by Holt, 4, by Everett 0; base hits, Hadley and Isler; Umpire Mr. Kelly.

A&M had an up-and-down season in 1904, finishing with a record of 10–12, playing a schedule that included prep schools and a professional team. On Easter Monday, April 2, 1904, in a wild, free-scoring game, Syracuse beat A&M 12 to 11. The Tuesday issue of the *News and Observer* reported, "It was a pretty game of baseball yesterday, when A and M was defeated by Syracuse by only one run majority." While this article still lacks a byline, it is unlikely the same writer as the previous year, as the descriptions and writing are less flamboyant, and except for labeling plays and hits as "pretty," the article contains many familiar phrases such as a struck-out batter "fanning." Missed swings are no longer referred to as punches, and it would be 80 more years before fans would understand another possible meaning when the writer notes that "Moon walked."

> The Syracuse team scored ten runs in the first and second innings. Burrill went out on a fly to Hadley, Ward hit by pitched ball, and Baker reached first safe but on wild throw by McIntire. Ward scored; Curtis out fly to second, but on Ruterford's safe hit coupled with bad throw to cut off man at home Wilbur scored. Keenan hit to center; Moon walked, and Hefferman put out safe single scored Ruterford and Keenan. Burrill hit to right field and Ward fanned.
> In the second inning Baker was given free pass; Wilbur got to first on error; Curtis bunted and with three men on base Ruterford scored; Baker on slow hit to first which he outran. Keenan put a pretty hit in center and scored Wilbur and Curtis; Moore fanned. Hefferman next up tapped out a pretty two-base hit and scored; Ruterford and Burrill scored; Keenan on his safe single to center, Ward went out short to first. Here A and M pulled together and in the third inning scored three runs, thus: Miller, after McIntire went out on fly to short, got to first on error; Asbury walked and Howell

The Easter Monday Baseball Game

The 1904 North Carolina A&M baseball team, coached by future governor (center, back row) O. Max Gardner (1929–1933). The "Farmers" lost their Easter Monday game on April 2, 1904, to Syracuse in a wild 12–11 contest (courtesy R.G. Utley).

went out on fly to right field; Hadley hit to left and scored Miller; McLaurin, with two men on bases, knocked out a pretty bagger: Asbury and Hadley scored.

In the fourth inning A and M scored another run. Springs reached first on pretty running and on wild throw went to second; Brockwell and House did not reach first but on wild throw of catcher to third to cut off Springs who was headed for that base allowed Springs to score.

In the seventh inning Asbury scored after reaching first on a pretty single to left field on Hadley's and McLaurin's singles in the eighth inning Brockwell and Miller scored on Howell's slow ball to second. The ninth inning again was good for the tall-enders. McLaurin walked; Knox hit to left; Springs safe on first while Knox was cut off at second; Brockwell singled and scored McLaurin and Springs; Shannonhouse out at first base; Miller singled; Asbury safe on first and scored Brockwell and Miller and the scoring for A and M closed when Asbury was cut off at second on Howell's hit to second. The visitors scored two runs after battery change was made by A and M. They scored Ward in the first inning, thus: Ward got to first by sac-

Living in the Dead Ball Era

rificing Burrill at second. Baker came to bat, hit a slow ball to Springs who cut him off at first and in the mix up Ward was allowed to score. In the eighth inning they too scored their last and winning run when Keenan, the first man up, knocked out a pretty home run down the foul line in left field.

The lineup was as follows:

Syracuse: Burrill, 3B; Ward, C; Baker, 3B; Wilbur, 1B; Curtis, C; Ruterford, SS; Keenan, LF; Moore, RF; Hefferman, P.

A and M: Miller, SS; Asbury, 2B; Howell, LF; Hadley, CF; McLaurin and Shannonhouse, P; Knox, 2B; Springs, C; and 1B; Brockwell, C; McIntire, 1B.

Score:

	R	H	E
A and M.	11	10	6
Syracuse	12	5	7

Battery: A. and M., McLaurin-Shannonhouse and Brockwell; Syracuse, Hefferman and Curtis.

There is no mention of attendees or attendance for this game.

Under the direction of Coach Richard Crozier, Wake Forest College was beginning to develop a competitive baseball program. While this team did not compete in the Easter Monday baseball game, their young pitchers would be the linchpin for the squad that would return to the Classic in 1907 (courtesy Wake Forest University).

The A&M boys had a more successful season in 1905, concluding the season with a 10–5 record. They were, however, unable to overcome North Carolina's spitballer in the only Easter Monday contest between the two teams. The *News and Observer*'s April 25 article on the April 24, 1905, Easter Monday game is the first extensive account of the social celebration that the game had quickly become. It begins with a headline and multiple subtitles, as was the convention of the day's journalists. Occasional misspellings, especially of players' names, are rampant in this enthusiastic article. Most of this article has been included, as it seems if not quintessential to the sport journalism of the day, at least representative of what would follow in the next couple of decades of game coverage. There are several first mentions here: one is the attendance by students from the various Raleigh colleges, and the other is the description of the conveyances that brought the overflow crowd that eventually spilled from the available seating to the areas along each foul line. Not only are this writer's descriptive powers superior, but his conclusions are also marvelous, as he suggests after describing the crowd and the atmosphere at the game: "Spring was there with both feet and base ball had arrived."

SITTON'S SPIT BALL SCORES A SHUT OUT
University Lands A&M Four to Nothing.
A GALA DAY CROWD
Fifteen Hundred People, Including
Hundreds of College Boys and
Girls, Lend Excitement, Dash
and Enthusiasm to Fine
Contest

University 4: A&M 0. And thereby hangs a tale.

It was a perfect day, the semi-holiday of Easter Monday. It was a game that was either "corking" or "kerfectly" grand accordingly as the adjective came from one of the hundreds of college students or from their fair sisters of the B.F.U., the St. Mary's School, or Peace institute.

All these were there in force: a special train full of rampaging youths from the university, flying colors, rooting systematically, wild after a while with the knowledge of victory; the A&M College, en masse, valiant to the end; delegations from Wake Forest and other colleges, drawn Raleighwards by the athletic event of the season: and rooterettes, hundreds of them, banked on the bleachers in a riot of hats, lavish of giggles and hand-clappings, inspiring of heroic diamond deeds and side-line witticisms.

The tiers of seats were collegiate to a nicety. Flags fluttered from fair hands. Megaphones spoke the defiance of brazen lungs. Locks loosened by enthusiasm fluttered almost like the colors in the breeze. The applause rolled to the accompaniment of feminine soprano. The players slid and batted and dived for bases in clouds of dust. The much abused welking [*sic*] rang and rang again. It was base ball at its best, delirium at its topmost pitch, beauty at its most daringly enticing.

A great day — a great game.

An Overflowing Crowd

The crowd included almost everybody. They were all there. For hours before the game the laboring street cars pulled slowly to the grounds, packed to overflowing with laughing women, smoking men, moving chariots of color. At almost every corner the cars stopped and dismayed crowds stood for a moment until the impossible came to pass and room was made somehow for the additions, the women sitting sometimes three deep in a seat, the men holding on to projecting portions of the cars' anatomy by tooth and nail. Carriages rolled along beside and past the belabored cars, filled with maidens and their college friends, old-time sports from the city, college youths smoking big cigars and important with the fate of Alma Mater strong upon them. At the ground the people simply overflowed. There was not a square inch of space on the seats when the game was called — and still they came! Men, women and girls. They spread themselves along the side-lines, banked in clusters in the field, filled every point of vantage. In the middle the diamond gleamed with its red clay like a scalped section of a tulip bed. The people stood about it like the frame to the play. The players, by contrast with the dimensions of their audience, looked like nimble ants as they swarmed over the ground in practice. The ball — that little white sphere on which two thousand hearts were set — flicked across the space of green and yellow li[k]e a comet of the sunlight. The people, on a holiday looked and gossiped and cheered and sang. Spring was there with both feet and base ball had arrived.

College Song and Banter

From the sidelines the rival rooters cheered and gave college yells and sang the college songs. All was as it should be. Megaphone fiends bellowed hoarse taunts when thrown across the separating diamond, took good on the opposite side, while the answering shout along was audible from whence they came. Amid the preliminary the grandstands palpitated with ribbons and flowers and maintained a strict neutrality except in color. But presently the University started up a mixture of a song, half-fymn [sic], half-carol, with a touch of serenade about it:

Peace to you, St. Mary's too!
Oh, BFU, peace to you!
St. Mary's too!

The A&M's were somewhat stunned by this but took it out in "Rah, Rah, Rahing" everything in petticoats on the field, and in the middle of the tumult somebody called time.

The Potent Mr. Sitton

Instantly there was quiet. The University players trotted briskly to the field. The umpire took out a brand new white ball. Eskridge, of A&M, a stalwart, gamy-looking chap took position at the bat. Sitton, of the University, faced him. Mr. Sitton made some passes with his arms, uncurled, there was a gleam of white, a thump when the ball hit the catcher's glove and Mr. Eskridge was leaning on his bat as the result of a vicious stab at the ambient — or was it ambulatory — air! Twice more did Mr. Eskridge bite at the point at which he thought the gleaming ball was located and twice more missing, sat down upon the bench.

Whereupon the University howled delightedly and the A&M responded with cat-calls as a damper to the previous enthusiasm.

The experience of Mr. Eskridge was the motif of the game. It was Sitton's day. Man after man went down before his curves. Of the 27 A&M men retired during the nine innings, he struck out seventeen, put out one, and threw out five to first base. He allowed only four hits, scattered through as many innings, two of them made by one man. The A&M batters could not remotely solve his curves nor calculate his speed. Several of them struck out three times out of three times at the bat, several others retired twice each by the three strike route. Mr. Sitton was all there with the goods. What curves he doesn't know are not in the book. The crowd has read of the spit ball. Mr. Sitton showed it in all its glory. Behind the cover of his protecting glove he could be seen to work ominously his salivary glan[d]s.

"Watch out, watch out!" would yell the A&M stands in chorus, "spit ball coming."

Sometimes it came and sometimes it didn't because Mr. Sitton alone of all the watching hundreds knew whether or not he really spat. And little difference it made whether it was a spit or a spit-fire. The sphere was as elusive in one event as the other to those of the white and red who banged their willows into the air in vain.

An Exciting Game

The game throughout was exciting, filled with good plays, risky situations, and fine fielding. A&M played hard, sometimes brilliantly. But her players could not bat, especially the "spit ball," which would come like a rifle bullet and then halt on a sudden: it was no go. Having some men on bases the University managed to score two runs in the fourth and two more in the seventh inning. A&M never had any real chance to cross the rubber, though twice her men reached third base. There were no earned runs, in the technical sense. As a matter of fact the University deserved her victory and earned every bit of change she got out of the controversy.

Follows the way the game went, play by play, from start to finish.

The Game in Detail

First Inning: A and M to the bat. Eskridge strikes out. Ashbury goes out, pitcher to first. Hadley retires, short to first.

University: Winston out on difficult catch of foul by Hadley. Stem takes first on pretty hit between short third. Cheshire sacrifices from pitcher to first. Stem takes second. Worth goes out on a fly to center.

Second Inning: Both Knox and Heath struck out. Drake gets pretty hit into short left field. Lattimore struck out.

University: Gudger singled to left. Thompson went out a fine foul caught by Hadley. James got base on balls. Sitton hit by pitcher takes first, the bases being full with Winston up, the University hopes were high but he could do nothing but pop a fly to Ashberry at third, retiring the side.

Third Inning: Harris struck out. Staples struck out; Eskridge retires pitcher to first.

University: Stem went out, second to first on a pretty stop and throw by Staples; Hadley gathered Cheshire's fly; Worth went out on fly to centre.

Fourth Inning: Ashbury flew to centre. Hadley hit with ball took first, and a moment later stole second.

Knox was next up, hit a liner to first who caught it and retired Hadley who had run towards the third on the play.

University: Grudger, after striking a dozen fouls, some of which tore through the line of rooters like shrapnel fire, went out on a fly to centre. Thompson hit a scorcher past first base which went over the red gulch, he

The Easter Monday Baseball Game

taking three bases. James hit to first who retired Thompson trying to come home on the play. Emmerson hit an easy one to pitcher who threw to first who muffed the ball rolling far down the field.

James made the circuit on the play but was put back to third on a ground rule on the play. Emerson taking second and Sitton then going to second. Winston then went out, pitcher to first, retiring the side. Score: University 2, A and M, 0.

Fifth Inning: Heath out, pitcher to first: Drakel [sic] hits little one in front of plate and beats out the throw to first: Lattimore struck out by Winston muffed the third strike, whereupon Lattimore took first and Drake second (although he was clearly out, there being a runner on first at the time.) Drake then stole third base and Lattimore went to second. At this point, the University woke up, entered protest and Lattimore was declared out. Harris struck out.

University: Stem flew out to Drake: Cheshire went out pitcher to first: Worth flew out to right.

Sixth Inning: Staple struck out: Eskridge went out, pitcher to first: Ashbury hit a pop fly which Cheshire muffed: Hadley struck out.

University: Grudger out, third to first: Thompson out third to first: Winbourne, (taking place of James) pops fly to Knox.

Seventh Inning: Knox put out by pitcher on hit along baseline: Heath struck out: Drake got base on balls and stole second: Lattimore struck out.

University: Emmerson out short to first: Sitton hit hot one to third who failed to handle: Winston hit by pitched ball: Stem hit to centre who caught ball, threw to second, who made error. Sitton taking third and Winston second on the play. Cheshire put in a pretty hit to right. Sitton and Winston both scoring on the play, the latter through low throw of Knox, trying to catch Sitton at the plate. Wo[r]th went out on liner to third. University 4, A and M, 0.

Eighth Inning: Harris struck out: Staples struck out: Estridge struck out.

University: Grudger struck out: Thompson went out short to first, Knox making nervy catch of low throw: Winbourne out, short to first.

Ninth Inning: Ashbury struck out: Hadley struck out: Knox took three bases on smash to red gulch (this hit might have been caught or stopped had right-fielder Thompson of the University not been engaged at the time in talking to certain young things from the B.F.U., who were fringing on the right field garden.) Heath, however hit to Stem, who retired the side. R. Thompson's flirtations not having cost the run they might easily have done.

News and Observer coverage of the 1906 game included a preview article, proof that the game was taking on increasing significance as both a local and regional event. Trinity College, later to be Duke University, makes its first appearance in the series.

Baseball Monday.

Tomorrow afternoon at 4 o'clock one of the most interesting games of the season will be played at the State Fair Grounds, the contesting teams being from the A and M College and Trinity College.

The day being a holiday and one of general celebration a big attendance is assured, for all know of the standing of the two teams and about what may be expected in the way of baseball.

The locals will be glad to learn that the A and M team is again in its regular form, Steele, McCathran, and Thompson having recovered, and are back at their old positions. The team was exceedingly crippled last week by the absence of Frank Thompson behind the bat, who was suffering from a broken finger, gotten in the Trinity game of ten days ago. He is now behing [*sic*] the bat and playing his usual game.

Trinity has been meeting with unlimited success during the season so far, and her victory over Harvard yesterday sounds big. We have not yet learned Trinity's line-up, but A and M's will be as follows:

McCathran, pitcher: Thompson, catcher: Fox, 1st base: Knox, 2nd base: Eskridge, short stop: Staples, 3rd base: Steele or Harris, left field: Shuford, center field: Farmer, right field. Game called at 4 P.M. Admission 50 cents.

The game coverage article again begins with a title and three subtitles.

TRINITY TRIMS BOYS IN GRAY
A&M's Only Score a Home Run
TRINITY SIX RUNS
A Game Full of Errors but Relieved from Dreariness by Good Box
Work and Some Stirring Scenes When Home Runs Were Made

The tone of this report is decidedly critical, and one can see that writers of the day did not withhold their opinions or feelings about a poorly played game. In this contest, won 6–1 by the Trinity College team, 15 errors were committed, and this time, inclement weather could not be blamed for the poor play. The game also included some exciting hits, two of which went for inside-the-park home runs, and again featured an

The Easter Monday Baseball Game

audience comprised of students from the Raleigh area girls' schools as well as the two participating colleges.

Offsetting the good looking score there is an error column, and in this there are eight charges against Trinity and seven against A and M, figures tell of poor baseball playing. It is no fun to sit out a game where ragged field work, muffled flies, wild throws and fumbled balls give one that tired feeling. There were few stolen bases, no double plays, and it was only the splendid battery work, home runs and two triplets that raised the thermometer of the game.

In the game, there were ten base hits made by Trinity and four by A and M. Pitcher McColtran struck out nine. The home runs were made by Eskridge for A and M, and by Smith for Trinity, while Hutchi[s]on and Smith for Trinity each blasted the leather for three baggers. Only one earned run is credited to A and M, this being Eskridge's home run, while Trinity has two earned runs, these being by Smith and Hutchison.

With Umpire Noble, of the University in charge, the Trinity men, who have as their coach Mr. O.H. Stocksdale, once of Raleigh's professional team and a splendid ball player, too[k] the first turn at the bat. Johnson fanned, and Smith swatted out a triplet, scoring on a passed ball. Justus walked, went to third on a wild pitch, and was left there as Clement fanned and Webb flew out to the pitcher. A and M began the game sky-rockety in going up, but came down with a dull thud, as Eskridge led off with a clean home run, lambasting the ball in deep right, but that was A and M's only run. Harris out, second to first, Farmer with a fly in right and Shuford second to first ended the inning.

In Trinity's second Luter fanned, Wrenn batted to Eskridge at short and Fox at first let the ball get away as he and the runner collided. As Wrenn tried to steal second catcher Thompson threw wild in that direction, the ball went on, centre fielder Shuford didn't stop it, so Wrenn kept on running and scored, with three errors giving the score. Flower went out on a fly and Hutchinson was put out by Fox at first unassisted. In its half A and M with three men up failed, Thompson fanning, Knox flying out to short and Fox dying on a foul fly to the catcher.

In the third neither side scored, though Justus, of Trinity, reached first on Eskridge's error, the ball going under him, but was caught trying to steal second. In A and M's half Staples fanned, McCathran reached on second's error, but was caught trying to steal second. Eskridge hit in left. Harris hit in right and Eskridge went to third, but Farmer was out, second to first.

In the fourth A and M piled up errors. For Trinity Clement was safe on Eskridge's wild throw to first and went on to second on a passed ball. Webb bunted, but was safe, pitcher McCathran failing to catch Clement at third. Suter batted to the pitcher who caught Clement off third. Wrenn was out second to first. Flowers batted to Staples and a wild throw put him safe on second, two men scoring. Hutchinson was out, pitcher to first. In its half A and M failed, though Knox reached first on a wild throw by pitcher Clement.

In Trinity's fifth Johnson made a single, Smith fanned, Justus was out, pitcher to first and Clement fanned. In its half A and M failed, Staples and McCatharan fanning, Eskridge getting a hit to right and stealing second, and Harris swatting the air.

In the sixth Webb put a fly in deep left, which Harris misjudged, so Webb trotted three bases, Harris redeeming his misplay by catching Suter's fly back off third after a hard run, it being prettily done. Wrenn fanned, and Flowers flew out in centre. In A and M's half Farmer was out on a foul, Shuford reached first on second's fumble, Thompson hit the air, Knox got to first on a wild throw from third, and Fox was out second to first, leaving two men on the bags.

In the seventh for Trinity Hutchison started in with a hit, Johnson fanned, Smith landed Hutchison and himself by a home run, Justus fanned, Clement hit in right and Webb went out pitcher to first. For A and M Staples fanned, McCathran and Eskridge went out short to first.

In Trinity's eighth, with Steele taking Shuford's place for A and M at centre Suter was out, second to first, Wrenn got to first on Staple's error, Flowers hit in left, Hutchinson fanned, and Johnson flew out to the pitcher. In A and M's half there was nothing, though with two down, Steele got to first on a wild throw from third and stole second, Thompson flying in right.

In the ninth for Trinity Smith as pitcher to first, Justus reached first on Eskridge's error, went to second on a passed ball. Clement was out second to first, and Justus scored on Webb's hit in left, while Webb was caught at second. In A and M's half Knox reached first on Short's error and was retired at second when Fox batted to Short. Staples fanned and McCathran was out, second to first.

The following day, this short article appeared in the *News and Observer*, indicating how socially important the Easter Monday game had become. The arrival of automobiles from faraway Durham was a big story, and the reader will likely recognize the names of some of these families.

The Easter Monday Baseball Game

Visitors from Durham

Two automobile parties yesterday from Durham to attend the Trinity and A and M ball game.

In Mr. A.B. Duke's automobile were Misses Bebra Dula and Caroline Fuller of New York, Miss Mary Duke of Durham: Messrs. Guy L. Winthrop of Yale University: George B. Cooper of Henderson: Angier B. Duke, J.N. Cole, Jr., and E.B. Lyon, of Durham. With Mr. George Lyon in his automobile were Messrs. Claiborne Carr, William Carr, and L.A. Tomlinson.

The 1907 Easter Monday game is the first to mention the use of special trains for access to the game. This announcement article appeared in the Friday, March 29, *News and Observer*. A&M had another successful baseball season in '07; led by Captain Frank Thompson, they completed a 14–8 record and went 2–1 in games with their Wake Forest rivals.

BASEBALL TRAIN

Seaboard Will Fix for It from Wake Forest Easter Monday

The Seaboard Air Line is going to fix it so that all who wish to come here from Wake Forest to the ball game on Easter Monday in Raleigh between Wake Forest and the A and M College teams can do so conveniently.

A round trip rate of 75 cents from Wake Forest is announced, and for the return trip to Wake Forest, the shoo-fly will not leave Raleigh until 5:30, so as to give ample time to see the game, which will begin at three o'clock. It will be a big game and there will be a big crowd here to see it.

A second, more detailed article appeared in the following day's paper.

TO THE EASTER GAME

Big Crowds Coming on the Seaboard Monday.

The ball game on Monday between the teams of Wake Forest College and A and M is going to attract a great crowd from along the Seaboard Air Line.

Special rates have been made for that day for the round trip, and from the points named will be: Henderson, $1.25: Kittrell, $1.25: Louisburg, $1.25: Franklinton, $1.00: Youngsville, 90 cents: Millbrook, 25 cents.

The game will be called at three o'clock and the "shoo-fly" will be held till 5:30 so that all who come may enjoy the contest through the last inning.

The article that appeared in the Tuesday, April 2, *News and Observer* was much briefer than the two previous years. With the buildup and story about the train, one would think an extensive game coverage article would have emerged. This was also the first of many Easter Monday games to be played in Raleigh between cross-town rivals Wake Forest and A and M. There is as much room dedicated to a discourse on the cold, "soggy" weather as is given to what must have been a very exciting 8–7 contest.

> WAKE FOREST TRIMS A & M.
> The Score Was Eight to Seven.
> A COLD DAY GAME
>
> It takes more than cold weather to freeze out baseball enthusiasm, and a big crowd here saw the Easter Monday game between A and M and Wake Forest, in which by eight to seven Wake Forest was a winner at the Fairgrounds yesterday.
>
> The day was cold and windy, not one to develop much in the line of baseball playing, so there was not much of high class playing, the numb fingers making it impossible to handle the ball properly. Despite the weather the teams went at their work with a will, but errors would come, and the score would continue to climb, while the temperature went down.

The writer suggests that the wet ground led to a number of errors in this contest and the unfortunate absence of what he referred to as "fast playing."

> As far as results go, the game was really won by Wake Forest in the third inning, for it was then that the visitors piled up five runs to their credit. With one gained in the second and with two more coming later on the eight runs were made by which Wake Forest trimmed the Cadet team which could only get as high as seven in the game.
>
> From the very start it seemed that Wake Forest had A and M at its mercy, but in the fifth inning, A and M made a spurt and picked up a little, but it was to no avail, as it never gained a lead.

The writer offers accolades for " batting work" to Temple and Thompson of A and M and to J. Turner and Hambrick of Wake Forest who hit exceptionally well "in the face of the weather."

The traditional Easter Monday celebration at North Carolina A&M changed dramatically on April 1, 1907. On that Easter Monday night the Alpha Epsilon chapter of Pi Kappa Alpha sponsored the second of many PiKA Balls that, in future years, would become the centerpiece of social activities not only at North Carolina A&M but also for the entire Raleigh area.

The invitation reproduced in the March 29, 1907, edition of the *News and Observer* lists names (patronesses), some of which are significant in the history of North Carolina State.

EASTER GERMAN
Given by the Pi Kappa Alpha Fraternity of the A and M College

Very attractive invitations have been issued, reading as follows:

The pleasure of your company is requested
At the
Annual Dance
Given by
Alpha Epsilon Chapter
Of the
Pi Kappa Alpha Fraternity
On the night of
Easter Monday, April 1st, 1907
Olivia Raney Hall,
Dancing ten till one
Music by Third Regiment Band

Patronesses: Mrs. Jas. A. Higgs, Mrs. D.H. Hill, Mrs. T.K. Bruner, Mrs. Sherwood Higgs, Mrs. F.L. Stevens, Mrs. B.S. Skinner, Mrs. W.C. Riddick, Mrs. Jas. McKimmon, Mrs. W.T. McGee, Mrs. A.F. Bowen, Mrs. Franklin McNeil, Mrs. A.W. Gnox, Mrs. Jas. H. Pou, Mrs. Julian Timberlake, Mrs. C.G. Latta, Mrs. Paul Lee.

Committee: George F. Bason, chairman; W.R. Marshal, A.J. Beall, D.H. Hill, Jr., J.T. Springs, E.J. Carpenter.

Articles on the early occurrences of the PiKA Ball often referred to them as germans, another term for a large dance or cotillion. The performance consisted of a series of dance figures led by a conductor or leader. The popularity of the "german" increased during the last quarter of the nineteenth century, and it almost always appeared on the programs of private balls.

Two articles associated with the 1908 game ran in the Sunday, April 19, *News and Observer*, the first a brief announcement regarding the special train schedule, and the second a full-blown preview of the game. Note that the preview says the game will be "called" at 1 o'clock, but the article announces the time as 4 P.M. instead and the first at the school's new athletic field.

>BEST BASE BALL GAME OF SEASON
>Wake Forest and A & M Play Tomorrow
>BOTH ARE CONFIDENT
>The Game Will Be Called at 1 O'clock.
>Sexton and Temple Will Pitch.
>Student Body from Both Colleges Will Root for Respective Teams!

Tomorrow afternoon at 4 o'clock on the new athletic field, the A & M and Wake Forest teams will cross bats for the second time this year. The first game was won by A & M by the close margin of one run. The game Monday will prove equally as exciting.

Sexton will twirl for the A & M and "Big" Temple for Wake Forest. These two pitchers are about evenly matched, and it will be Greek against Greek.

The Wake Forest team is the strongest in years and was only beaten by Guilford 1 to 0, while Guilford defeated the A & M and the University 4 to 0.

The Wake Forest boys are coming to Raleigh tomorrow confident of winning, as the whole student body will be behind them here rooting for their success.

The A & M team will be there with the "mustard plaster," and expect to stick it to the visitors.

This will be the best game played in Raleigh this season and will be witnessed by the Wake Forest student body and the A & M student body, the three girls' schools and everybody in Raleigh, as Monday is a half holiday.

The game will begin promptly at 4 P.M.

>Special Seaboard Train

The Seaboard Air Line Railway will run a special rate shoofly train from Norlina on account of this game, with the following rates:

Round trip rate from Norlina, Oxford and points north of Henderson, $1.25.

From Henderson, $1: from Kittrell and Franklinton, 75 cents: from Louisburg, $1: from Youngsville and Wake Forest, 50 cents: from Neuse, 35 cents: from Milbrook, 25 cents.

The train will leave Norlina at 7:30 A.M.: Oxford, 7:05: Henderson, 8:02: Louisburg, 7:50, arriving at Raleigh at 9:35 A.M.

Returning the train will leave Raleigh at 6:30 P.M.

The Easter Monday Baseball Game

The article describing the game appeared in the Tuesday, April 21, edition of the *News and Observer*.

ERRORS COST WAKE FOREST THE GAME
Defeated By A & M in an Exciting Game.
SCORE FOUR TO THREE
Game Won by A & M in the Second Half of the Ninth Inning —
Witnessed by 2500 People — Playing of Both Teams Magnificent.

Despite their record and an anticipated victory, the A&M team was able to defeat J.R. Crozier's elite Wake Forest team. In its hard-fought Easter Monday defeat of Wake Forest, the play is described as perhaps the most exciting to have taken place at the new athletic grounds. The contest only lasted an hour and a half and is described as an intensely exciting affair that "was of thrilling interest to the enthusiast." Attendance for the game was approximately 2,500, which was said to have been "the largest number that ever attended a game in Raleigh." Wake Forest led in the scoring, making two runs in the second inning, A&M also scored in this inning, adding a third run in the next, Wake Forest tying the contest in the sixth. The game remained tied until the second half of the ninth, when damaging errors on the part of Wake Forest's first baseman and pitcher allowed A&M to tally the deciding run.

> Sexton pitched for A and M, Temple for Wake Forest, and although Sexton struck out 11 and Temple but three, yet Temple did magnificent work in short circuiting the liners from the bat and putting men out on first. Wake Forest displayed excellent ability to play ball, having the strongest team that institution has had in years, and except for the fatal errors in the ninth, a tenth inning would have been played to determine which was the victorious team.

Although the game was a close one, the A&M batting was termed "outstanding." A&M's hitters connected for a number of two-base hits and would have won easily but for what the writer called "the remarkable alertness and swiftness of Wake Forest's fielders, who managed some difficult skyscrapers." A "beautiful" highlight of this game was a double play by Hamrick to Jones for the Wake Forest nine.

"Mr. J.W. Thompson umpired the game."

Game by Innings

First Inning: The game began with Wake Forest at the bat, Freeman striking out, Dawson being thrown out at first and Hamrick striking out. In the second half A and M did not reach first, Abernethy being caught on a foul to first, and both Fox and Harris being thrown out at first by the third baseman.

Second Inning: Hammond was at the bat for Wake Forest, reaching first on an error by the third baseman. Temple hit to first going to second on an error by the first baseman, and Hammond scored, leaving Temple on third. Benton struck out. Couch was struck by the pitcher and went to first. Josey met the ball, dispatching it through pitcher and shortstop to centre field, scoring Temple. Couch was put out on second and White struck out.

Farmer was at the bat for A and M and hit safe to first. Council sacrificed with a bunt to let Farmer make second, and the latter stole third. One of the sensational features of the game was Thompson's two-bagger, sending Farmer across the home plate. The centre fielder, by a difficult play, prevented Thompson from making a home run, putting the bat to second just as Thompson arrived, and playing was suspended for several minutes in an argument over the umpire's decision, Thompson having been called safe at second. Seifert directed the ball to right field and made second on a wild throw to first, Thompson reaching home. Black was out on a foul to catcher, and Sexton struck out.

Third Inning: Freeman got a hit and went to first, going to second on Dawson's sacrifice: Hamrick struck out and Hammond was beat by the ball to first.

Abernethy bunted safely to first for the farmers. Foy was put out on first and Harris took the tie away from the visitors with a two-bagger, scoring Abernethy. Farmer and Council were thrown out at first.

Fourth Inning: Temple and Benton struck out and Couch was denied the glory of the best hit of the game by A and M's centre-fielder, who caught a fly that went nearly to the fence.

Thompson nearly duplicated Couch's feat, being caught out by Wake Forest's centre-fielder. Seifert and Black were put out by pitcher to first.

Fifth Inning: Josey's fly to left field was caught and White was struck by a ball from the pitcher, going to first. Freeman was thrown out at first and White was put out on second.

Sexton struck out, and Wake Forest's short stop and second baseman prevented Abernethy and Fox from reaching first.

Sixth Inning: Wake Forest tied A and M in this inning, the tie not being broken until the ninth. Dawson was at the bat, but was thrown out by second to first. Hamrick hit to right field, making first. Hammond sent a liner through pitcher and short-stop, making second and sending Hamrick to third. Temple placed the ball between center field and second, scoring Hamrick, leaving Hammond on third but to no avail, as Benton and Couch struck out.

Harris' fly to left field was muffed, but Farmer's attempt to sacrifice resulted in a ball popped up to catcher, and Harris was doubled at first. Council got to second on a hit to the right field. Thompson was out on a fly to first.

Seventh Inning: Josey struck out: White was caught out on a fly to second, and Freeman's fly to centre field was caught.

As brief work was made of A and M in this inning. Seifert struck out, Black was thrown out by third to first, and Sexton was caught out by the pitcher.

Eighth Inning: Dawson was thrown out by second to first: the short stop caught Hamrick's fly and he did the same thing for Hammond's.

Abernethy was out by a fly to short-stop. Fox was thrown out at first by the third baseman, and Harris put a fly into the hands of the centre-fielder.

Ninth Inning: At the beginning of the ninth it was believed there must be another inning to decide the contest. Wake Forest was quickly retired, Temple being thrown out at first by the third baseman, Benton striking out and Couch, the last hope, giving a foul to first."

Farmer was at the bat for the home team, and reached first on an error, beginning the rally that won the game for A&M. Temple's wild throw to first after Council bunted allowed Farmer to get all the way to third and Council to advance to second. Finally, Thompson singled to center field, scoring Farmer with the winning run.

On Easter Sunday, April 19, 1908, the *News and Observer* carried the following social article:

FRATERNITY DANCE

The annual Easter German of the Pi Kappa Alpha fraternity will take place in Pullen Hall Monday night commencing at 9:30 o'clock. A large number of out-of-town college men will be present.

The following participated in the game for Wake Forest — Temple, Hamrick, James, Freeman, Dawson, Hammond, Benton, Couch, White and Josey.

In 1909, the Ball was included in the Social Calendar listing in the April 11 *News and Observer*. Again, the dance was slated for 9:30 in Pullen Hall.

From the *News and Observer*'s weekly social calendar printed on Easter Sunday, April 11, 1909: "With the closing of Lent Raleigh social events come fast on the other. Some of those to take place this week are: Monday Ball game, A and M versus Wake Forest. Pi Kappa Alpha dance, Pullen Auditorium."

The elaborate pregame write-up in the Easter Sunday edition of the paper included separate photographs of A&M's starting lineup: Sexton, P, Fox 1B, Bost 2B, Seifert 3B, Harsell SS, Harris (Captain) LF, Freeman CF, Brown RF, and Council behind the plate. Wake Forest's projected lineup was also listed: Pope P, Harris C, Edwards 1B, Benton (Captain) 2B, Hammond 3B, White SS, Leggett LF, "Kid" Dawson CF, Beam RF.

Tuesday's article that summarized the game, though less effusive than in years past, suggests another successful well-attended event.

THE FARMERS BEAT BAPTISTS
Largest Crowd Assembled Since Last Easter
IT WAS FIVE TO TWO
There Was a Great Crowd to Witness the A and M–Wake Forest Game Yesterday and Until the Eighth Inning the Baptists Were Ahead, But the Tables Were Turned.

The writer notes that the A&M 5–2 victory was the best-attended Raleigh contest since the Easter Monday game of the previous year. A&M outplayed the Wake Forest nine from the standpoint of both strong hitting and pitching. He described the game as a hard-played one with the runs being scored in clumps. The Wake Forest men scored their two runs in the fourth inning, and all the A&M runs were scored in the eighth. Up until the eighth, the A&M squad had suffered from what he called "hard luck," and it looked like they may be destined for another loss at the hands of their rivals.

> Wake Forest was at the bat first. Three men came up, and everyone went out at first base. A and M got one hit, but nothing to count. In the second inning, three Wake Forest men came up, one going out at first, another by knocking a fly to Brown, another by playing Casey. A and M got a hit in this inning, but could not make it count. A sacrifice hit settled one man, and fly-outs two more. In the third inning, neither side did anything but go out.

The fourth inning sent Wake Forest into the seventh heaven. Leggette struck out, but Edwards made up for his with a two-base hit, which went just a little out of Freeman's reach. Benton was hit by a pitched ball, and got his free pass. Dawson struck out. Hammond got to first by an error, and Pope finally made a hit which scored Edwards and Benton. Sexton then struck out another man, the third in this inning, and sent Wake Forest to the field. A and M hit well in this inning, but again scored nothing.

In the fifth inning, neither side distinguished itself. The sixth was most equally uneventful, with the honors to Wake Forest to the extent of one hit. In the seventh inning, only three men faced Sexton, and only three faced the Wake Forest.

The game turned around for A&M in the eighth inning. First the visiting team was retired in order. For A&M, Seifert started out with a drive which bounced high and counted for a two-bagger, and Sexton made a sacrifice hit. Freeman followed with a hit which scored Seifert and Brown with another. Next, Council was struck by a pitch and lay on the ground for several minutes while the crowd waited uneasily. But he stayed in the game and finally took first base; however, he thought better and was replaced by a pinch-runner. Then Harris connected on a double and scored two men. Black followed Harris's double with another one, and the score was five to two. Two fly-outs finished the side. In the ninth inning, Wake Forest made one hit but nothing more, ending the game in just over an hour and a half.

				R	*H*	*E*
Wake Forest	0 0 0	2 0 0	0 0 0	2	4	4
A. and M	0 0 0	0 0 0	0 5	5	9	4

SUMMARY: Runs by Edwards Benton, Seifert, Freeman, Brown, Council, Harris. Two base hits, Edwards, Council, Seifert, Black, Harris. Bases stolen, Dawson, Beam, Black 2, Freeman, Harris, Hartsell. Bases given by Pope 1, by Sexton 1. Hit by ball by Pope 1, by Sexton 1. Struck out by Pope 4, by Sexton 9. Sacrifice hits, Black, Sexton. Time of game, 1:35. Umpire, Mr. Brenig.
Attendance was listed as 1,500.

The Sunday, March 27, 1910, edition of the *News and Observer* ran an ad for the Easter Monday ball game and a short article promoting both a track meet with Guilford College and a baseball game with Wake Forest. The Saturday paper also advertised special train rates as in the two previous years. In addition, the Raleigh and Southport Railway offered round trips from Fayetteville and Fuquay. A separate article promoted and previewed the baseball game. Finally, the game article appeared in the Tuesday, March 29, edition.

A & M DEFEATED WAKE FOREST 8 TO 2
Game Won by Cadets by Fine Playing
ATTENDANCE OVER 2,000
Breaks the Record for Crowds at the College Games—
Sexton Strikes Out Twelve Men, the Record for the Season.

A beautiful game was yesterday's contest between Wake Forest and A and M, the players from both colleges putting their best into the game, but A and M was too strong for the visitors, though the playing of Wake Forest showed that it is to be a factor in the season's series of college games. The

This classic Easter Monday shot was taken at the March 18, 1910, game. The new dormitories rise in the background to Riddick Field on the Raleigh campus. Attendees included A.B. Duke and other original "tailgaters" (courtesy R.G. Utley).

The Easter Monday Baseball Game

score was 7 to 2 [note discrepancy with headline]. Wake Forest securing both its runs in one inning, and batting like that throughout would have made the score different. A and M got eight hits, Wake Forest seven, but there were too many errors by both teams, A and M making four and Wake Forest six. Sexton did the best pitching of the season to date, striking out twelve men, and Carter, for Wake Forest, had two of A and M's giants go down before him.

The crowd at this game was estimated to be around 2,000, making it the largest to ever attend a college game in Raleigh. According to the writer, every seat in each grandstand was occupied, and hundreds of fans stood along the sidelines throughout the festivities.

Besides the great number of college girls and boys at the game, adding to the gaiety and merrymaking of the event, there were many visitors from other points, all the surrounding towns being represented in the crowd that saw the game. Five touring cars, bringing thirteen persons, came from Henderson, making the trip in two hours and forty minutes, returning to Henderson at 8:30 last evening.

Game by Innings

Wake Forest, first — Beam fanned; Britt out, third to first; Lee out, short to first.

A and M, first — Freeman, base on being hit by pitched ball. Brown popped out to pitcher; Black singled to left and Freeman caught at third; Black caught off first.

Wake Forest, second — Utley, first on error of short; White struck out; Daniel struck out; Utley stole second; Futrell fanned.

A and M, second — Robertson first on error of second; Seifert advanced Robertson to second on sacrifice; Hartsell, clean hit to centre and Robertson scored; Hartsell went to second on error of catcher; Bost went out, second to first and Hartsell went to third; Hartsell scored on error of third; Ross out, third to first.

Wake Forest, third — Carter went out, third to first; Riddick, first on being hit by pitched ball; Beam struck out; Britt flew out to first.

A and M, third — Sexton out, pitcher to first; Freeman base on balls, caught trying to steal second; Brown out, pitcher to first.

Wake Forest, fourth — Lee first on error of second, stole second; Utley first and Lee out at third; White struck out. Daniel first on error of second, and Utley went to second; Castlow (substitute for Futrell) fanned.

Living in the Dead Ball Era

The 1910 North Carolina A&M baseball team defeated Wake Forest in their Easter Monday game by a score of 8–2. Back row, left to right: J.L. Springs (manager), Bost, Riddick, Stafford, Council, Freeman, Ross, Frank Thompson (coach). Front row, left to right: Black, Hartsell, Dave Robertson, Sexton, D.W. Seifert, Brown, Speer. Dave Robertson went on to a major league career, including an appearance in the 1917 World Series (courtesy R.G. Utley).

A and M, fourth — Black out, second to first. Robertson walked; Seifert, clean hit to right for one sack and Robertson caught at third; Hartsell first on error of first, and Seifert went on to third; Speer (substituted for Bost); Hartsell stole second; Speer fanned.

Wake Forest, fifth — Carter first on scratch hit; Riddick out pitch to first; Carter advanced to second; Beam flew to second; Bratt flew to right, pretty catch.

A and M, fifth — Ross fanned; Sexton flew to left; Freeman walked; Brown singled to left and Freeman stole third; Brown stole second; Black flew to centre.

Wake Forest, sixth — Lee out second to first; Utley out pitch to first; White landed in right for two bags; Daniel fanned.

A and M, sixth — Robertson out second to first; Seifert first on being hit by pitched ball, stole second; Hartsell base on being hit by pitched ball; Seifert third on error baseman and Hartsell went to second; Speer singled to right and scored Seifert and Hartsell and took second on throw home; Ross first on fielder's choice while Speer made third and home on error of third baseman; Ross out catcher to third; Sexton out short to first.

Wake Forest, seventh — Castlow out pitcher to first; Carter singled to left; Riddick fanned; Beam flew to first.

A and M, seventh — Freeman singled to centre; Brown made first but Freeman was out at second; Black flew to left and Brown went to second on error of first baseman; Robertson out second to first.

Wake Forest, eighth — Bratt flew to centre; Lee first on infield hit; Utley went to second and Lee to third on errors of shortstop; White singled through short, and Lee and Utley scored; White stole second and third; Daniel struck out; Castlow fanned.

A and M, eighth — Seifert flew to left; Hartsell singled to left, second on wild pitch; Speer base on balls; Ross first on error first baseman; Hartsell went to third and Speer to second; Sexton singled but made third on error of left fielder, scoring Hartsell, Ross and Speer; Sexton caught off third; Freeman out second to first.

Wake Forest, ninth — Carter out pitcher to first; Riddick struck out; Beam singled to centre; Bratt hit to centre and Beam advanced to second; Lee flew to third.

The game, marred by ten errors, was played in an hour and fifty minutes.

Dave Robertson, who played in the Easter Monday games of 1910, '11, and '12 for A&M, was signed by John McGraw, manager of the New York Giants of the National League in 1912. He made his major league debut on June 5 of that year.

In the "dead ball era" the left-handed Virginia native won the 1916 home run title outright, and tied with Williams of the Chicago Cubs for leading home run hitter with 12 in 1917.

He played in the 1917 World Series when his team lost to the Chicago White Sox 4 games to 2. In 1922 he was a member of the World Series champion New York Giants. Robertson spent nine years in the major leagues with the New York Giants, Chicago Cubs, and Pittsburgh Pirates.

After that he played minor league ball from 1923 to 1931 for Richmond, Norfolk, and York. He died in 1970 at the age of 89 in Virginia Beach.

Although Wake Forest lost this game, their newly formed Athletic Alumni Association had stabilized their sports programs, and this team, again led by Crozier, after a weak start (Crozier was still coaching the basketball team when the season began), finished second in the state.

Wake Forest	AB	R	H	PO	A	E
Beam, l.f.	5	0	1	3	2	1
Bratt, 1b	5	0	1	10	0	2
Lee, s.s.	5	1	1	1	1	0
Utley, r.f.	4	1	0	0	0	0
White, 3b	4	0	2	4	2	2
Daniel, 2b	4	0	0	1	4	1
Futrell, c.f.	1	0	0	1	0	0
Carter, p.	4	0	2	1	2	0
Riddick, c.	3	0	0	2	2	0
Castlow, c.f.	3	0	0	1	0	0
Total		2	7	24	13	6

A&M	AB	R	H	PO	A	E
Freeman, c.f.	2	0	1	1	0	0
Brown, r.f.	4	0	1	0	0	0
Black, 3b.	4	0	1	1	2	0
Robertson, 1b.	3	1	0	11	0	0
Seifert, c.	3	1	1	12	0	0
Hartsell, s.s.	3	3	2	1	1	2
Bost, 2b.	1	0	0	0	0	2
Ross, l.f.	4	1	0	0	0	0
Sexton, p.	4	0	1	0	5	0
Speer 2b.	2	2	1	1	1	0
Total		8	8	27	9	4

SUMMARY: Struck out by Sexton, 12: by Carter, 2. Base on balls, off Sexton, 0; off Carter, 3. Two base hits, White. Wild pitch, Carter. Umpire, Upchurch. Time, 1:50.

1911–1920

The state having increased its population by another 400,000, the next decade would prove to be a busy one that began with the state legislature removing the authority for capital punishment from the individual counties and replacing hanging with the electric chair as the means for execution. A new antitrust law forced the American Tobacco Company to split into four companies, allowing for more competition in one of the state's largest industries.

The Easter Monday Baseball Game

In 1915, the North Carolina Highway Commission was established to maintain and build a state highway system, and Mount Mitchell became the first official state park.

Developments on the international scene also began to affect the Tarheel State. In 1915, the state's National Guard units were deployed along with U.S. Army troops to the Mexican border to fight the Mexican outlaw, Pancho Villa. Two years later, as a result of World War I, three training camps were built in the eastern part of North Carolina. Camp Bragg near Fayetteville would eventually become Fort Bragg, one of the largest military installations in the world. Among North Carolina's contributions to the war efforts were the massive shipments of roll-your-own tobacco, the entire Bull Durham crop having been purchased for the purpose of supplying Europe-bound troops.

Late in the decade, work began on the first of several hydroelectric

The 1911 North Carolina A&M team, champions of the South, earned a record of 15–3 and won their Easter Monday game 6–0 for former star and coach Frank Thompson before 2,000 fans. Back row, left to right: J.W. Sexton (captain), H. Hartsell, Riddick, Dave Robertson, Stafford, Council, Bost, Frank Thompson (coach). Front row, left to right: Black, Brown, Steer, Ross, D.W. Seifert, Freeman (courtesy R.G. Utley).

dams to be built in the western part of the state on the Catawba River. A devastating flood had hit the area in 1916, making it necessary to better control the Blue Ridge watershed. The result of this new source of power was, of course, a watershed of growth in the region.

On the national scene, Congress passed the Sedition Act, which made it illegal to write or say anything against the war effort. This law produced the most severe restrictions on freedom of speech in the country's history. As the U.S. military operations succeeded in breaking the German lines in France, leading to a late autumn armistice, a huge influenza epidemic hit North Carolina, causing over 13,000 deaths.

Remarkably, the Easter Monday Baseball Classic survived all this upheaval and tragedy, and in fact became even more important as a diversion during this decade.

The new decade of Easter Monday baseball games was greeted by a substantial preview article in the Sunday, April 16, 1911, *News and Observer*.

WAKE FOREST VS. A & M
Big Game to Take Place Monday on A & M Grounds
There Will Be a Big Attendance at This Game, as There Is Keen Rivalry Between the Two Teams, and the Contest Is Expected to Be a Hot One.

The game that interests Raleigh most is the Wake Forest vs. A & M contest. On Monday afternoon, after the great throng of spectators will have witnessed the great State inter-collegiate track meet in the morning, in which Carolina, Wake Forest and A & M will strive for honors, the great baseball contest will be pulled off between Wake forest and A & M. With ideal weather conditions, baseball fans are predicting that this attraction will draw a greater crowd to West Raleigh at 2:30 P.M. than has ever been seen in that hustling part of the city. When one considers that there has already been some gatherings of considerable size, it is hard to conceive of what magnitude and proportions this hilarious, baseball fiendish crowd will assume.

The Meredith girls will be present en masse to cheer on their brothers of Wake Forest. They have always been loyal for their denominational college, and it is right that they should be so. The visiting team will be stimulated and cheered on to victory by these sympathizing girls. The young ladies of Peace and St. Mary's will overrun the bleachers, presenting a solid mass of

The Easter Monday Baseball Game

white, and those new Easter bonnets so dear to their hearts. Incidentally, this solid phalanx of laughing, blushing, gushing jolly crowds of girls will be another attraction for a part of the population at the contest. Carolina will send a large following over to cheer their men on to victory in the track meet. They will be present to witness the titanic struggle between the close rivals. The whole student body of Wake Forest will be present to support their team. Added to this, the 500 A & M students, there will at least be 2,000 students present, hardly leaving room for the Raleigh and outside people.

But why all this gathering? Because two great colleges have each a great team that will oppose each other. The loyal alumni and supporters of each expect to see their team win. For several years, these two teams have been pitted against each other with about equal strength. A & M has been the victor on most of these occasions. This year the two teams are strong again; if anything, Wake Forest has a better team than formerly. One game has already been played which resulted in A & M's favor by a slight margin. But the game is so uncertain that no one can make a prognosis of the outcome with any degree of certainty. The final result is always veiled in mystery until the umpire declares the last man out in the ninth inning.

Wake Forest has determined that for one time they are going to win from A & M. When those boys once make up their minds to do a thing, nothing can stay them. Every energy will be put forth, the best of tactics will be brought to their command, and the skill and drill of previous months will be exhibited with precision. Everything points to one of the greatest playing machines ever seen on the home grounds.

And what is A & M doing to oppose this? They have a record behind them of only one game lost. Wake Forest already defeated this season to urge them on. But the Red and White is not relying on past victories to win this one for them. They are fully aware that a formidable adversary will oppose them, and that they will have to bring all the baseball knowledge and skill to their command if they ever expect to win. Farmer, A & M's crack center fielder will be out of the game, on account of a broken hand, received in the Richmond game last Tuesday. Outside of this, the team is in the very pink of condition, and the classy article of ball they exhibit will be of the stellar variety. It is just a toss up as to who will pitch for A & M, Stafford and Robertson are both reliable. Stafford, as an A & M pitcher, has not lost a game. Robertson has already defeated Wake Forest.

The writer concludes that, at fifty cents admission, the game is a great value for fans of all stripes and that the level of enthusiasm will be like at no other area event this spring. This flamboyant piece, though containing useful information about the competing squads, is little more than a commercial endorsement. One would have to wonder how much of an effect the focus of local media on the Easter Monday event had on its ascension as a cultural and social requirement or obligation.

The article on Tuesday, April 18, about the game told a different story, one of dominance, both at the bat and on the mound.

FARMERS SHOW WAKE FOREST HOW
The Great Annual Easter Monday Game
THE SCORE WAS 6 TO 0
Robertson Pitches a Fine Game, Allowing Only One Hit and Striking Out Eleven — Two Three Baggers and Two Two Baggers the Features

As in the previous year, two thousand passionate fans made their way to the game from "various parts of the state." By this time, the local female colleges had chosen their favorites, the Meredith girls being naturally inclined to side with their denominational brothers at Wake Forest. The traditional colors for the two schools had already been established, as it was noted that in the stands there was a great deal of the red and white as well as the black and gold. Most of the local Raleigh fans pulled for the A&M team, who were often referred to as the Farmers. "The game was at no time dangerous for the Farmers and their timely hits, two of which were three baggers and two more two baggers brought them six runs before the long last inning was played."

As in the game of the year before, the future Major Leaguer, Robertson starred for A&M, this time tossing a brilliant, one-hit shutout:

> Robertson was on the mound for the Farmers and as usual pitched a good game. The Wake Forest boys were unable to find him but for one hit, which was a scratch hit. He also struck out eleven of the visitors, while Underwood and Smith together stuck out eight of the Farmers. The stick work was another feature of the Farmers' side of the game yesterday, for Robertson and Hartsell each rapped out a three bagger while Farmer and Seifert pounced on Underwood for a two bagger each. Only twenty-six [?] faced Robertson in the nine innings. He had good support, too, for only one error was charged against his fielders, this being against Williams for holding his foot on first when second threw Correll's grounder to him. Wake Forest was charged with four errors, two of which were by the second baseman.

The Easter Monday Baseball Game

In the first the Farmers lost a good chance to score when Farmer was safe on third baseman's error and Brown followed with a sacrifice. But Williams and Hartsell fanned.

In the second Utley hit a slow one to left infield and beat it out before the catcher could field it. Stringfield then sacrificed. Brown flied to shortstop and Correll fanned.

A & M started the fun in the second, when Robertson lifted a beauty to right field, which looked good for a home run or a three-base hit, but a strong wind checked it, and the center fielder clasped it in the glove in a pretty running catch. Seifert then hit one which bounced over the pitcher's head and went to center field. He then stole second, and Ross landed a nice single in right field. Seifert scored when catcher muffed right fielder's throw to the plate. Patton and Speer then fanned.

The Farmers lost another good chance to score in the third inning. Farmer, first up, landed a two-bagger in left garden, and Brown, the veteran sacrifice, again put his man another base with a nice little bunt. With Farmer on third, Williams fanned and Hartsell flied to center field.

In the fourth the Farmers claimed another tally. Robertson whipped out a three-bagger to left field and scored on Seifert's two-bagger. Ross followed with a sacrifice, but Patton fanned and Speer grounded to first.

In the fifth Correll was awarded first base, but "Dutchie" Seifert was too quick for him and caught him before he reached second, catcher to short.

It was in the fifth that the Farmers played havoc with Underwood's curves, batting him out of the box. He started ball rolling when he gave Farmer a free ticket; then second muffed Brown's grounder, and Williams singled, filling the bases. Hartsell was just at the right time next when brought them all in with his three-bagger to center field. Robertson followed with a long drive to right field, who gathered it in but Hartsell came in before the ball was fielded. Another hit was made by Ross in this inning but no more scoring was done.

Beginning with the sixth inning Smith was substituted in the box for Underwood by Wake Forest. He proved more effective, allowing only one hit and no more runs.

In the seventh Robertson hit one to third and beat it out. He then stole second but Seifert and Ross went out second and third to first.

The 1911 Wake Forest team was a disappointment to its fans, though its Athletic Association announced at the end of the season that it had turned a profit. Their main problem was that their captain, Utley, who was expected to be the top pitcher in the state, had injured his shoulder at the beginning of the season and was relegated for the season to first base. The North Carolina State team, on the other hand, finished one of its finest seasons at 18–3, defeating their rivals twice.

Wake Forest	AB	R	H	PO	A	E
Faucette, c.f.	4	0	0	3	0	0
Betts, 2b.	4	0	0	0	3	2
Turner, c.	3	0	0	9	0	1
Utley, 1b.	2	0	1	11	1	0
Stringfield, s.s.	2	0	0	0	0	0
Brown, 2b.	3	0	0	0	0	1
Correll, r.f.	2	0	0	1	1	0
Mills, l.f.	3	0	0	0	0	0
Underwood, p.	2	0	0	0	4	0
Smith, p.	1	0	0	0	0	0
	26	0	1	24	9	4
A&M	AB	R	H	PO	A	E
Farmer, c.f.	4	1	1	1	0	0
Brown, r.f.	2	1	0	0	0	0
Williams, 1b.	4	1	1	8	0	1
Hartsell, s.s.	4	1	1	4	2	0
Robertson, p.	3	1	2	2	3	0
Seifert, c.	4	1	2	11	2	0
Ross, l.f.	3	0	2	0	0	0
Patton, 2b.	4	0	0	1	2	0
Speer, 2b.	3	0	0	0	2	0
Tucker, 3b.	1	0	0	0	0	0
	32	6	9	27	11	1

Score by innings:
```
Wake Forest   0 0 0   0 0 0   0 0 0   0
A&M           0 1 0   1 4 0   0 0 0   6
```

The 1912 Easter Monday game took place on April 8 and was covered in the April 9 *News and Observer*.

WAKE FOREST WERE THE LOSERS
In Annual-Easter Baseball Game Agricultural and Mechanical Team Victors
THE SCORE WAS THREE TO ONE
Two Thousand Persons Witnessed Game — Colors of Both Colleges Were Greatly in Evidence — Students Vied with Each Other in Rooting — Many Out-of-Town People at the Game

The Easter Monday Baseball Game

In what was called "a fast and closely contested game," A&M won the annual Easter game from Wake Forest in what was once again deemed "one of the largest crowds ever assembled on the ball field to see an intercollegiate baseball game." Considering the buildup to the past few games, this article was rather spare, mostly directed by an inning-by-inning account of the low-scoring affair.

The game was snappy from the start to finish and the utmost of good humor prevailed between the rival rooters whose stentorian yells could be heard, vying with each other as to who could make the most racket, being marred only once by a scrap started by two too-happy partisans and which looked for a while like a free-for-all fight, being finally stopped by those who wanted to see the game and by the aid of a liberal dose of cold water. Cates for the visitors was replaced by Smith in the third inning, all of A & M's runs being made off of Cates. Stafford for A &M pitched fine ball only allowing three hits, two of those coming in the second inning, when Wake Forest scored their only run.

The features of the game were Hartsell's stop of Stringfield's grounder past third in the second inning; Farmer's catch of Faucette's hit to deep center; Speer's catch of Turner's foul fly; Page's one-hand catch of Speer's wild throw to first and Hartsell's stop of Stringfield's hit over second, although he threw wild to first.

Both teams fielded well, only three errors being made by A & M, and two by Wake Forest.

There was about 2,000 present completely filling the grandstand and bleachers near the grandstand, and partially filled the right field bleacher being a mass of color, A & M and Wake Forest mixed.

The game by innings:

First—Wake Forest: Faucette fanned; Parker hit to Hartsell, who fumbled, Parker safe; Stafford threw to Page, who muffed it, Parker going to second, and in trying to stretch it to third base was thrown out; Bean out, second to first.

A & M: Farmer went to first on error by short, going to second on a passed ball. Seifert sacrificed, Farmer going to third base; Seifert out, pitcher to first; Hartsell was hit by the pitcher, and stole second base; Patton hit one to center, Farmer and Hartsell scoring, Patton going to second base. Jaynes hit to right field and Patton was thrown out at the home plate trying to score on the hit.

A & M, 2; Wake Forest 0.

Second—Wake Forest: Correll singled over third base; Utley sacrificed, going out, second to first; Correll going to second; Tuner hit one for two bases, Correll scoring; Billings hit one to left field, which Robertson gathered in; Springfield hit a fast one, which Hartsell fielded beautifully, throwing him out at first.

A & M: Stafford walked; Page sacrificed, going out, pitcher to first; Stafford going to second; Speer popped up a foul fly to third; Farmer hit in right field for two bases, Stafford scoring; Seifert hit to left field and Farmer was out on the throw in, when trying to score.

A & M 3; Wake Forest 1.

Third—Wake Forest: Cates fanned; Faucette hit one to deep center, being gathered in by a fancy catch by Farmer; Parker walked and stole second; Bean fanned.

A & M: Cates is replaced by Smith; Hartsell singles between short and third; Robertson fans; Hartsell is caught off first; Patton fans.

Fourth—Wake Forest: Correll goes out by a long fly to left field; Utley out, short to first; Turner goes out on a fine catch by Speer of a foul fly.

A & M: Jaynes fans; Stafford out on a fast play, third to first; Page fans.

Fifth—Wake Forest: Billings out on a close one, second to first; Stringfield out, pitcher to first; Smith out on a fast stop by Speer and a good one-handed catch by Page of Speer's throw.

A & M: Speer goes to first on error by first base; Farmer walks; Seifert sacrifices, advancing both runners, going out, pitcher to first; Hartsell wings at one which hits his finger, rolling in front of the plate, going out, pitcher to first; Robertson pops up to first.

Sixth—Wake Forest: Faucette hit a hot one to Stafford who gathered it in with one hand; Parker hit a high one to Hartsell; Bean hit a hot one to Stafford, who fielded it, throwing him out at first.

A & M: Patton out, second to first; Jaynes fans; Stafford out, pitcher to first.

Seventh—Wake Forest: Correll fanned; Utley out on a pop up fly gathered in by Speer; Turner out, short to first.

A & M: Pages fans; Speer fans; Farmer hits a high one to first.

Eighth—Wake Forest: Billings out on a snappy play, third to first; Hartsell made a magnificent stop of Springfield's hit over second, but threw wild; Smith hit to Hartsell who cut off Stringfield at second, Smith going to first; Faucette hit one for two bases, Smith going to third. Parker dribbled to first, going out.

A & M: Seifert popped up to third; Hartsell fanned; Robertson fanned.

The Easter Monday Baseball Game

Ninth—Wake Forest: Bean out, second to first; Correll out, pitcher to first; Utley out on a pop fly to Page.

Wake Forest	AB	R	H	PO	A	E
Faucette, c.f.	4	0	1	0	0	0
Parker, 2b.	3	0	0	0	1	0
Bean, r.f.	4	0	0	0	1	0
Correll, l.f.	4	1	1	0	1	0
Utley, 1b.	3	0	1	11	1	0
Turner, c.	3	0	1	11	1	0
Billings, s.s.	3	0	0	0	0	1
Stringfield, s.s.	3	0	0	2	2	0
Cates, p.	1	0	0	0	1	0
Smith, p.	2	0	0	0	4	0
	30	1	4	24	12	2

A & M	AB	R	H	PO	A	E
Farmer, c.f.	3	1	1	1	0	0
Seifert, c.	2	0	1	1	0	0
Hartsell, s.s.	3	1	1	1	4	2
Robertson, l.f.	4	0	0	2	0	0
Patton, 2b.	3	0	1	1	4	0
Jaynes, r.f.	3	0	1	0	0	0
Stafford, p.	2	1	0	1	3	0
Page, 1b.	2	0	0	14	2	1
Speer, 3b.	3	0	0	3	2	0
	25	3	5	24	15	3

Score by innings:

							R	H	E
Wake Forest	0 1 0	0 0 0	0 0 0				1	3	2
A & M	2 1 0	0 0 0	0 0				3	5	3

As the importance of the dance increased, so did the coverage in the local press, as indicated in this article from the Tuesday, April 9, 1912, *News and Observer*.

FRATERNITY DANCE
Enjoyable Event Last Night Attended by Many

The annual dance of Alpha Epsilon chapter of the Pi Kappa Alpha fraternity was held in Pullen Hall last night. Dancing began at 9 o'clock and lasted until 1 A.M. Mr. C.A. Steadman led the dance with Miss Ernestine Nuttall, of Rockingham. The german figures occurring with every third dance were unusually well planned and executed, the many dancers making a beautiful scene. There were about fifty couples, who declared that the occasion was one of the most enjoyable they had ever attended.

The favors were small silver change purses for the ladies and brass-bound cards for the order dancing for the gentlemen. On the cards appeared the names of the patronesses, which were as follows: Mesdames, D.M. Hill, M.T. Norris, J.I. Johnson, John McDonald, Julian Frasier, W.T. McGee, C.C. Wright, A.W. Knox, Clee Lee, W.C. Riddick, Franklin McNeil, James H. Pou, C.G. Latta, John A. Clark, Herbert B. Norris, Jr.; W.G. Peace, James McKimmon, Ella Harriss, James Boylan, A.C. Hinton. A list is also of the Fratres in Urbe appeared...."

In 1913, Wake Forest finally broke through with a win over A&M. The Tuesday, March 25, edition of the *News and Observer* reported yet another exciting, well-attended game. In accomplishing this victory, Wake Forest defeated a fine A&M team, who, led by Coach Dr. Fred Anderson, had defeated their other rivals at Carolina in the first contest between the two schools in seven years. By the end of the season, Wake Forest had accomplished one of its finest efforts to date, finishing with a 21–3 record and as State champions.

BAPTISTS DEFEAT
OLD TIME HOODOO
Thirteenth Game Gives Them
Another Beautiful
Victory.
GREAT WORK BY BOTH
Correll, Gift of Baptists, Bats in
Both and Edwards Stars—
Big Crowd Witnesses It.
Wake Forest 4: A and M 2.

This game was the thirteenth one of the series, and only the second time that Wake Forest was to emerge victorious.

The game won by the Baptists at Riddick Field was one that the reporter called "a game of marked excitement." He also noted that the contest ran somewhat long for one of such "fast play," partially because of what he referred to as the "elongated Mr. Smith, whose mysterious underhand heave kept him ever on the safe side, was chiefly responsible...." He added that the opposing pitcher, Russell, "held the ball but momentarily and pitched a very creditable game."

He explained that it wasn't really a pitchers' duel, and that "the

The Easter Monday Baseball Game

The 1913 Wake Forest team won the Easter Monday Classic and turned in one the school's finest seasons to date. Players included: PL Carter, manager; F.M. Thompson, coach; G.M. Billings, captain and shortstop; L.W. Smith, pitcher; H.H. Cuthrell, pitcher; J.R. Lowe, catcher; H.F. Faucette, center field; P.M. Utley, first base; M.L. Parker, second base; C.L. Stringfield, third base; G.W. Edwards, left field; L.C. Gooch, right field. Gooch, whose minor league scouting report ironically rated him low on intelligence and leadership, would return after a pro career to coach Wake Forest to a national title game and a regional title game (courtesy Wake Forest University).

virtue of the contest was its universality of play. Hardly a man failed to fill in well at some time. Some shown [sic] with real glossiness." He complimented the outstanding arm of the Wake Forest catcher, Lowe. "Not a Farmer, not even Arehle, the Ty Cobb of the A and M had the temerity to try second. Lowe whipped the men off the bases and literally tied the men on bags."

> There were errors but those who made them lived them down. Edwards and Gooch sinned grievously, otherwise the Farmers might have been blanked. But Edwards and Gooch hit when it was becoming and aided greatly in the size of the score. The little freshman in the left balliwick [sic]

made three of the six hits and Gooch put Russell in the hole with a bunt that sent a runner to third.

Correll for the A and M fielded beautifully and hit hard. His hot singles went through and tallied both runs. Correll is Wake Forest's gift to the Farmers. He was their great source of strength. Farmer was fleet on the base paths and Terry at first took everything. He has shown himself a great first sacker, but has not put his weight often against the ball.

Billings at short is one of the fastest men ever seen in that position. He juggles sometimes but he gets the ball from any position and throws quite well whenever he picks it up. Both Billings and Parker took difficult Texas Leaguers. Utley had no special chance to shine.

The Crowd

The crowd was typical. It was not only large, but not so demonstrative as it has been. It wasn't even so stirred as that one last year when Wake Forest broke a succession of defeats and hammered out a victory of 4 to 2. The Baptists sat in the left wing and sang ominous sounds while the Farmers on the right uttered their potent rahs. Sandwiched between them were the college girls whose "ruthers" were well-divided. The Meredith women rose often in their spring shoes and shouted. They were with their Christian brethren.

There wasn't a fight of fists. There wasn't any chance to get up one. The decisions were all in the open and clear. There was no room for kicking. Wake Forest played so tightly that there was no opportunity to penetrate the defense. There was but one man left on base. A&M had few chances to get on and when it did, Lowe knocked his man off.

Team Toted

When Correll drove a clout to deep center and Faucette stabbed it, the twenty-sixth man had been retired. The game was over, almost. Four hefty boys picked Coach Frank Thompson up and started off. But Winston hit safely to center. The boys dropped their load. Britton flew out to center and the Baptists were carried from the field. After Thompson came stringy Smith who had let the Farmers down with four hits. And each of the nine players was borne to a carriage.

But for Correll, the present of Wake Forest to the Farmers, there had been no score for the locals. He smashed two hard ones that gave no license to tally, but they did. One of these went through Edwards, the freshman left fielder, who took Correll's place.

The Easter Monday Baseball Game

And Mr. Edwards was a worthy successor. He beat Correll on hits and pulled down some whizzing liners. The exchanges are worthy of mention. By plays the game went something like this:

First Inning

Faucette skies to Patton and Parker is retire nice stop of Page to first. Gooch out, flying to Terry.

A and M — Smith takes the mound and Farmer first up, walks. Patton bunts and Lowe throws him out at first. Farmer going to second. Correll hits through Billings and Edwards, scoring Farmer and takes third. Lowe whips him out by a beautiful throw to third. Winston flies to Parker, who is nicely tackled by Faucette. One hit, one run, one error. Score A and M 1, Wake Forest 0.

Second Inning

Wake Forest — Lowe goes out, Page to Terry. Edwards singles to right and steals second and is later caught. Utley fouls high but Winston drops it and he flies out to deep left. One hit, one run.

A & M — Britton fans. Terry is thrown out by Stringfield. Jaynes fans.

Third Inning

Billings flies high to Patton. Stringfield drives hotly into Correll's hands. Smith out, Britton to Terry.

A & M — Page hits long fly to Faucette. Russell grounds from Stringfield to Utley. Farmer is retired by Billings on a dead run.

Fourth Inning

Wake Forest — Faucettes swings twice and takes the bench. Parker flies to Winston. Gooch hits single through right and goes to third. He is sent back on ground rule to second. Lane Fans. One hit, one error, no run.

A & M — Patton hits to Stringfield, who fumbles it. Lowe throws badly to first and Patton gets second. Correll hits single to Gooch, who make costly error and Patton scores. Winston is thrown out by Billings in fast fielding. Britton fans. Terry flies out to Faucette.

Fifth Inning

Wake Forest — Edwards hits safely to center. Utley hits fierce single to center, Edwards going to third. Captain Billings flies to short right and Edwards scores. While Winston fusses with Caddell, Utley takes third.

Stringfield drives deep one to center and Utley races home. Smith ends it, grounding from Britton to Terry. Two hits, two runs, no errors. Score: A & M 2 Wake Forest 2.

A & M — Jaynes fans. Page flies to Parker. Russell bats the ball against himself and is out on strikes.

Sixth Inning

Wake Forest — Faucette fans. Parker strikes out. Gooch fouls high to Winston, who drops it. And Russell fans the side, the "big end."

A & M — Farmer gets on first by error of Billings. Patton bunts and Utley stops him, Farmer going to second. Correll fouls to Lowe. Winston out to Parker.

Seventh Inning

Wake Forest — Lowe drives terrific liner over Correll, who pulls it down. Edwards fans. Utley is thrown out from Page to Terry, making long one-hand stab.

A & M — Britton hits out grounder to Billings, but Lowe's terrible right catches him off first and he warms the bench. Terry is thrown out by Stringfield to Utley. Jaynes pops up to Smith.

Eighth Inning

Wake Forest — Billings fans. Stringfield takes advantage of Patton's transgression and gets on. Smith strikes out. Edwards caught stealing.

A & M — Page out, Stringfield to Utley. Russell is thrown out by Billings. Farmer goes out on grounder in front of the plate.

Ninth Inning

Wake Forest — Faucette opens with a single to center. Parker bunts and Terry misses it, both safe. Gooch bunts and moves Faucette to third. Gooch out at first. Lowe is walked, bases full. Edwards hits to center and scores Faucette and Parker. Utley is out bunting to third. Edwards doubled at second. Two hits, two runs. Score A&M 2: Wake Forest 4.

A and M — Patton hits it nearly to left fence, but Edwards gets it. Correll hits line drive to right center, good for a triple, but Faucette spears it with one hand, a great stop. Winston singles to center. Final score. Wake Forest 4: A and M 2.

As was often the case during this period, the narrative ends abruptly with the final out of the last inning without any conclusion or summary.

The Easter Monday Baseball Game

A & M	AB	R	H	PO	A	E
Farmer, c.f.	4	1	0	1	0	0
Patton, 2b	2	1	0	5	0	2
Correll, l.f.	4	0	2	3	0	0
Winston, c	2	0	1	9	1	0
Britton, 3b	3	0	1	1	2	0
Terry, 1b	3	0	0	7	0	1
Jaynes, r.f.	3	0	0	1	0	1
Page, s.s.	3	0	0	0	4	0
Russell, p	3	0	0	0	1	0
	27	2	4	27	8	4
Wake Forest	**AB**	**R**	**H**	**PO**	**A**	**E**
Faucette, c.f.	4	1	1	4	0	0
Parker, 2b	3	1	0	3	0	0
Gooch, r.f.	2	0	1	0	0	1
Lowe, c	3	0	0	6	3	1
Edwards, l.f.	3	2	3	1	0	1
Utley, 1b	2	1	1	9	0	0
Billings, s.s.	2	0	0	2	4	1
Stringfield, 3b	2	0	0	1	3	1
Smith, p	3	0	0	1	0	0
	24	5	6	27	10	4

The following article appeared on the social page of the *News and Observer*, Friday, March 21, 1913:

DANCE EASTER MONDAY

The Alpha Epsilon Chapter of the Pi Kappa Alpha fraternity will give their annual dance in Pullen Hall at A. and M. College Easter Monday night. Invitations will be issued the latter part of the week.

The dance is always one of the most enjoyable of the spring dances given at the college and it is always one of the largest attended. The members of the chapter have done a great deal to make the dance a success and they are engaged at present looking after decorations of the hall. The dance will be led by N.S. Lachicotte, one of the senior members of the fraternity. He will be assisted by some of the Pi Kappa Alpha alumni.

The preview of the 1914 game predicted a probable easy victory for A&M, with Wake Forest only returning a few players from its 1913 squad. The article appearing in the Tuesday, April 14, *News and Observer* depicts a wild, high-scoring game, far from a pushover for A&M. The Wake Forest nine this year, though, would prove to be a hard-luck team, losing close games all season, including the three against their cross-town rivals and their two with Carolina.

A & M TAKES GAME FROM FORESTERS
Both Teams Batted Fiercely and Played Loosely in Field,
Score Eleven to Eight

The A&M nine did win, building a huge lead that caused many fans to leave early, but Wake Forest mounted a comeback that fell short. A&M's Coach Anderson could not have been pleased with the letdown. The game was played before what was described as an "immense crowd."

The writer calls the game a "weird exhibition." In the fourth, when the locals had piled up four runs and were plastering the precarious pill of Mr. Moore, the people began to leave. They prophesied a 10 to 0 defeat. In the fifth the visitors took a brace. They had two on and nobody out. They pushed the runners up a notch and a hot single sent both across.

> Coach Thompson thought a moment about a battery change, but did not make it. Correlle for A & M opened the local half with a furious drive into the bleachers. He stopped at second. He stole third and Winston cut Stringfield's feet off. Patton and Hodgin were easy infield outs and Wheeler doubled over center field scoring Winston. Gammon singled through second and registered Wheeler. Russell hit it in the same place and scored Gammon, but Russell drew up late at second.

Even after the A&M men tallied four more runs with five hits, the Wake coach elected to leave Moore in the game, apparently thinking nothing could be done to help with their team trailing 8–2.

However, at this point, the Wake batters began to take advantage of the A&M pitcher's wildness:

> The visitors had caught onto Russell who was wild and ineffective. Billings went to first on Russell's error and Ferree sent him to second on a hot single. Daniel fanned. Russell threw it over Winston's head and Billings scored. Whitley went in for Eure at second and singled to center, scoring Ferree. Moore bunted into Gammon's hands. Trust burns Liverman up. Stringfield out short to first. Two runs scored.

A&M threatened again in the seventh, but their rally was cut short by a Wake Forest double play:

The Easter Monday Baseball Game

Patton hit it into Stringfield's hands in the last of the seventh but Hodgin was safe on Whitley's error. Wheeler made it on slow work of second and Gammon took first on a drive to that bag. Russell hit a high bounder to second and Wheeler scored. Farmer went out Whitley to Hensley and Liverman grounded unassisted. Three runs.

Wake Forest scored three in the eighth. With one down, Whitley sent a double into the bleachers. Moore fanned. Trust hit to short and reached first on a wild throw. Ferree scored. Trust went down while Russell slept. Stringfield popped high to third and Gammon dropped it, Whitley and Trust scoring. Hensley flew out to second.

Correlle batting 800 sent a whizzer to center. Winston drove savagely at Stringfield who made the play of the day, recovered, shot Winston out at first and caught Correlle on the return to third. Hodgin flew to left.

Lee for Wake Forest pounded the ball into the bleachers and rested on second. Billings flew to Farmer and Ferree went out from second to first. Daniel scored Lee on a fine drive to left, but Whitley fanned. Relief at last came. But it was a hitting game and Russell has rarely fared worse.

A&M	AB	R	H	PO	A	E
Farmer, 1b	4	0	0	11	0	0
Liverman, cf	3	2	1	1	0	1
Correlle, lf	5	2	4	1	0	0
Winston, c	4	1	1	9	2	0
Patton, rf	5	0	1	0	0	0
Hodgin, 2b	5	1	0	3	3	0
Wheeler, ss	4	2	1	1	5	0
Gammon, 3b	3	3	2	1	0	1
Russell, p	4	0	3	0	1	1
	37	11	13	27	11	3

Wake Forest	AB	R	H	PO	A	E
Trust, cf	5	2	3	2	0	0
Stringfield, 3b	4	0	2	1	3	1
Hensley, 1b	5	0	0	15	1	1
Lee, lf	3	1	2	2	0	0
Billings, ss	5	1	0	1	0	2
Ferree, rf	4	2	2	0	0	0
Daniel, c	5	0	2	2	2	0
Eure, 2b	2	0	0	0	2	0
Whitley, 2b	3	1	2	1	3	1
Moore, p	4	1	1	1	4	0
	40	8	14	25	15	5

SUMMARY:

A&M	1	0	2	1	4	0	3	0	0	11
Wake Forest	0	0	0	0	2	2	0	3	1	8

Two base hits, Corrrelle 2, Stringfield, Lee, Whitley, Wheeler. Sacrifice hits, Farmer, Winston, Stringfield. Stolen bases, Liverman, Corrrelle, Winston, Patton 2, Gammon, Trust, Stringfield 2. Struck out, by Russell 7, by Moore 2. Bases on balls, off Russell 3, off Moore 2. Hit by pitched ball, Liverman. Double plays, Stringfield to Hensley to Stringfield, Wheeler to Hodgin to Farmer. Passed ball, Daniel. Wild pitch, Russell. Left on bases, Wake Forest 9, A & M 7. Umpire, Kauffman. Time of game, 1:47.
Attendance, 1,480.

The 1915 Easter Monday baseball game was greeted by an extensive article previewing the game, and then one detailing a gigantic surprise Easter Sunday snowstorm.

SNOWFALL IN THE STATE WAS NEARLY A BILLION TONS
Weather Sharp C.M. Heck Makes Some Interesting Calculations on Blizzard
RALEIGH RECEIVED ABOUT 130,000 TONS
Ten Thousand of the Largest Coal Cars Would Have Been Required to Carry Away What Fell in This City; Obelisk Twice as High as Washington Monument Could Have Been Built Out of Raleigh Supply

The article described Raleigh as "cut off from communication with the rest of the world, telephone, telegraph, electric light wires hanging in tangled masses around snapped poles; completely obstructing many streets; car system, demoralized; and streets themselves standing rivers of half-melted snow; this is the condition into which the severest snow storms on record for the month of April has plunged Raleigh. After groping, working and hoping for a whole day, there is scant promise that Sunday will furnish much relief."

The game preview article in the Sunday paper, however, noted:

Old Sol is a wonder. Yesterday morning he arose and the snowy whiteness of the earth threw back his rays with wonderful brilliancy. Then he got busy and Mr. Snow began a retreat almost as hasty as his advance. In the meantime, the A and M athletic authorities and the boys of the college have been busy, and, at some mysterious time, all the snow has been raked off the baseball park and the warm sun of today will make the diamond as firm as a hearth it is expected.... The hundreds from out of town who come here

H.E. Winston, catcher and captain of the 1915 North Carolina A&M baseball team is pictured here. Winston was the starting catcher for A&M in four Easter Monday games from 1913 to 1916 (courtesy R.G. Utley).

each year have sent word by the vanguard that they are coming, doubly full of the holiday spirit of enthusiasm.

The game went on as detailed in this Tuesday, April 6, article:

TOO MUCH JAYNES FOR WAKE FOREST
West Raleigh Collegians Win 5 to 0 from Their Ancient Adversaries
ELIIS PITCHES NICELY
Only Six Hits Garnered Off His Delivery, But Bad Break in Sixth Inning His Undoing; Jaynes Allows Only Four Hits and Makes Three Singles Himself

Despite the incredible snow event and the miraculous reversal of weather conditions, the rival teams managed to play a nearly perfect game for the first five innings. This was amazing, considering that the field must have certainly been a mess. Despite the weather, a large crowd estimated at 1,500 managed to attend what turned out to be a pitchers' duel, and it was not until the last four innings that the A&M team, now referred to as the "Techs," was able to get to Ellis, the freshman Wake hurler.

For five innings there was a battle royal with A and M held helpless before the curves of Ellis and the lightning work of the Wake Forest infield and outfield. Time and again, Lee and Trust in the outfield and Billings in the infield, and outfield too, brought rousing cheers from the grandstand and bleachers by some magnificent catch or sensational stop. Nor was A and M far behind in the sensational. Wheeler was going like a streak of lightning. Hodkin was playing airtight, twice Gammons made feature stops near the third sack and Thrash prevented Wake Forest from scoring by going behind the lower end of the football bleachers and jerking the pellet out of the atmosphere, while a Wake Forest man was racing toward home with a score, had he missed it. At the same time they were breaking good for Johnson at first and he was turning hits into outs. "Mig" Billings, in the fourth went back to third base and made what looked before he did it like an impossible catch of Gammon's Texas leaguer.

The Horseshoes Take Legs

Thus far the sensational first five innings. Then came that fateful sixth and the "monkey" got hold of Wake Forest. The first Tech batter singled. Holding let one drop and the runner went to second. The batter was walked. Then came the bad break for Ellis; next up hit a quick bounce to the pitcher. With an almost sure double and a chance for a triple play he dropped the ball from his hand and was forced to throw to first, advancing the two runners. The next A and M batter rolled one to the infield. Ellis disregarded the man coming from home and threw wild over first, two scoring. Another misplay followed and Winston counted with the third run. When the side was retired the "pep" had already gone from the Wake Forest batters and they were unable to get a new start for the concluding innings. A and M failed to get anything that looked like a hit in the seventh. In the eighth, "Hero" Jaynes got his third single and scored on Winston's timely double to left. Another miscue and A and M had scored their fifth tally and tied the game up in a sack.

The A&M pitcher, Jaynes, was the star of the game, both at the plate and on the mound. While pitching a complete-game, four-hit shutout, he also collected half of his team's six hits. For the visiting team, left fielder Lee was cited for fielding honors in a game in which he made three running

Front page of *Raleigh Times*, with coverage of Raleigh's record-breaking Easter Weekend blizzard of 1915 (courtesy R.G. Utley).

catches. Remarkably, considering the weekend weather, there were only three errors committed in the contest.

No box score is available for this game.

									R	H	E
Wake Forest	0	0	0	0	0	0	0	0	0	4	2
A and M	0	0	0	0	0	3	0	2	0	5	6	1

Attendance: around 1,500

In 1916, the longstanding Easter Monday baseball series between Wake Forest and A&M was interrupted for a year. Instead of playing each other, A&M played the Raleigh Capitals of the Class D North Carolina

State League, and Wake Forest traveled to Winston-Salem to play the Winston-Salem Twins, members of the same Class D league.

In a pregame write-up Easter Monday, April 24, 1916, the *News and Observer* stated: "Wake Forest has been the opponent of the Techs for several years past, but strained athletic relations now exist between these two institutions, and it was decided that the game should be played with the Raleigh (professional) leaguers."

At this point we do not know what caused the strained relations of 1916. Conjecture brings up three possibilities: (1) relationships between the student bodies of North Carolina A&M and Wake Forest (2) the transfer of Lee Correll from Wake Forest to North Carolina A&M after Correll had played one year of baseball for the Baptists and (3) outstanding football and baseball star Frank Thompson who became A&M baseball coach, immediately after graduation, for the 1909, 1910 and 1911 baseball seasons. And then he became head baseball coach at Wake Forest in 1911, 1912 and 1913. Movements of players and coaches between rival schools can easily cause "strained relations."

The article also gave A&M credit as the undisputed state champions of college baseball in North Carolina. The case for the championship was built on the premise that A&M defeated Trinity twice; Trinity defeated Wake Forest, who in turn beat UNC; and A&M was undefeated except for the game against Baltimore of the International League. One has to wonder how the championship race would have turned out if A&M and Wake Forest had played their Easter Monday game.

There was no doubt that this was one of A&M's finest teams. Jack Dunn, manager of the Baltimore Orioles of the International League, stated while in Raleigh during the spring training season that the A&M team was the best college team he had ever seen in action. The A&M team, led by pitcher Bill Evans, defeated the Raleigh professional team by a score of 4 to 2. By August of that summer, Evans, a native of Reidsville, North Carolina, who had transferred from Elon College was pitching for the Pittsburgh Pirates, where he worked the mound for three years. His son, Bill Jr., played for North Carolina State in four Easter Monday baseball games in the 1940s.

A & M	AB	H	O	A	E
Hodgin, 2b	5	2	1	2	1
Wharton, rf	4	1	0	0	0
Wheeler, ss	5	0	2	0	0
Winston, c	4	0	17	1	0
Correll, cf	4	2	2	0	0
Brittain, 1b	4	4	5	1	0
Evans, p	4	0	0	3	0
Thrash, lf	4	1	0	0	0
Sullivan, 3b	4	0	0	1	0
	38	10	27	8	1

Raleigh	AB	H	O	A	E
Russell, cf	5	0	3	1	0
Duncan, rf	3	3	0	0	0
Busch, ss	2	0	1	2	1
Roberts, lf	3	0	4	0	0
Yealsley, 3b	3	0	3	3	0
Williams, 1b	4	0	8	0	1
McCord, 2b	3	0	5	4	0
Carson, c	4	0	3	0	0
Munoz, p	3	0	0	1	0
Parham	1	0	0	0	0
	31	3	27	11	2

```
A&M      0 0 0   0 1 1   2 0 0   4
Raleigh  0 0 1   0 1 0   0 0 0   2
```

Runs, Hodgin, Brittain, Wheeler, Sullivan, Duncan. Three base hit, Wharton. Stolen bases, Wheeler, Brittain 2, Duncan. Base on balls, off Evans 4; off Munoz 1. Struck out by Evans 16; by Munoz 2. Wild pitch, Evans. Passed ball, Winston. Hit by pitched ball, Busch, Duncan, McCord. Double Play, Russell to Busch. Left on base, A&M 10; Raleigh 8. Time: Two hours. Umpires J. Sherwood and Upchurch. Attendance: 2,100.

In 1917, the two teams returned to their traditional Easter Monday game. In a short preview article on Monday, April 9, the *News and Observer* announced, "Weather permitting, the annual Easter baseball classic between Agriculture and Engineering College and Wake Forest College teams will be staged on Riddick Field at 3:30 o'clock and promises to draw an assemblage of college fans equal to previous year's attendance figures."

The article continued: "Both Manager Hartsell, of the Techs, and manager Billings, of the visiting club, have their players in fine condition for the fray." Note how often former players have now begun to appear in leadership roles.

The next day's paper ran the following game story:

TECHS LOSE THEIR ANNUAL CLASSIC
TO WAKE FOREST TEAM
Baptists Emerge Victor in Exciting Easter Game by 3 to 2

The article begins with this wonderful use of personification amidst a meandering sentence that seems to take on a life of its own: "A large crowd of alumni, students, supporters, ordinary fans, overcoats, and Easter flowers at Riddick Field yesterday saw Wake Forest cop the classic Easter clash from Agriculture and Engineering College in a game replete with all the thrills and heart-rending disappointments characteristic of college baseball, and marred by a doubtful decision of the umpire in the last and crucial inning." Wake Forest won the 1917 game 3–2 as their teams began to gain traction in the rivalry.

> The Techs warriors made more errors and hit for fewer bases than did the Baptists, so arithmetically figured they were due to lose. The one earned run of the game is to their credit, however, and they staged a mighty comeback towards the end of the game that was good enough to win. The Tech technique technically speaking was a fiasco in the early innings. They did everything to the pill which they should not have done. They juggled it when it rolled to them; they threw it wildly about; they muffed it when they should have squeezed it; and they caressed it fondly when the opposition was rounding the bases. In the first six innings, they thus presented Wake Forest with three runs, for though Baker was hit pretty hard, he was invincible in the pinches. Meanwhile, Monsieur Franks, on the mound for the Baptists, had everything his own way, and but once did he have to pitch himself out of a hole. He was first scored on in the eighth inning, and when the last half of the ninth began, he was two counts in the lead.
>
> The ninth round that brought so many palpitations to the hearts of the Black and Gold rooters and which increased so profoundly the profane vocabularies of the Red and White supporters opened for the Techs with Wheeler wielding the willow. The fast favorite responded to the soulful appeals from the bleachers by sending a grounder near first base which Cox found too hot to handle quickly. After Miller had made two vain attempts to bunt, Wheeler stole second; on the next ball Miller singled to right, and went to second when the ball was relayed to third to catch Wheeler. With

The Easter Monday Baseball Game

two on and nobody down, Generalissimo Billings, with strategy a la Hindenberg, beckoned the Veteran Franks, whose bombs had showed signs of failing to burst in the previous inning, from the box, and called on his officers reserve training corps for a Southpaw now known to fame as Austin. This lad came modestly and prayerfully to the mound to face Davis, put in for Thrash because the fast center gardener is supposed not too strong against lefthanders. Pitch-hitter Davis wasted little time before he slashed one of Austin's offerings over first base near the right field line. Wheeler and Miller ambled home, and Davis cavorted to third.

The home club bleachers went wild; Business Manager of the Agromeck McGeachy and Captain Hodgin ecstatically decided to recommend that Betty Howe put a matrimonial barrier forever between Davis and conscription; and the crowd was leaving the field when umpire Pillien announced that the ball was foul. The rooters dejectedly and ominously sought their seats again, and all was over, for Davis then struck out, and the next batter in an endeavor to bunt lifted a pop fly to Cox who doubled Wheeler on third.

Wake Forest scored all their runs in three innings: the third, sixth, and seventh.

With two down in the third, Captain Cox lifted a fly to the bushes in right field, on which he should have had three bases. Miller, however, after recovering the sphere, relayed it wildly to Thrash, and while the latter was chasing the pill in right field, Cox came home. Cox scored again in the sixth on two weird plays. He hit a hard line drive to right near the foul line, which Miller knocked out in an endeavor to catch, Cox taking second. Herndon lined out to third, but Ellis lifted a short fly between center and left. Castelloe muffed it after a long run, and Thrash recovered it, but held the ball while Cox came home.

In the seventh, Duncan, having advance to third on a couple infield groundouts, scored on a wild pitch.

In this article, there is even a mention of a veteran of the series returning as a leader in the cheering section for his team.

When the last of the eighth came round, "Gin" Rand, '16, recently returned from the border, assumed the leadership of the cheering in his National Guard uniform. His memory of the old yells has been considerably influenced by the army atmosphere, and they called loudly for an abandonment of watchful waiting on the part of the players. With one down, Lewis suddenly decided that the locals' bats had been used long enough for ornaments, and poked a single into left field. Heins was called out on strikes, but Hodgin singled to left, Lewis being held on second. Wharton shoved a long hit to right, and Lewis came home but Hodgin was caught at the plate by a good margin. The tale on the ninth has been told.

The article concludes with perhaps the most perplexing tidbit of information offered during the series. Was the scorekeeper betting on the opposing team? "The Techs official scorer left the bench surreptitiously in the ninth inning to settle some financial matter that seemed to stand in his favor, and a few minutes later it is supposed he went into the Wall Street Show of Despond; he never came back. His following, however, is guaranteed to be practically correct."

During this abbreviated season, the Wake Forest team was a bit of a disappointment, finishing with a .500 record, but they did make a pitch for the State title by defeating A&M twice and Carolina in the lone contest between them. Coach Hartsell's A&M team went 6–5 against college competition, 0–2 against pro teams, and canceled a part of their season due to war preparations.

Wake Forest	*AB*	*R*	*H*	*PO*	*A*
Duncan, ss	5	1	1	4	1
Leggett, 3b	4	0	2	3	1
Carlyle, 2b	5	0	0	3	3
Cox, 1b	4	2	1	8	1
Herndon, lf	4	0	0	1	0
Ellis, rf	4	0	0	2	0
Franks, p	4	0	1	0	5
Harris, cf	2	0	0	1	1
Vassey, c	4	0	2	5	3
Austin, p	0	0	0	0	0
	36	3	7	27	15

Techs	*AB*	*R*	*H*	*PO*	*A*
Hodgin, 2b	3	0	1	1	4
Wharton, 3b	4	0	2	2	3
Wheeler, ss	4	1	0	1	3
Miller, rf	4	0	3	0	0
Thrash, cf	2	0	0	2	0
Oastelloe, lf	3	0	0	2	1
Johnson, 1b	3	0	0	13	0
Lewis, c	3	1	1	6	1
Baker, p	2	0	0	0	3
Walker, p	0	0	0	0	0

The Easter Monday Baseball Game

Techs	AB	R	H	PO	A
DeBerry, p	0	0	0	0	0
	28	2	7	27	15

Wake Forest	0 0 1	0 0 1	1 0 0	3
Techs	0 0 0	0 1 0	0 1 0	2

The name State College is first used in the preview to what turned out to be an epic 14-inning battle between the two rivals in 1918. This State team, led by top-flight pitchers DeBerry and Murray, finished the season with an 11–5–1 record. Although they defeated Wake twice later in the season, they were not so lucky on Easter Monday.

WAKE FOREST WINS BIG EASTER GAME
Victorious Over Old Rivals, State College, in 14-Inning Diamond Battle

After battling for three hours and thirteen innings, the Wake Forest batters finally broke through for two runs in the top half of the fourteenth inning to secure a second straight victory over their Easter Monday rival, 3–1. While State College used three pitchers, Ellis, who had pitched very well in the game two years before as a freshman, pitched the entire game, striking out nine Tech batters and walking no one. Ellis was also a star at the plate in the decisive inning. The game, a marathon one at a time when games rarely went more than two hours, was well-attended as usual and described as "a contest that furnished one of the most exciting exhibitions seen here in several seasons."

> The game was long drawn out, but the spectators who cared nothing for supper and the evening arrangements were rewarded by an exhibition hard to equal on college diamonds in this section. The Techs secured their lone run in the third inning and Wake Forest tied the count in the fourth. Then for nine innings both teams were held scoreless by the opposing pitchers after they have been turned back upon every attempt to get within threatening distance of the plate. Several times each team seemed on the verge of staging a rally but each time the consistent defense of the fielders held the hitters in check.

Kesler Starts Rally

After trying in vain to produce the necessary rally that would bring victory, Wake Forest started its half of the fourteenth with a rush when Kesler singled to center. Pittman sent him to second with a bunt and was safe himself at first when Murray booted the ball. Brewer then walked and loaded the bases. Ridge lifted a fly near the left foul line and Johnson dropped the ball which gave the visitors one run. This run, as it developed later, would have been enough to win the game, but Wake Forest was not satisfied. Pitcher Ellis followed with a single to center and another runner crossed the plate, but a throw to the plate caught Brewer trying to score. Holding and Cox tried to send two more runners home but the former skied to right and Cox fanned for the third out.

The Techs began their fourteenth inning with a great handicap to overcome and were unable to bother Ellis' offerings sufficiently to save them from defeat. After one out, Davis singled to left center, but White and Pinch-hitter H. Lewis did not have the power to start a rally, and the game broke up amidst victorious yells from the Wake Forest students and followers.

Techs Score First

State College dented the rubber first by scoring a run in the third inning on Pressly. The locals bunched three successive doubles by DeBerry and hits that inning but were able to duplicate the bunching of hits only once more — in the sixth frame when a pretty double play executed mostly by Holding spoiled a chance for probable more runs. The Techs never threatened the visitors but twice during the entire game and were unable to solve Ellis' curves for any appreciable hitting. Both teams secured the same number of hits, but the visitors were able to bunch five at needed times.

The fielding on the part of both teams was spectacular and strong. The Baptists went through the entire game without an error while the Techs had three recorded against them and two were costly. Both infields gave the pitchers support seldom seen among college players and time after time players were robbed of seemingly sure hits. Ridge, Gurley, Woodall and Kesler were the bulwarks of the defensive and the work of those infielders could not have been better. Of course, First Baseman played his usual corking, good game but another first baseman by the name of Davis also won admiration for his smooth playing. This player had harder chances than Cox and he handled himself in fine style, scooping bad throws and keeping the visiting players off the base.

In the outfield Bill Holding, who is still at Wake Forest with his added athletic ability, was the star of the game and his conferences with Pitcher Ellis and Coach MacDonnell had a steadying effect upon the visiting team more than once. Herndon and White, the latter playing centerfield for State College, cut off hits by pretty catches.

Credit to Ellis

However, regardless of the splendid playing of both teams, the credit for the Wake Forest victory belongs to Captain Ellis whose effectiveness in the box turned back the Techs every time they attempted to threaten and whose hit in the 14th inning placed the game in the refrigerator for his team. Ellis pitched a beautiful contest from beginning to end and was better at the last than when he started. He gave no base on balls, fanned nine Techs and held the locals to four hits in the last seven frames.

Ellis was opposed by Deberry and Murray, the latter going to the rescue of Deberry in the 13th after he had allowed a hit and then walked a batter. Deberry was master of the Baptists with the exception of the fourth when they bunched three hits and for the five innings he pitched he allowed only an infield hit. Many doubted the wisdom of removing Deberry even if he did become a little unsteady in the 13th.

A large crowd of 1,500 was announced, and many of them would return again as the two teams were scheduled to play twice more during the 1918 campaign.

Wake Forest	AB	R	H	PO	A	E
Ridge, ss	7	0	1	0	6	0
Ellis, p	7	0	2	1	2	0
Holding, cf	7	1	1	7	1	0
Cox, 1b	6	0	2	12	2	0
Herndon, lf	6	0	1	5	1	0
Blanchard, c	6	0	1	10	0	0
Kesler, 3b	6	1	1	1	4	0
Pittman, 2b	5	1	1	5	3	0
Brewer, rf	3	0	0	1	0	0
	53	3	10	42	19	0

State College	AB	R	H	PO	A	E
Pressly, lf	5	0	2	2	0	0
Gurley, ss	5	0	0	3	9	1
Johnson, 3b	6	0	2	1	1	1
Floyd, rf	5	0	0	2	0	0
Davis, 1b	6	0	2	12	0	0
White, cf	5	0	1	3	1	0
Lewis, E. c	5	0	1	11	1	0
Woodall, 2b	4	0	0	8	3	0
DeBerry, p	4	1	2	0	1	0
Murray, p	1	0	0	0	0	1
Lewis, p	1	0	0	0	0	0
	47	1	10	42	16	3

Wake Forest	0 0 0	1 0 0	0 0 0	0 0 0	0 2	3
State College	0 0 1	0 0 0	0 0 0	0 0 0	0 0	1

SUMMARY: Two base hits, Holding, Deberry, Pressly. Stolen bases, Herndon, Johnson, E. Lewis 2. Sacrifice hit, Pittman. Base on balls, off DeBerry 3; off Murray 1. Struck out by Ellis 9, by DeBerry 2, by Murray 2. Passed ball, Blanchard. Double plays, Woodall to Gurley to Davis, Herndon to Blanchard, Holding to Pittman to Cox to Holding. Left on base, Wake Forest 13, State College 9. Hit by pitched ball, White, Pressly, Floyd, Woodall. Time 3:05. Umpire, Mr. Kauffman.

On April 21, 1919, State College returned to Easter Monday winning form in a game that was attended by the "entire Wake Forest student body." One of the stars for State in this game was leadoff hitter Dick Burrus, who collected two hits, stole three bases, and scored on a perfectly executed squeeze play. After playing for State, Burrus played for six seasons for Philadelphia and Boston, collecting over five hundred hits and finishing with a .291 career average. The son of a sea captain and a native of Hatteras, North Carolina, Burrus had his most promising season in 1925, when he batted .340 and led the league's first basemen in fielding. Unfortunately, he was injured that season and never able to produce again at an elevated level.

George Murray, the State pitcher, also spent parts of six seasons as a big league pitcher, winning 20 games while playing for the Red Sox, Yankees, and Senators. Murray, a Charlotte native who was nicknamed "Smiler," continued to pitch into the late '30s. He accumulated 160 wins in his minor league career, experiencing his greatest success pitching for the Class A Dallas teams, where he was called the Clark Gable of Dallas. After his playing career, Murray spent several years as an umpire before going into business.

The 1919 version of the State College team was somewhat disappointing, finishing with a 12–11 record, splitting games with Wake Forest. Although Murray's pitching was outstanding in the Easter Monday game, his work was less than stellar earlier in the season. During the winter, the pitcher had been run over by a truck and had not fully recovered when the season began.

Playing a briefer schedule, Coach Carlyle's Wake 9 finished with an 11–4 record and laid claim to the state championship, the first time since 1913.

The Easter Monday Baseball Game

STATE COLLEGE IS VICTORIOUS AGAIN
Wins Easter Classic from Wake Forest by Count of Four to Three

State College was the winner in the 1919 game by a score of 4–3. While no specific attendance number was recorded, it was noted that it was one of the largest if not the largest crowd ever at State's Riddick Field.

Though the game was well played and filled by outstanding catches, for the reporter, the most impressive part was the size and enthusiasm of the crowd. The "pretty baseball weather" combined with the holiday spirit to draw "fans and fannies" from all parts of the region. Among the colleges well represented were Wake Forest, Meredith, Peace and St. Mary's, while alumni of both contesting colleges garnered a large share of the audience. Numerous autos parked around the playing field made the scene resemble a typical conference game.

Murray Effective

"The Techs won the game by more fleetness on the paths and bunching long hits in one inning together with the effectiveness of George Murray." A local hurler, Murray was mostly responsible for the victory and only had one difficult inning "when the visitors made all their runs—and was master of the game throughout the balance of the contest." Outside of the second and third innings, Wake Forest was held to only two hits. They came in the sixth and ninth innings.

"Sack" Barnes, moundsman for Wake Forest, also pitched a nice game but he was continually in trouble and allowed Tech runners on bases in every frame. His most effective work was in the pinches, but there was one pinch in which he failed to emerge at the best end. This was in the sixth inning when State College rallied for enough runs to capture the contest.

In the field, Wake Forest was led by the play of Ellis, Duncan, and Whitehurst, the latter of which made an outstanding running catch. "Duncan, at short, and Ellis, at second, played a wonderful fielding game and scooped up grounders that seemed impossible. In the second Ellis made a pretty one-hand stab of Murray's wicked bounder and threw the runner out." Blanchard was the top hitter for the Baptists, reaching on a single and a double in his four at-bats.

"Pretty" Catch by Park

Two of the highlights for State College were a tremendous catch by Park and the outstanding base running by Burrus. "Burrus got to first three times, stole three bases and executed a nice squeeze score. It was his fleetness that gave the Techs their first run. Park's catch was the prettiest seen on the college diamond in some time. He had to race to the embankment in center for Blanchard's deep drive in the eighth inning and then fell as he caught the ball after a hard run." Park also smashed a triple in the sixth that started the game-deciding rally.

"The Techs were first to score. They secured their initial marker in the opening frame when Burrus gave a nice exhibition of fleetness on the paths." He began the rally by beating out a grounder to first, and was credited with an infield hit. Next, he stole second and was able to reach third on Blanchard's first passed ball. "With P. Johnson at the bat, Burrus made a dash for home. Johnson fouled the ball. On the next pitch Burrus again sprinted for the plate and Johnson bunted." Kesler had no choice but to throw to first for the out, allowing Burrus to score.

Baptists' Runs in Third

"In the third inning the Baptists sent their supporters into the realm of joy by annexing three runs which put them into the lead. The visitors had missed a glorious opportunity to score in the second when a double by Blanchard and single by Kesler went for naught as the other three outs were easy. However, in the third Pittman, after one out, scratched a hit at short. Barnes then hit to Sipe, who tossed to second for a force-out." When Black failed to cover the bag, both runners were safe. Pittman advanced to third on the play. Barnes then stole second while Blanchard struck out. "Kesler did better and dropped a wicked bounder in front of the plate. He beat Murray's throw to first and Pittman scored while Barnes hurried to third." Kesler then stole second, after which Ellis hit a grounder that went through Burrus's legs, scoring both Barnes and Kesler. "Ellis was thrown out at second after the throw to the plate and Wake Forest's run-getting was at an end."

The Easter Monday Baseball Game

TECH'S BIG FRAME

"State College's big inning and jubilant occasion was the sixth frame when the Techs secured the three runs that gave them the victory." Park began the inning with a huge triple to right field. Johnson, P. followed with a base on balls and immediately stole second. Johnson, W. with third and second occupied and no outs, missed his best chance of the season to clean up. He didn't. "The Sorrell top catcher whiffed the azure three times and sat down discouraged. George Murray then hit the chance of winning his own game and also fell down." He struck out as well. With two out, Wake Forest fans were more cheerful. Pressly, however, upset all calculations by doubling near the foul line in left field. Park and P. Johnson scored and the count was tied. Hudson followed with a fast grounder which went through Ellis, at second, and Pressly touched the rubber with what proved to be the winning run. Black ended the rally by striking out. During State College's big inning, Barnes managed to strike out three men, but also walked a batter and allowed both a triple and double.

HAD FEW CHANCES

"Wake Forest had only one chance to score after the third frame. That was in the sixth when runners were on second and first with only one out. Gwynn flied to Sipe at short and White hit to the same infielder, who tossed him out at first. In the ninth, White scratched a hit to short after two out but Austin, a pinch hitter, gave Pressly an easy chance in left field."

State College had runners on the bases in every inning and had several opportunities to score other than the first and the sixth. "In the second, Pressly registered an infield hit and stole second after one out. Hudson then flew to Ellis and Black was thrown out by Duncan. In the fourth, Murray tripled to center after one out, but was caught at the plate on an attempted squeeze play."

The style of play in this game is indicative of the era. With ten stolen bases, sacrifices, a squeeze play, and another attempted one, the teams made the most of their combined thirteen hits. Nineteen nineteen is typically seen as the end of the dead ball era, and the long ball and the power game would soon become a part of the Easter Monday series.

The two rival teams were yet to play their third game of the baseball series on May 5. The game would mark the end of the Tech's 1919 season.

Wake Forest	AB	R	H	PO	A	E
Duncan, ss	4	0	0	0	4	0
Pittman, 1b	4	1	1	10	0	0
Barnes, p	4	1	0	0	1	0
Blanchard, c	4	0	2	8	0	1
Kesler, 3b	4	1	2	0	2	0
Ellis, 2b	3	0	0	2	3	1
Gwynn, cf	3	0	0	1	1	0
White, lf	4	0	1	2	0	0
Whitehurst, rf	3	0	0	1	0	0
Austin	1	0	0	0	0	0
	34	3	6	24	11	2

State College	AB	R	H	PO	A	E
Burrus, 1b	3	1	2	9	0	1
Park, cf	4	1	1	2	0	0
Johnson, P., 3b	2	1	0	0	1	0
Johnson, W., c	4	0	0	9	1	0
Murray, p	3	0	1	2	1	0
Pressly, lf	4	1	2	2	0	0
Hudson, rf	4	0	0	0	0	0
Black, 2b	3	0	0	1	3	1
Sipe, ss	3	0	1	2	1	0
	30	4	7	27	7	2

Wake Forest	0 0 3	0 0 0	0 0 0	3
State College	1 0 0	0 0 3	0 0	4

SUMMARY: Two base hit, Blanchard, Pressly. Three base hit, Murray, Park. Stolen base, Burrus 3, Kesler 2, Johnson, P., Johnson, W., Pressly, Hudson, Barnes. Sacrifice hit, Johnson, P. Base on balls off Barnes 1. Struck out by Barnes 7, by Murray 7. Passed ball, Blanchard 2, Johnson, W. Hit by pitcher, Murray, Ellis, Gwynn. Double plays, Gwynn to Pittman. Left on base, Wake Forest 6, State College 6. Time 1:45. Umpire, Mr. Doak.

The result of the 1920 game, as reported in the April 6, *News and Observer*, was the biggest one-sided affair in the history of the Easter Monday series. Coach Holding's 12–6 club, which lost the state title by percentage points, had no trouble figuring out the State College pitchers. Despite this devastating loss, Coach Fetzer's charges completed a highly successful 16–6 campaign, avenging themselves twice against Wake Forest. They were again led by the pitching of DeBerry and Murray, now upperclassmen.

BAPTISTS CLEAN UP OLD RIVALS
Annual Easter Game Is Runaway Victory for Wake Forest College
STATE COLLEGE GOES DOWN BY SCORE OF 27 TO 6
Thirty-five Hundred People Brave Cold Wave and Wake Forest Student Body Almost to a Man Sees Old Gold and Black Triumph; Baptists Show Hitting Punch

Perhaps what happened in 1920 signaled the beginning of the live ball era. Certainly everything that Wake Forest swung at seemed to come to life. As the writer so eloquently describes, "Wake Forest started something with the first ball Deberry put over the plate in the first inning and kept it up until the last. When the score was counted the visitors had scored twenty-seven times to the six for State College, had pounded out thirty hits and had quit because they were tired, the crowd was leaving and it was getting mighty cold and almost dark." No time is listed for this game, but it must be assumed that it was one of the longer ones of the series and reason enough to enforce some kind of mercy rule.

Despite the cold weather, a huge crowd assembled for the spring classic:

> Fully 3,500 spectators braved the chilly blasts that swept across the field and jammed the stands to capacity. Long before the hour set for playing the crowd began to gather, and when Umpire Barney called the game at 3:45 the overflow attendance made ground rules necessary. Peace, St. Mary's and Meredith were well represented, a section of the concrete stands being reserved for the fair visitors. The Wake Forest student body, almost to a man, was present and kept the air filled with snappy yells and college songs.

On this day, State College was mostly noted for their lack of representation both on the field and in the stands. Not that the Techs had anything to root for, but either the majority of the West Raleigh aggregation was spending the holidays at home or they soon gave up the job as a hopeless proposition. The team seemed to respond to the lack of support by giving no reason to make it otherwise.

Having so often been on the losing end of the rivalry, it would seem that Wake Forest had decided to exact revenge all in one game.

It was a great game for those who wanted to see Wake Forest get revenge on the Techs for any games they may have lost to them in the years that have gone, and the Baptist contingent, which was here in large numbers, had the best time of their lives. But there is no joy in West Raleigh over the results, for the State College aggregation was unable to do anything with Barnes. He worked underhand ball that looked like any high school boy could hit, but the opposing batters missed it inches off the mark and looking foolish when they recovered balance. Barnes seemed to have everything he needed and plenty in reserve. Up to the final inning he struck men out when he pleased, and there was mighty little safe hitting. In the final frame, he loosened up and allowed some of the second string men who came in for a little fun to get some hits to their credit.

Wake Forest Hits at Will

Both pitching and fielding were huge problems for State College:

Deberry who was warmed up for the game started off badly and got no better. Wake Forest hit almost at will, clouting the ball all over the field and to the embankment in left and into the hedges on the outskirts of the field. Two and three bases were the rule, but some of the visitors were content with singles. Going became so bad for Deberry in the fifth inning that he was relieved after Wake Forest team had batted around. Floyd took his place and retired the next two men, but Wake Forest soon got on to his delivery and hit him just about as hard. Black finally finished up the game for the home team, and he was also easy picking.

Support of the State College pitchers was dismal. Even though many balls were hit out of the reach of the fielders, they managed to commit an amazing ten errors and made none of the spectacular defensive plays that the series had always featured.

None of the State pitchers had very good support in the field. On the other hand, though he allowed seven runs on eleven hits, Wake Forest's Barnes kept the State batters in check, striking out thirteen.

The weather grew colder as the game advanced, and Easter crowds, dressed for the occasion, shivered through half the game and then gave it up as a bad job. Some of the more hardy ones, and some who had been on good terms with the weather man and knew the cold wave was coming, took their overcoats also, remained with the joyous Wake Forest crowds until the end of the game.

State	AB	R	H	PO	A	E
Faucette, 1b	5	2	2	10	1	1
Gurley, c	3	0	0	4	0	0
Parsons, c	2	0	0	4	0	1
Wood, 2b	3	0	1	1	1	0
Black, 2b-p	1	0	0	1	1	0
Johnson, J., p-3b	4	1	2	2	2	2
Norwood, cf	3	1	1	2	0	0
Routh, cf	1	1	1	0	0	0
Zackary, rf	1	0	0	0	0	1
Murray, rf	2	0	0	2	0	0
Kirkpatrick, lf	5	0	3	0	0	1
Sipe, ss	3	0	0	1	3	2
DeBerry, p	2	0	0	0	2	1
Floyd, p	2	0	0	0	2	0
Castello, 2b	2	1	1	0	1	0
	39	6	11	27	13	9
Wake Forest	AB	R	H	PO	A	E
Stringfield, ss	8	3	4	1	2	0
Jennette, cf	7	5	4	1	1	0
Ellis, 2b	7	3	4	4	1	0
Duncan, 1b	7	2	3	7	0	0
Johnson, lf	6	2	3	0	0	1
Ragsdale, rf	7	4	5	0	0	0
Kosler, 3b	6	2	2	0	2	0
Boylin, c	5	2	1	13	2	0
Wake Forest	AB	R	H	PO	A	E
Barnes, p	7	4	4	1	0	0
	60	27	30	27	8	1

```
           Wake Forest   2 0 1   2 7 3   12 0 0   27
           State         0 1 1   0 0 0    0 0 4    6
```

SUMMARY: Two base hits, Barnes, Stringfield 2, Kesler, Kirkpatrick. Three base hits, Jennette, Barnes, Ragsdale, Johnson, J. Bases on balls, Off DeBerry 0, off Floyd, 1, off Barnes 1, off Black 0. Hit by pitched ball, Barnes. Struck out by DeBerry 3, by Barnes 13, by Floyd 1, by Black 2. Left on base, Wake Forest 9, State 8. Stolen bases, Faucette, Kirkpatrick, Jennette, Ellis, Ragsdale. Sacrifice hits, Johnson, Kosler, Boylin. Umpire, Mr. Barney of Buffalo.
Attendance: 3,500.

THE ROARING TWENTIES

1921–1930

Despite all the devastation of war and illness, North Carolina managed to add another 350,000 people to the population. The state began the decade known as the "Roaring '20s" as the second most industrialized state in the South. The three top industries, tobacco, textiles, and furniture, now produced a billion dollars in revenue annually.

The decade began with the passage of two important pieces of legislation. First, the 18th Amendment, which prohibited the sale of alcohol, was passed. Later in the year, over the objection of North Carolina's legislators, the 19th Amendment, allowing women the right to vote, finally received the two-thirds majority necessary to make it a law.

At the state level, plans were made to build a highway system which would connect the seats of each county with quality roads. In High Point, the Southern Furniture Exposition Center opened, and by mid-decade, North Carolina had become the leading manufacturer of wood furniture. In 1924, the state surpassed Massachusetts in textile production value. The shift from an agrarian economy to an industrial one accelerated as roads are improved and access to electricity was increased.

Union activity in the textile mills began in earnest toward the end of the decade. The Loray Mill strike of 1929 resulted in the tragic deaths of the Gastonia police chief and the legendary activist Ella Mae Wiggins. A decade that included many improvements in education, industry, and individual rights ended with the Wall Street crash and the beginning of the Great Depression.

The first Easter Monday game of the new decade was an epic affair. First it was rained out; then the following week, a twelve-inning tie was stopped by darkness; and finally the following Tuesday the tie was broken in a low-scoring eleven-inning battle.

RAIN PUTS SPEEDY END TO BALL GAME
State College, Wake Forest Battle Barely Commenced; Spectators Drenched

Even with a large crowd present, the first attempt was doomed by a spring downpour:

> One minute before the scheduled time for calling the annual Easter Monday baseball game between State College and Wake Forest, the rain storm which had been impending broke. Living up to the tradition that an Easter Monday ball game must be played, regardless of weather conditions, the battle was commenced. However, after one-third of one inning had been run off, the downpour became so furious that no tradition, even one which had survived two snows and sundry ordinary rains could defy it.
>
> Failure to play the game was a keen disappointment to what would have undoubtedly been the largest crowd ever to see a college baseball game in Raleigh, and not a few of the would be spectators received the drenching of their lives. Hundreds, who would have been late arrivals turned back on their way to the park, while hundreds of others, more weatherwise, scanned the heavens, were duly warned, and stayed at home. An even larger contingent, running into the thousands, had not moved over from the motor-cycle races at the State Fair Grounds. [This is the first mention of such an event on an Easter weekend.]
>
> But in spite of all these considerations, close to 3,000 fans were in the park when the first drop of rain fell. That drop was the signal of departure for a goodly percentage of the crowd. They were speedily joined by an ever increasing number, but several hundred of the faithful stuck it out only to rue their optimism. When the deluge broke, all those without automobiles, and well enclosed automobiles at that, were in for the wetting of their lives. They rushed out of the park like drowned rats and sought shelter in dormitories and other college buildings, but there was not enough shelter available to go around, or at least a number of the seekers were not sufficiently acquainted with their surroundings to enable them to find it. Nobody stayed out through all the rain, but fifteen minutes after it began they were still milling around by the hundred....

COLLEGES BATTLE TO A TWELVE INNING TIE
Darkness Ends Play Off of State–Wake Forest Game With Score Standing 3 to 3

EACH CLUB SCORES ONE TALLY IN FINAL FRAME
Game Stand Off Between Better Pitching of Murray and Baptists' Superior Support

The better support of Wake Forest was a perfect stand off for the better pitching of Murray yesterday and after twelve innings of bang up baseball, with each club scoring its third run in the final stanza by way of an added thriller, darkness yesterday put an end to the State College Wake Forest baseball game and the series now stands just where it did before the deluge of Easter Monday. [Note: in this game, the coaches, Utley and Doak, served as umpires.]

The two clubs will resume the fray this afternoon at Wake Forest. Johnson is expected to start for Wake Forest, with Austin a possibility, while Curtis will do the pitching honors for State....

So finally, eight days after Easter Monday, the game was decided in a contest that took place at Wake Forest instead of the traditional location at Riddick Field on the State College campus.

WAKE FOREST BEATS STATE IN ELEVENTH
Blow to Road by Ellis Gives Baptists Decision by Margin of One to Nothing

JOHNSON AND CURTIS BOTH IN GREAT FORM
Two Youngsters Allow Only Three Hits Apiece Over the Entire Eleven Innings

by JONES.

When the 1921 game was finally completed, it stood in stark contrast to the contest of the year before. While Wake Forest once again took the measure of their rivals, they did so as a result of fine pitching rather than relentless hitting: "Wake Forest, April 5 — After pitching a masterly game up to the eleventh inning, Curtis today made the fatal mistake of grooving one for Ellis, with the result that said Ellis drove the horse hide out into the street which had been fenced off as a part of the outfield, scoring Stringfield from second and giving Wake Forest the game by margin of one to nothing."

Jones, whose byline appeared here for the first time, noted: "The game was a fitting sequel for yesterday's twelve innings without a decision, as far as thrills are concerned. But, it was a much better brand of baseball that was served up here this afternoon."

The Easter Monday Baseball Game

After the marathon game of the previous afternoon, the coaches each went with a freshman pitcher:

Murray and Barnes, two far famed veterans were replaced today by two men in their first year of college baseball, Curtis and Johnson, and how those youngsters did pitch! It would be a carping critic indeed who assumed to draw any invidious comparisons between them or to take from the glory of one in order to add to the prestige of the other.

Each pitched a perfect brand of ball for the orthodox distance and though Curtis weakened in the eleventh, he was somewhat the victim of circumstances and made the mistake of giving Ellis one where he wanted it per instructions from the bench. Three hits apiece were what they allowed during the entire eleven innings, and even that does not tell the whole story. Faucette's blow was the veriest of scratches, which might have been charged up to Kesler, while S. Johnson's bingle bounced off of Blue's shins. Each youngster also displayed remarkable control, allowing just four bases on balls, equally divided between them. In addition, however, Curtis hit one batsman and Johnson also had somewhat the best of it in strike outs, whiffing twelve to seven for his opponent.

State was only able to advance a runner as far as third base once in the seventh inning, when future major leaguer Redfearn reached second on Stringfield's wild throw to first and then stole third.

Wake Forest waited even longer to get a runner, but when that station was finally reached in the ninth inning only poor base running prevented the Baptists from winning the ball game then and there. S. Johnson started off the inning by driving one against Blue's shins for a bingle. The State infield then had a momentary collapse, and chalked up the only error accredited to the Techs during the game. Curtis made a wild throw on Stringfield's bunt and after Jeannette had popped up in an effort to sacrifice, another bobble, this time by Redfearn filled the sacks with only one out.

At this juncture, Coach White sent in Duncan to hit for Barnes. The ex-captain delivered with a fly to left field on which Johnson could have easily scored, but the pitcher was overcautious and hugged the sack. All three runners were stranded for the best Ragsdale could do was a popup to the infield.

But the next time the Baptists started something they saw it through. Twas in the aforementioned eleventh frame. Stringfield drew a base on balls and was sacrificed down. Curtis got into a hole with Ellis, getting two balls and three strikes. A shout came from the State bench to "groove it." So Curtis did, Ellis landed on the offering and another ball game became history.

Aside from the pitchers, Johnson, the State College third baseman was the bright and shining light of the game. He collected two clean bingles on a day when hits were exceedingly scarce and accepted five chances without a semblance of an error. But smart infield plays were the rule rather than the exception for the entire outfit one each side. Stringfield, who along with Johnson, promises to be a unanimous choice for the All-State team made one error, but he also did some splendid work.

The makeup game was destined to join the celebrated history of this rivalry as one of the "hardest fought" in the long series of "closely contested affairs" between the neighboring schools. Though another contest between the two was not scheduled, Jones suggested that one, possibly two more contests might be added to the schedule to determine which team was the best.

Box score for the first game, which ended in a tie:

Wake Forest	AB	R	H	PO	A	E
Stringfield, ss	4	1	1	1	4	0
Jennette, cf	5	0	1	6	0	0
Ellis, 2b	5	0	0	4	1	0
Ragsdale, rf	5	0	0	0	0	0
Kesler, 3b	5	0	0	5	0	0
Johnston, lf	3	1	1	2	0	0
Armstrong, 1b	5	0	1	8	1	1
Hollowell, c	5	0	2	9	0	0
Barnes, p	5	1	0	1	4	0
	42	3	6	36	10	1
State College	AB	R	H	PO	A	E
Faucette, 1b	6	0	0	14	1	0
Kirkpatrick, rf	6	1	2	3	0	1
Norwood, lf	6	2	2	1	0	0
Johnson, 3b	5	0	2	2	3	0
Weathers, lf	5	0	1	1	0	1
Redfearn, ss	5	0	1	2	3	1
Murray, p	4	0	2	0	2	1
Blue, 2b	2	0	0	1	1	0
Arthur, 2b	1	0	0	0	2	0
Tolar, 2b	0	0	0	0	0	1
Parsons, c	4	0	0	12	1	0
Costelloe	0	0	0	0	0	0

The Easter Monday Baseball Game

State College	AB	R	H	PO	A	E
Floyd	1	0	0	0	0	0
	45	3	10	36	13	5

Wake Forest	0	1	1	0 0 0	0 0 0	0 0 1	3
State College	1	0	0	0 0 0	0 1 0	0 0 1	3

Summary: Earned runs: Wake Forest 1; State College 2. Two base hits: Johnston, Kirkpatrick 2, Norwood 2, Johnston 2, Weathers. Sacrifice hits, Stringfield 2, Jeanette, Ellis, Ragsdale, Weathers, Murray. Double play, Stringfield to Ellis to Armstrong. Base on balls, off Barnes 4, off Murray 2. Struck out by, Barnes 8, Murray 9. Hit by pitcher, Stringfield. Passed ball, Parson. Left on bases, Wake Forest 10, State College 8. Time 2:47. Umpires Utley and Doak (team coaches also).
Attendance: 3,500.

Replay the next day:

State College	AB	R	H	PO	A	E
Faucette, 1b	4	0	1	14	0	0
Kirkpatrick, rf	3	0	0	1	0	0
Norwood, lf	4	0	0	2	0	0
Johnson, 3b	4	0	2	1	4	0
Weathers, lf	4	0	0	2	0	0
Redfearn, ss	4	0	0	1	4	1
Blue, 2b	4	0	0	3	4	0
Parsons, c	4	0	0	7	0	0
Curtis, p	4	0	0	0	3	1
	35	0	3	31	15	2

Wake Forest	AB	R	H	PO	A	E
Stringfield, ss	3	1	0	3	4	1
Jeanette, cf	4	0	0	0	0	0
Ellis, 2b	4	0	1	1	2	0
Barnes, 1b	3	0	0	13	0	1
Ragsdale, rf	4	0	0	0	0	0
Kesler, 3b	4	0	0	1	3	0
Johnston, lf	4	0	1	1	0	0
Hollowell, c	3	0	0	11	4	0
S. Johnson, p	1	0	1	0	4	0
Duncan, 1b	1	0	0	3	0	0
	31	1	3	33	17	2

State College	0 0 0	0 0 0	0 0 0	0 0 0
Wake Forest	0 0 0	0 0 0	0 0 0	0 1 1

Summary: Earned runs, Wake Forest 1. Two base hits, Ellis. Sacrifice hits, Stringfield, Jeanette. Base on balls, off Curtis 2; off S. Johnson 2. Struck out by S. Johnson 12; by Curtis 7. Stolen bases, Ellis, Johnston, Faucette (2), Redfearn. Hit by pitcher: Hollowell. Left on base: State College 4; Wake Forest 7. Time 2:35. Umpires: Utley and Doak. Attendance 1,500.

The 1922 game was previewed twice in the *News and Observer*, once in an article that detailed the history of a tradition begun in the '90s and now over twenty years old. The second article noted the importance of the game in regard to the eventual state championship, noting that the only game of similar significance was the Carolina-Virginia game, played annually in Greensboro. This article is the first to refer to the West Raleigh team as North Carolina State and to give a detailed comparison of player and team statistics.

In 1922, Coach Hartsell led a largely inexperienced group of State players to a successful 13-7 record, including this game. Wake Forest, under Coach Hoge, ended their season at 12-9. Their losses included games against two minor league teams, two games with State, and their one contest against Carolina.

STATE COLLEGE IS VICTOR IN ANNUAL EASTER GAME, 4-2
Wake Forest Outhit and Outfielded in Game Containing Good and Bad Ball
RUTH FEATURES WITH FOUR HITS IN A ROW
Four Thousand People See Game Which Requires Two Hours and 25 Minutes

In the 1922 game, State College regained their footing as the dominant team in the rivalry. The State team won the game in the field and at the plate in the latest episode of the Easter Classic in a game described as a mix of good and bad baseball and "riotous confusion." The final score was 4 to 2.

Poor fielding and strong hitting kept both pitchers in constant trouble. Each team left nine runners on base, which resulted in many missed opportunities and tense moments. "What was none too good a ball game at best was further marred by intermittent bickering over the decisions of Umpire Pete Holland, who was assigned for the 1922 season by the Piedmont League, but released by President Bramham (of the National Association of Professional Baseball Leagues) before the opening game on the ground of further investigation of the record of Holland, who has worked in several leagues."

Four Thousand See It

A record four thousand fans attended the game and stayed to the end although it "dragged on" for nearly two and a half hours. "Both student bodies were on hand in force and were augmented by mass delegations from each of the three girls' colleges."

All four runs scored by State College were unearned, but the West Raleigh team combined enough strong hitting with the errors to knock Stanley Johnson out of the game by the sixth inning. John Caddell, who had resigned as the Wake Forest coach before the season began, returned to the bench to direct the Baptists' efforts for this game.

Buck Edwards, the Wake Forest right fielder who came on in relief with two on and one out, "retired the side and breezed from the remainder of the game safely, although yielding two base hits in the ninth."

"Harry Curtis, who was Hartsell's [the State College coach] pitching selection," got into a serious jam in the first inning when he hit a batter, walked another, and eventually gave up a run. But after that, the tall right-hander kept the runners off the bases "except in the fifth, when the Baptists bunched doubles for their second marker."

Ruth Blossoms Out

Interestingly enough, bearing in mind who was the star of the national baseball scene at the time, the top player for State College this day was Rufus Ruth. State's leftfielder, who had not done well all year, had a breakout game, going four for four, scoring two important runs, and making two exceptionally difficult catches in left field. As the writer noted, "'Babe' burst yesterday with all the brilliance of an August sun at high noon."

> Though each threatened constantly, neither club scored except in the first and fifth frames, each team counting a warmly disputed run in the opening chapter and the Baptists counting on one more in the fifth, only to take the field and make three errors, which combined with the same number of hits, gave the Techs a lead of 4 to 2, the same standing until the end of the argument.
>
> A hit batsman, a base on balls and Blue's error on Armstrong's bunt placed the first three Wake Forest runners on the bases without any of them having had a legal time at bat.

In this game, there was no shortage of controversial calls. "The situation looked dubious indeed for the Techs, but only one runner scored and that lone tally produced a lively argument. Edwards, the fourth batter up set a precedent which remained unbroken during the entire afternoon by going out. Poole was next up and batted one to Redfearn who sent the ball home in ample time to beat the runner. The big question was whether Parsons touched the plate." The umpire and some of the spectators believed the runner beat the throw, but all of the State College fans and others more neutral in their sympathies believe that the runner was clearly out.

Curtis Settles Down

"The argument over, Curtis settled down to real pitching. Barnes forced Ellis at the plate due to the latter's slow work, and Albritton retired the side by striking out."

The controversy continued in the State half of the inning. "State evened the count in its half with somewhat shorter work. Ruth began the game with a slashing single to left, was sacrificed to second from that bag when Johnson cut loose a wild pitch, Dennis not knowing the ground rule and loafing on the job of getting the ball back." This particular ground rule was made more complicated by a division of passed balls into two classes, and it caused another huge argument from the visiting team.

"Neither club threatened again until the fourth when Saxe Barnes lashed out a triple with one out, but scoring was prevented by two neat fielding plays, Ruth making a running catch of a liner to left and holding the runner at third." Redfearn continued his brilliant play at shortstop, catching a line drive as he slid across second base to end the inning.

"In the fifth the Baptists had more luck when they scored on a double, a steal and a hit. In the bottom of the frame, with the contest still up in the air," the Techs mounted the biggest rally of the afternoon. The team batted all the way around, scoring three runs and leaving the bases loaded.

It was an afternoon of surprise hitting as well.

Parsons, rated the weakest hitter on either club, began the inning with his first of two hits and took second when Albritton kicked the pill. Curtis then walked and the fireworks started on the next batter, Ruth beating out an infield and Saxe Barnes throwing the ball away. The play put Curtis on third and in an effort to keep him there, Dennis held the ball too long after dropping Norwood's third strike and the bases were choked.

They did not remain so long, for the Baptists had not finished erroring, nor had State desisted from hitting.

Johnson hit a line drive single and Curtis scored. Ruth, however, was nearly picked off third with Norwood a long way off base as well at second. But Barnes dropped the ball, and both runners made it back safely. Redfearn sent the third run home by a grounder to short for the first out of the inning, and while the bases were again filled when Holland walked, the next two batters were easy outs, and the scoring for the day ended.

More Anxious Moments

But anxious moments were still abundant. Wake Forest threatened seriously only once more, when Small, who had relieved Edwards in right field, singled and took third when Lassiter failed to see the throw to catch the runner off the bag. The ball was thrown away again when returned to the diamond and Small went home, only to be sent back, after another argument, on the ground rule which makes an overthrow to first or third base a dead ball. Small stayed on third despite Ruth's error in dropping a fly ball, and the Baptists' last chance was a matter of history.

Edwards came in in relief after Parsons and Ruth had singled in the sixth and struck out four of the eight hitters that he faced, but allowed two hits, between strike outs, in the ninth.

"Another argument with the umpire was precipitated in the seventh, when Parsons was cut off first, the umpire being unable to see the play because the bag was in the way."

Wake Forest	AB	R	H	O	A	E
Stringfield, ss	3	1	0	0	4	0
Ellis, 2b	4	0	1	5	0	0
Armstrong, 1b	3	0	0	9	1	0
Edwards, rf, p	4	0	0	0	0	0
Poole, cf	4	0	0	0	0	0

Wake Forest	AB	R	H	O	A	E
Barnes, 3b	4	0	2	1	2	2
Albritton, lf	3	0	0	1	1	1
Dennis, c	4	0	0	7	1	1
S. Johnson, p	2	1	1	0	2	0
Small, rf	2	0	2	1	0	0
	33	2	6	24	11	4

N.C. State	AB	R	H	O	A	E
Ruth, lf	5	1	4	1	0	1
Norwood, cf	2	0	0	3	0	0
R. Johnson, rf	4	0	1	1	0	0
Redfearn, ss	3	0	0	2	1	0
Holland, 3b	3	0	0	1	2	0
Lassiter, 1b	3	0	0	11	0	0
Blue, 2b	4	0	1	0	3	1
Parsons, c	4	1	2	7	0	0
Curtis, p	2	1	1	0	4	1
	30	4	9	27	12	3

```
Wake Forest   1 0 0   0 1 0   0 0 0   2
N.C. State    1 0 0   0 3 0   0 0 0   4
```

Earned runs: Wake Forest 2; N C State 0. Two base hits: S. Johnson, Ellis. Three base hits: Barnes. Sacrifice hits: Armstrong, Norwood (2), Stringfield, Curtis. Base on balls off: Curtis 1, off S. Johnson 4. Struck out: by Curtis 6, by S. Johnson 4, by Edwards 4. Stolen bases: Stringfield, Ellis. Hit by pitcher: Stringfield (by Curtis). Wild pitch: S. Johnson. Passed balls: Parsons. Left on base: Wake Forest 9; N C State 9. Umpire: Holland.
Attendance: 4,000.

"War Cry Rings in Baptist College, 'On to Raleigh,'" the detailed 1923 Easter Monday preview article proclaimed in the April 2 *News and Observer*. And the writer who predicted that the NC State boys would be evenly matched with the undefeated Wake Forest nine was correct.

N.C. State and Wake Forest Battle to Sixteen Inning Tie 6–6
Sensational Rally Saves Baptists in Ninth Inning
Pitcher Stanley Johnson Hero as He Shows Way with Double
    RALLY CAME SUDDENLY WITH STATE UNAWARE
Wake Forest Threatened to Win in Fourteenth but State Rallied"

In a marathon game which saw each team send 57 batters to the plate, the two old rivals fought to a sixteen-inning 6–6 tie. The game was described as one "replete with thrills as any ever witnessed on the Riddick Field."

"Both teams brought the spectators to their feet on two thrilling occasions with spectacular rallies when both White and Red and Old Gold and Black came from behind apparent defeat to tie the score and fight again."

Wake Forest seemed doomed to lose this contest and trailed 5–2 when they began their last at-bat in the ninth inning. In fact, "the fans were filing from the grandstands with heavy hearts to begin the saddened return trip to the Baptist Halls of Learning."

"But as they filed with downcast eyes—crack—came the sound of willow wood on horse's hide and when they turned eager eyes toward the diamond they saw Pitcher Stanley Johnson hugging second base." On the following play, usually reliable State shortstop George Redfearn had bobbled Arnette's grounder and "hope rose again in Baptist hearts for Johnson was on third and Arnette was at first."

Pinch Hitters Save Game

Wake Forest relied on some timely hits by pinch hitters:

Coach Phil Utley then called [them] in and they did their stuff. Small hitting for Coward ripped out a single to left, and as Stanley Johnson crossed the plate the throng went wild. Castellos pinch hitting for Jones forced Small at second, but Arnette crossed the plate and the crowd raved.

Then gloom fell over Wake Forest for Castellos was thrown out at second by several feet when he attempted to steal and but one more out stood between Wake Forest and defeat. Two men were down and nobody on.

Richardson, pinch hitting for Curtis took a worthy cut and singled. Then Poole shot a line drive to center field and the ball grazed Correll's glove as he reached for it, and then fell harmlessly to the ground as bedlam broke loose in the Baptist stands and Richardson running wild, crossed the plate with the tying run. State College held a council of war.

The scoring ended when Stringfield lifted a fly ball to left field.

Baptists' Great Chance

Wake Forest had a chance to clinch the game in the fourteenth inning when Grearson began the inning with a double and scored when Jimmy Allen threw wildly to first after fielding Poole's grounder. "State immediately tied the game when Curtis singled, took second on a fielder's choice and scored when Greason in an attempt to double Correll at first threw the ball over the first baseman's head."

From there on out, neither team could score, and the game was eventually called on account of darkness. Unlike the course of action in a previous year, no additional play took place to decide the outcome.

While the 1923 Wake Forest team got off to a great start, they ended their season with a rather ordinary 11–8–1 record. After a similar start, the State squad finished 13–7–1, and lost the state championship to Carolina, who swept their three games.

Buck Redfearn, the State shortstop and Asheville native, went on to play several years with multiple minor league organizations. In 1928, he broke through with the Chicago White Sox, where he played for two years as a utility infielder.

Wake Forest	*AB*	*R*	*H*	*O*	*A*	*E*
Greason, 2b	7	1	2	2	0	1
Poole, cf	6	0	0	4	1	0
Stringfield, ss	5	0	1	4	4	4
Clark, lf	5	1	2	2	1	0
S. Johnson, rf	5	3	1	1	4	2
Arnette, 2b	7	1	2	1	3	0
Coward, c	3	0	0	5	2	0
Small, rf	4	0	2	1	0	0
Jones, p	3	0	1	0	1	0
Boylin, c	3	0	0	5	1	0
D. Curtis, 1b	3	0	0	10	0	0
Richardson, 1b	5	1	1	4	0	0
Castelloe,	1	0	0	0	0	0
	57	7	12	39	17	7

State	*AB*	*R*	*H*	*O*	*A*	*E*
Ruth, lf	6	2	2	2	0	0
Gladstone, 2b	7	1	3	3	2	0
R. Johnson, rf	6	0	0	3	1	0
Correll, cf	6	2	2	2	0	1
Redfearn, ss	6	0	2	4	5	1
Faulkner, c	7	0	3	8	4	6
Holland, 3b	5	1	0	2	1	0
Lassister, 1b	7	0	3	23	0	0
H. Curtis, p	4	0	1	0	3	0
Allen	3	0	1	0	3	1
	57	6	17	47	19	9

The Easter Monday Baseball Game

Wake Forest	0 0 0	0 0 0	2 0 3	0 0 0	0 1 0	0 6
State	0 2 3	0 0 0	0 0 0	0 0 0	0 1 0	0 6

SUMMARY: Two base hits: S. Johnson, Greason, Small, Redfearn, Lassiter. Three base hits: Clark. Sacrifice hits: R. Johnson (2), Redfearn, Holland, Gladstone, Stringfield. Double plays: Curtis to Redfearn to Lassiter. Base on balls: off Jones 0; off Curtis 5; off Allen 0. Struck out: by Jones 1; by S. Johnson 1; by H. Curtis 5; by Allen 2. Stolen bases: Ruth (2). Hit by pitch: S. Johnson, Clark, Curtis. Passed ball: Coward. Left on base: Wake Forest 8; State 7. Time 2:55. Umpire: Duke Dunon.
Attendance: 4,000.

In 1924 another close game was predicted. "With teams evenly matched and with supporters of each side confident of victory, N.C. State and Wake Forest will clash at Riddick Field, West Raleigh today in the annual Easter Monday classic which the two teams have staged from time to time since the memory of the oldest freshman at either institution." This was the first of sixteen seasons for Coach Chick Doak of State, for whom their current field is named.

> Largest Throng Sees State Win Easter Monday Classic, 4–1
> Six Thousand People See Techs Down Baptists, 4–1
> Wake Forest Cracks Under the Strain in the 6th Inning After Tying Score
>   JIMMY ALLEN HERO FOR STATE COLLEGE
> Pitching Captain Holds Baptists to 4 Scattered Hits and Never Weakens

As the series moved into the mid–'20s, the baseball game reached the zenith of its popularity. On what was described as a "sun-swept, wind-blown field," the teams battled in another low-scoring affair before a reported 6,000 fans on the State campus at Riddick Field. While the play of the State College club was certainly responsible for the 4–1 victory, the weather did seem to play the part of a tenth player.

"It was the wind that seemed to pave the way for State's victory for as a great gust of smoke from a passing engine was sweeping over the diamond in the sixth inning with the score tied and State just coming to the bat, there rang out the resounding crack of sturdy hickory against resilient horsehide and a round white sphere sped into the midst of the smoke cloud as 'Dutch' Holland started around the sacks."

When the ball reappeared, it landed in between the Wake Forest center and right fielders, allowing Holland to register a standup triple.

At this point, Wake's Coach Garrity decided to change pitchers from Staney, the team captain to Sam Jones.

"But it was too late. Church was out."

Honor to Allen

State's pitcher and team captain, Jimmy Allen, was the star of the game as he "hurled a marvelous game and kept the Wake Forest batters knocking the balls in the air. He never pitched a steadier game in his life and showed no signs of cracking under the strain. He was going just as good in the ninth as he was in the first."

Allen pitched so well that in the first six innings he allowed no bases on balls or runners left on base. For the game, Wake Forest could only muster four hits. "Three of these were doubles and one of them led to the only Baptist score of the game when Wake Forest knotted the count in the sixth. Martin opened the frame with a long drive to center that was carried this way and that by the wind and finally bounded off Charlie Shuford's glove as he was breaking his back trying to follow the contortions of the pellet. Martin held up at second."

Gladstone Leads Batting

"Gladstone was the big noise for the Techs at the bat getting three singles out of four times at bat. Al Johnston drew three passes out of four times at bat."

Martin was the top hitter for Wake Forest, garnering two of the above-mentioned doubles in his three trips to the plate.

"If there is any such thing as an outfielders' duel, this game was it. Al Johnston for State and Edwards for Wake Forest out-doing each other in brilliant running catches of the most sensational variety. Edwards made three hard catches while Johnston got five."

Best Team Won

"There is little doubt that the team that was best yesterday won the ball game. State had the edge over Wake Forest all the way and from the first inning it was apparent that the outcome was merely a matter of the

Baptists holding out against heavy odds and of staving off the big break. They managed to do this up until the sixth inning but then the foreseen happened and the game was put on ice."

While Wake Forest committed two errors, the State team played errorless ball for the afternoon. State collected ten hits off the two Wake Forest pitchers and stole three bases. The battery of Allen and Johnson held the Wake runners in check for the game.

In a rare mention for this series, which had by this time become quite contentious if not outright controversial, the umpiring was labeled as "exceptionally good," with "both Mr. Duncan and Mr. Henderson making it through the game "without a wrangle."

This State team proved to be one of the best on record, finishing with an 18–4 record and taking the state and South Atlantic championships, quite a start to Coach Doak's career. Coach Moore's Wake Forest nine was a tremendous offensive squad, scoring ten or more runs in six of their twenty games and finishing with a very respectable 13–7 record.

Wake Forest	AB	R	H	O	A	E
Small, lf	4	0	1	2	0	0
Greason, 2b	4	0	0	1	2	0
Poole, cf	4	0	0	0	0	0
Armstrong, 3b	3	0	1	1	2	0
Arnette, ss	3	0	0	2	4	1
Edwards, rf	3	0	0	3	0	0
Martin, 1b	3	1	2	12	0	1
Hood, c	2	0	0	1	0	0
Staney, p	1	0	1	0	2	0
Jones, p	1	0	0	0	2	0
	28	1	5	22	12	2
N.C. State	AB	R	H	O	A	E
Correll, lf	4	0	0	3	0	0
Gladstone, 2b	4	0	3	2	1	0
C. Shuford, cf	5	0	2	1	0	0
Johnson, c	4	0	0	4	0	0
Johnston, rf	1	0	0	5	0	0
Lassiter, 1b	4	0	0	6	1	0
Holland, 3b	3	2	2	3	1	0
Gilbert, ss	3	1	2	3	0	0
Allen, p	4	1	1	0	4	0
	32	4	10	27	7	0

Wake Forest	0 0 0	0 0 1	0 0 0	1
N.C. State	0 1 0	0 0 3	0 0	4

The Roaring Twenties

SUMMARY: Two base hits: Martin (2), Shuford, Armstrong. Three base hit: Holland. Sacrifice hits: Gilbert, Hood, Staney, Correll. Double plays: Greason to Arnette to Martin. Base on balls: off Allen 0, off Staney 4, off Jones 1. Struck out: by Allen, 3, by Staney 1, by Jones, 0. Stolen bases: Gladstone, C. Shuford, Gilbert. Passed balls, Hood. Left on base: Wake Forest, 2; N.C. State, 11. Time: 1:40. Umpires: Henderson and Duncan.
Attendance: 6,000.

The 1925 game featured a huge dispute over whether certain players for each team were eligible to play. The dispute hinged on whether they had played illegally for pay during the previous summer. It was a pretty common practice for semi-pro teams to pay the better college players under the table for a summer that improved their teams and an experience that often contributed to the development of the players. The key player in this controversy was Wake starting pitcher Vic Sorrell. Despite the protests of the State contingent, he went on to pitch a twelve-inning complete-game 5–4 victory for Wake Forest.

After a lengthy period in the minors, Sorrell made his debut as a major league pitcher at the age of twenty-seven. His career, in which he won nearly a hundred games, spanned ten years. Interestingly, after his career as a player, he became the North Carolina State baseball coach, a position that he held for a remarkable twenty-one years.

In the lead-up to the Easter Monday game, Wake's Coach Garrity had scheduled a variety of difficult games with professional teams that, though they show up as losses in the official record, were the reason the Wake Forest team had such a successful season. Led by the pitching of Sorrell and the batting of Simmons and Armstrong, who hit respectively for clips of .380 and .372, the team finished with a 13–7 record and, having lost only one game in state, were crowned North Carolina state champions. The N.C. State team that returned both Redfearn and Allen finished with an excellent 14–4 record. Two of their losses, however, were to Wake Forest, giving the Baptists the championship. In that year's *Agromeck*, the Easter Monday game is referred to as the Easter Monday tragedy.

Although the Wake Forest nine was heavily favored in this contest, the N.C. State team fought valiantly in a twelve-inning game in front of a record 8,000 fans. The following is an excerpt from the *News and Observer* article that summarizes this exciting game.

Last Ditch Rally

Eight thousand fans were screaming advice and encouragement to their favorites as Sorrell settled down to pitch himself out of his worst hole of the game. Johnson had merely to drive the ball beyond the precincts of the infield and the score would be tied. He had merely to single and the Tech rooters could have staged a jubilee. He grounded in the direction of Armstrong who threw the ball to catcher Hood for a force out at the plate. Holland hit to the flashy Greason who stepped on the second sack to end the baseball game.

And it was some game. Wake Forest should have scored in the first inning for the first three men up singled but Timberlake was out at second trying to stretch his blow. Greason singled and Hill caught him taking a nap off first. Small singled and died on base when Armstrong flied to Correll at center.

State started the scoring in the third inning when the Wake Forest infield blew up. Hill was safe at first on Riley's error. Correll sacrificed him to second. Gladstone hit to Timberlake who seemed unable to pitch the ball off the ground and Hill scored. Gladstone then stole second and scored on Johnson's infield hit as Timberlake kicked the ball toward the left field bleachers.

The Baptists lost no time in tying the score in the fourth frame as Small, Armstrong, Simmons, and Motsinger singled in succession. Some flashy fielding and some great pitching by Hill kept the Deacons from breaking loose altogether.

Baptists Take Lead

An attempt by Johnson to stage a double killing in the fifth gave the Baptists the lead. Timberlake drew a pass and Greason doubled sending Timberlake to third. Small fouled out to catcher Johnson and Armstrong was purposely passed filling the bases. Simmons then bunted to Lassiter who pegged to Johnson forcing Timberlake at the plate. Johnson shot the ball back to Lassiter in an attempt to get Simmons but as Simmons crashed into first in a cloud of dust and shoulders Lassiter dropped the ball and Greason who had never stopped running crossed the plate.

Greason opened the seventh with a two-bagger for another Deacon threat and took third on an infield out but Armstrong bunted a pop fly into Melver's hands for a double play. In the eighth Simmons led off with a two-bagger and Motsinger walked but Simmons was forced at third by Riley, Hood flew out to right and Sorrell forced Riley at second.

All Kinds of Fielding

Brilliant fielding features were notable by their absence although the infields of both teams at times showed flashes. Otherwise, both infields creaked rustily on their hinges. Motsinger had a chance to be a hero in the eighth inning when he got his gloves all over Holland's hit that went for a homer, but he could not hold to it.

There will be another game between Wake Forest and State College next Easter Monday, 1926, and we hope to live to see it.

Box score for this game is unavailable.

After the huge attendance at the 1925 game, preparations began in advance for what was expected to be an even larger crowd. "J.F. Miller, Tech athletic director, announces that by using the centerfield bleachers, which are located in the home run territory, approximately 10,000 spectators can be accommodated. If Sunday's bright sunshine holds through the afternoon, the largest attendance in the history of the game is anticipated by local officials." The athletic department opened an additional downtown ticket office for the convenience of those who wished to purchase advance tickets.

Player eligibility continued to be a point of contention in the series. In fact, there was an unusual amount of "interest in the game this year due to the fact that the management of the two teams have been somewhat at outs over the question of eligibility of members of both teams." Publicly, the Wake Forest coaches claimed that State's star pitcher Melver was ineligible because he pitched "summer ball," an infraction of the Southern Conference rules. As a result, Melver was "barred not only for this game, but for all time." State similarly protested the participation of Simmons and Sorrell, two of Wake Forest's top players. A review of the box score shows that neither player entered this game.

Wake Forest Wallops State in Easter Monday Classic, 10 to 3
RESPONSIBILITY FOR DEFEAT RESTS WITH WEAK MOUND WORK
Except for Third Inning Joyner Keeps Tech's Big Guns Silenced
STATE IS SLAUGHTERED FOR FIRST TWO INNINGS

At this point, the series does seem to have peaked in terms of popularity. While it was still wildly so, the expectations for a crowd of 10,000 proved to be overblown. Though 4,000 was a still a huge crowd for the era, this would remain a fairly standard number over the succeeding years. The increasing mobility of the students allowed them to travel home on this weekend, and in the area, the opportunities for other events were on the rise as well. What follows is an excerpt from the *News and Observer* article that describes this one-sided game:

> Standing out in bold contrast to the games of previous years when extra innings were required to decide the winner, the Demon Deacons from Wake Forest pounded the offerings of State College moundsmen to all parts of Riddick Field in the first two frames of the annual Easter Monday classic here yesterday and in those two innings sewed up the victory for the Baptists and in the minds of the four thousand spectators, substantiated their preseason claim to the best ball team in the Tar Heel State.
>
> After a week of argument as to who would take the mound for the visitors, K. Joyner was chosen, and with the exception of the second inning, he was master of the situation. In that period, by pulling out a single, a double, and a triple, the Techmen gathered their only runs of the day. Beal started the Tech tossing and was battered unmercifully. Hunsucker, who took his place, was wild, and only occasionally did Referee Marr's right hand go up. Morrison was sent in for the third assignment, and after warming up, pitched a good game. Shelton, the last of the tribe of hurlers, was warmed up but was never sent in to action.
>
> The greatest difference in the two teams was the relative strength of the moundsmen and state's inability to hit Joyner with telling blows.
>
> After the fourth inning, both teams settled down and the result was a good game of baseball, but it was the four before this that caused much wailing and weeping among the State supporters and gave the Demon Deacons their second Easter Monday win in as many years. Until the eighth when Riley's homer upset things for the Techs, Morrison was pitching a steady game. Three men crossed the plate after he took possession of the mound, one of who had been given a free pass to second by Hunsucker.
>
> For the first time this season, Wade failed to tally a home run during a game. One single in the eighth was the best that lanky outfielder could do.
>
> The oldest scribes at the college were at a loss to remember the last time that Jonah Morrison presented such a performance of slugging. This Tech hurler got a double and a single in two trips to the plate.

After two years of excellence, the State team fell on difficult times in 1926, losing both games to Wake Forest. They were, however, victorious twice over Carolina, giving them six straight wins in that series. The Wake Forest team finished 16–10 playing a difficult schedule and were crowned North Carolina state champions.

(Note: Play by innings omitted.)

Wake Forest	AB	R	H	O	A	E
Timberlake, cf	4	3	1	2	0	0
Greason, 2b	4	2	2	2	2	1
Clayton, ss	5	2	2	2	3	0
Martin, c	4	0	1	5	0	0
Holt, lf	3	1	1	3	0	0
Baucom, rf	4	0	1	1	0	1
P. Joyner, 3b	5	0	0	2	1	0
Riley, 1b	4	2	2	10	0	0
K. Joyner, p	3	1	1	0	5	1
	36	11	11	27	11	3
State	**AB**	**R**	**H**	**O**	**A**	**E**
C. Shuford, lf	5	0	0	4	0	1
Gilbert, 2b	4	0	0	3	4	0
Wade, rf	4	0	1	1	1	0
C. Faulkner, c	4	1	0	2	2	0
Harrill, 2b	4	1	1	11	0	1
Vick, ss	4	1	1	0	4	0
Austin, 3b	3	0	0	3	1	1
Kidd, cf	3	0	1	2	0	0
Heat, p	0	0	0	1	0	0
Hunsucker, p	1	0	0	0	0	0
Morrison, p	3	0	2	0	1	0
W. Shuford, c	0	0	0	0	0	0
Kirkman, ph	1	0	0	0	0	0
	36	3	6	27	13	3

```
Wake Forest   2 3 1   2 0 0   0 2 0   10
State         0 3 0   0 0 0   0 0 0    3
```

Summary: Two base hits: Martin, Harrill, Morrison. Three base hits: Greason, Kidd. Home runs: Clayton, Riley. Sacrifice hit: Baucom. Double plays: Austin to Gilbert to Harrill. Base on balls: off Beal, 1; off Morrison, 1; off Hunsucker, 2; off Joyner, 2. Struck out: by Beal, 1; by Morrison, 1; by Joyner, 5. Stolen bases: Greason (2), Martin. Wild pitch: Hunsucker, Morrison (2). Passed balls: C. Faulkner. Left on base: Wake Forest, 6; State, 6. Time: 1:50.
Attendance: 4,000.

One of the preview articles for the 1927 game listed the locations for advance ticket sales, now a very popular practice, and noted that Riddick Field could now "comfortably care for a crowd of 10,000, and good weather is expected to bring out a capacity attendance." There were three preview articles for this game, one which included a social calendar that announced the PiKA dance at 9 P.M. on Easter Monday.

BEAL AND JAMES CLASH IN MOUND DUEL IN CLASSIC
Baptists Score 5–4 Triumph After Twelve Innings of Hectic Battling
POOR WORK ON BASES CHEATS TECHS OF TIE
Pair of Technicians Go to Sleep on Paths on Outen's Long Clout and Double Play Ends Game: Kendall's Homer with One on in 7th Ties Score; Clayton Steals Home
by A.J. McKEVLIN April 19, 1927

This is the first article to appear under the byline of A.J. McKevlin, though it's likely that he may have been responsible for some of the earlier game coverage. His writing could be hyper-critical, even caustic, but as seen in this excerpt was generally entertaining if slanted a bit toward the home team.

Dumb base running by a pair of Technicians yesterday afternoon brought to an unfitting close the annual Easter Monday meeting of Wake Forest and State College on the diamond and ended the contests with the Deacons capturing a 5–4 victory in 12 innings.

A hectic game the greater portion of the way, with both teams showing lapses on the defense but with State taking the lead in this respect, the game was a nip and tuck affair. It was sent into extra innings when Billy Kendall hit for the circuit in the seventh after Beal had walked and knotted the score at 3–all. From then until the twelfth there was no scoring.

Kendall's Homer Ties It

The Deacons had tallied two markers in their half of the twelfth, and the Technicians failed to tie the score and lost a possible chance of victory in that frame because of poor work on the paths. With one out in the twelfth, Kendall was given life when Riley juggled Dowtin's throw of Ball's roller. Mayfield hit for Austin and slapped the first ball pitched to deep center for a triple.

Kidd was sent in to run for Mayfield and Matthews went in to hit for Harrell. The pinch-hitter sent a sizzler to the right of first, which Riley scooped up and on which Matthews gained an infield hit while Kidd held third.

Asleep at the Switch

Chink Outen stepped to the plate. The big catcher connected solidly with one of James' slants and it went on a line for right. Lassiter made a nice catch of the drive, but Kidd and Matthews had but one thought in mind. They were both off with the crack of the bat and went to the middle of the diamond and although Lassiter's throw-in to Riley was back at first to make it a double play and end the contest before Matthews had begun his return journey to first from the point 'twixt second and third where he had decided to reverse his direction.

It was a tragic ending for the State followers. Doped to lose the contest for various reasons and primarily because they had shown a lack of offense in other games, the Technicians fought gamely against the Deacons and with Rooster Beal more than holding his own with Ralph James on the mound, the hopes for a State victory had reached great heights.

The game was primarily a pitchers' battle. Beal and James squared off on the mound and the Technicians' captain hurled hitless ball for the first three frames. He gave up seven hits for nine bases during the game, while State collected ten hits off James for 15 bases. But two of the Deacons' five runs were of the earned type, while the Technicians held an advantage of one tally in this respect.

Beal enjoyed better control than James, but the latter shaded him in the matter of strikeouts with four to one for the Tech captain.

McKevlin listed the attendance at 5,000, a tic up from the previous year, but still quite shy of the expected 10,000.

Chic Doak's Technicians had a dismal year in 1927. They lost ten one-run games, were swept by Wake Forest and lost for the first time in four years to Carolina. Wake Forest had an excellent year, sweeping the three games with its rival and finishing with a 13–4 record.

Wake Forest	AB	R	H	O	A	E
Lassiter, rf	3	0	0	2	1	0
Dowtin, 2b	6	0	0	1	4	1
Clayton, ss	5	1	1	2	0	0
Holt, lf	4	0	0	0	0	0
Riley, 1b	4	1	1	14	1	1
P. Joyner, 3b	4	1	0	0	0	0
Furches, cf	4	1	0	3	0	0
James, p	2	0	1	0	0	0
Phelps, c	5	1	1	0	0	0
	37	5	6	22	6	2

The Easter Monday Baseball Game

N.C. State	AB	R	H	O	A	E
Kendall, lf	5	2	1	4	0	0
Austin, 3b	3	0	1	2	2	1
Harrill, 1b	5	0	1	19	0	0
Outen, c	6	0	0	1	1	0
Hovis, rf	4	0	1	1	0	0
McDowall, cf	4	0	1	0	0	1
Vick, 2b	5	0	1	2	4	0
Matheson, ss	5	1	1	0	0	0
Beal, p	4	1	1	0	0	0
Mayfield, ph	1	0	1	0	0	0
Matthews, ph	1	1	0	1	0	0
Kidd, c	0	0	0	0	0	0
	43	5	9	30	7	2

(Note: This box score was partially illegible.)

```
Wake Forest   0 0 0   0 1 2   0 0 0   0 0 2   5
State         0 0 0   0 1 0   2 0 0   0 0 1   4
```

SUMMARY: Two base hits: Clayton, Riley. Three base hits: Mayfield. Home run: Kendall. Sacrifice hits: Lassiter (2), P. Joyner, James (3), Kendall, Austin. Double plays: Beal to Vick to Harrill, James to Dowtin to Clayton to Riley, Lassiter to Riley. Base on balls: off Beal, 2; off James, 4. Struck out: by Beal, 1; by James, 4. Stolen bases: Clayton, Outen, McDowall (2), Vick. Hit by pitcher: Lassiter. Passed ball: Outen. Left on base: Wake Forest 6; State 8. Time 2:30. Umpires: Walt and Elliott.

In 1928, the attendance for the Easter Monday Classic had waned somewhat. A throng of 3500 people gathered on April 9 to watch an excellent performance by State College's Larry Allgood.

ALLGOOD HEAVES CLEVER GAME TO DEFEAT DEACONS
Tech Right-hander Is Real Good Most of Time and State Wins, 4 to 3
DOAKMEN BUNCH HITS TO SCORE IN 3 FRAMES
Allgood Messes Easy Out in Ninth to Fill Bases but Fast Double Play Nips Deacon Rally; Victory Is First for Techs in Easter Monday Game in Years
by A.J. M'KEVLIN

In his fifth year as a coach, the State teams are now referred to informally as the Doakmen. After the disappointment of the previous season, Doak pulled together a "surprise" team that went 12–6 and won the state championship. Led by "fence-rackin'" Captain Chink Outen and slow ball pitcher Larry Allgood, the Technicians dominated the in-state colleges, only losing once to Wake Forest.

In this game, the State team was led by the outstanding pitching of Larry Allgood, what McKevlin described as an "improved defense," and the team's ability to take advantage of each scoring opportunity. The final score was 4–3.

The triumph ended a succession of Deacon victories over the last several seasons. A crowd of 3,500 witnessed the hard-fought game at Riddick Field on State's campus.

> Allgood, a chunky right-handed hurler, did better work yesterday than he has ever turned in on the mound for the Technicians. He gave up but five hits, four of which came in the last two innings, but his pair of wild pitches gave the Deacons their initial run, the first counter of the game, and in the ninth he all but gave away the ball game. With runners on third and first and one out, Ott Person lifted a pop fly toward the third base foul line. Allgood committed the inexcusable error of trying to take the hoist himself, and when he crowded Seal, the latter was unable to hang on to the ball. This filled the bases, and a one-run Tech lead looked no bigger than a midget who sat on the Deacon bench and puffed nervously at a cigar. However, Key Joyner, who had taken over pitching duties for the Baptists in the eighth, sent a fast traveling grounder at Woodworth and it was tuned into a double play to end the game....
>
> **The Leaders**
> P. Joyner was the only Wake Forest player to manage more than one safe hit, while Outen and Woodworth led the Techs with a pair of hits apiece. Responsibility for the four State runs was spread across the lineup as Woodworth, Eatman, McDowell and Outen each drove in a run, while the only Deacon tally coming under the runs batted in column was sent home by Reynolds. Wake's other runs were unearned.
>
> Outstanding in the field for the Deacons were P. Joyner and Clayton, and for the Techs, the second baseman, Outen. Wake kept the game close on the strength of two outstanding double plays.
>
> **Techs Upset Dope**
> As usual there was a colorful crowd on hand for the game. New spring raiment of the fair fans gave to the stands every color of the rainbow and few others, while corsages dotted the crowd. It was a much better ball game than that of the year before, and to State fans it was a big day as pre-game dope had favored the Baptists as just about certain victors.

The Easter Monday Baseball Game

The Techs, however, went on the field and went about their business early in the game with a style and zip which made them look better than a State team has looked in a long time. It was a sort of omen of victory and players and Tech supporters seemed to sense this. And so the Techs went on out and won the ball game.

Amazingly, despite fifteen hits, four walks, and five errors between the teams, the game was played in an hour and a half.

Wake Forest	AB	R	H	O	A	E
Lassiter, cf	3	0	0	0	0	0
Kuykendall, c	3	0	1	4	0	1
Dowtin, 2b	4	0	0	4	0	0
Clayton, ss	2	1	0	2	4	0
Scarboro, lf	4	0	0	1	0	0
P. Joyner, 3b	3	1	2	3	4	1
Reynolds, 1b	4	0	1	7	1	0
Foust, rf	1	0	1	1	0	0
James, p	3	0	0	1	3	0
Phelps, ph	1	0	1	0	0	0
Dorsett, rf	0	1	0	0	0	0
K. Joyner, p	1	0	0	0	1	0
Person, ph	1	0	0	0	0	0
	30	3	6	23	13	2

State	AB	R	H	O	A	E
Woodworth, ss	4	2	2	1	3	0
McDowall, 1b	4	0	1	15	1	0
Outen, 2b	4	1	2	1	8	1
Eatman, c	4	0	1	4	1	0
Snipes, lf	3	0	1	3	0	0
Kidd, cf	3	0	1	0	0	0
Mayfield, rf	3	0	0	2	1	1
Seal, 3b	3	0	1	0	1	1
Allgood, p	3	1	1	1	2	0
	31	4	10	27	17	3

```
Wake Forest   0 1 0   0 0 0   0 1 1   3
State         0 0 0   1 0 0   0 1 2   4
```

SUMMARY: Two base hits: Snipes, Allgood, Phelps, P. Joyner. Sacrifice hit: Kuykendall. Double plays: James to P. Joyner to Clayton to Dowtin: James to Reynolds: Woodworth to Outen to McDowall. Base on balls: off Allgood, 4. Struck out: by James, 4: by Allgood, . Stolen bases: P. Joyner, Seal, Outen, McDowall. Wild pitch: Allgood (2). Left on bases: Wake Forest, 7; State, 3. Time: 1:30. Umpire: Walker.

For the 1929 season, Larry Allgood had been named the captain of the 1928 state champion Tech team and was expected to pitch before a huge crowd. By this time, however, Davidson and Carolina had also developed an Easter Monday rivalry, which pulled some of the fans away from the classic in Raleigh.

Anthony McKevlin reached new heights with his colorful description and lively narrative. This excerpt is a great example of the sports journalism of the era.

HOMER BY HORD PROVES MARGIN OF DEACON WIN
Circuit Clout in Seventh, Needless at Time, Finally Means Win
SANDY SHORE IS STAR FOR DOAK'S WOLFPACK
Shore Takes Slab After Allgood Is Bumped for Five Runs in Second; Relief Hurler Fans Nine and Leads State Attack; Catch by Hord Features
by ANTHONY J. McKEVLIN

"Runt" Hord, Wake Forest shortstop, hit a seemingly unnecessary home run in the seventh inning of the Deacons' Easter Monday battle with N.C. State College here yesterday but when it was all over that circuit clout was the margin by which John Caddell's charges counted a 7–6 victory over the local collegians before 4,000 fans.

Hord's blow was a powerful one, the ball cleared the high wooden bleachers in left field and was many feet inside the foul line. Incidentally, that homer produced the only score Wake Forest was able to put across in seven innings of trying against the offerings of one Sandy Shore, right-hander who was rushed to the relief of Captain Larry Allgood at the opening of the third frame. In the second inning the Baptists had played hide and seek with the Tech captain and the sum total of their All Fools' Day allies in that verse was five hits and as many runs, the attack being climaxed by a home run inside the park by Captain Al Dowtin.

Deacons Bump Allgood

Allgood was treated unceremoniously by the Deacons. They got a run in a queer first inning, the tally counting from second when Foust took a pitch for a third strike. The ball, which hit the dirt before it reached the plate, rolled to the bleachers and the batter pulled up at second. Lassiter had opened the inning with a blow down third which odd fielding by Freeman had turned into a hit. He had been forced on Furtado's true stop of Scarborough's slashing roller. Dowtin went out but Freeman errored Hord's roller to put Scarborough on second. Then came Foust's valuable strike out.

The Easter Monday Baseball Game

The five Baptist tallies in the second were all wool and a yard wide. Benton opened with a single and Gillespie duplicated. Lanning's neat bunt moved each up a base. Lassiter's hit scored Benton while Scarborough's safety counted Gillespie. Hero Captain Dowtin drove one to the far reaches of centerfield and beat the relayed throw home.

Gets Interesting Near Close

It wasn't much of a ball game until the Techs started putting on rallies in the late stages. It had all the earmarks of a walkaway in view of the early Deacon lead. But State, which had counted a run in the third on a walk to Woodworth and Shore's double, came to life in the seventh.

Clark, pinch-hitter, opened the lucky home inning with a single and was safe at second when Hord failed to touch after taking Lanning's throw of Woodworth's roller. Shore scratched a hit down third and the bases were filled. Umpire Lou Kearney called a balk on Lanning and Clark trotted home. Eatman's single to center scored Woody and Shore. Allgood forced Eatman and Hargrove doubled to left, but Snipes rolled to Reynolds.

The Wolfpack [apparently the first time this name appears] got two more in the eighth. Albright was safe to start things on Hord's error. Furtado hit to deep short and Hord's throw to second failed to nab the fleet Albright. Clark bounced to first and Woodworth rolled out, but Shore, who was the big noise all the way for State, dropped a hit toward left to send home two runs. Eatman walked but Allgood's best was a roller to Jit Benton, who threw out the runner at first in preference to taking the easy course and forcing Shore at third.

Hord Pulls Star Catch

Runt Hord contributed the winning blow for Wake Forest, and likewise he turned in the fielding feature of the afternoon. With two out and State runners on first and second in the fifth, Allgood slammed one on the nose and the ball seemed headed for a safe spot in left center. But Hord leaped in the air, stuck up his gloved hand, and came down with the ball. It was a great catch and apparently cut off a run.

Shore's Sure

Sandy Shore was the shining light in State College colors. It wasn't this lad's fault that the Techs lost. He pitched seven innings, allowed only three hits and one run, walked no one and fanned nine. At the bat he gathered a double and two singles in four tries, drove in three runs and scored another.

The Roaring Twenties

John Caddell went against the old laws of averages, pitching and whatnot when he selected Lanning, a southpaw to face Doak's raft of right-handed hitters. The Techs had eight right-handed swingers in action most of the time, but they didn't worry Lanning. Shore and Hargrove, both left-handed swingers, collected half of the State hits. Only in the seventh and eight were the locals able to bunch blows off the lanky portsider of the Deacons.

Twas a colorful crowd. The ladies were there in all their Easter finery and in this finery could be found any color of the rainbow and some others to boot. The Weather Man, although ever threatening to produce showers, thought better of it and let it go at threats.

As it turned out, 1929, after a run of really fine teams from both Raleigh schools, was an off year. Wake Forest managed to pull out a .500 season while State was just under .500, though they managed to gain a 2-1 edge in the season's rivalry games.

Wake Forest	AB	R	H	O	A	E
Lassiter, rf	5	1	2	0	0	0
Scarborough, cf	5	2	1	0	0	0
Dowtin, 2b	5	1	1	4	1	0
Hord, ss	4	1	2	1	4	2
Foust, lf	3	0	0	0	0	0
Dorsett, lf	1	0	0	0	0	0
Reynolds, 1b	4	0	0	14	0	1
Benton, 3b	4	1	1	2	2	0
Gillespie, c	4	1	2	5	2	0
Lanning, p	3	0	0	1	4	0
	38	7	9	27	13	3

State	AB	R	H	O	A	E
Woodworth, 3b	3	2	0	7	0	0
Melton, rf	1	0	0	0	0	0
Shore, p	4	1	3	0	3	0
Eatman, c	2	0	1	10	0	0
Allgood, p-rf	5	0	0	0	1	0
Averette, lf	2	0	0	0	0	0
Hargrove, lf	2	0	1	0	0	0
Snipes, cf	5	0	1	2	0	0
Albright, 2b	5	1	0	0	3	0
Furtado, ss	4	1	1	5	1	1
Freeman, 3b	1	0	0	1	0	1
Clark, 1b	2	1	1	2	0	0
Harris, ph	1	0	0	0	0	0
	37	6	8	27	8	2

The Easter Monday Baseball Game

Wake Forest	1	5 0	0 0 0	1 0 0	7
N.C. State	0	0 1	0 0 0	3 2 0	6

Summary: Runs batted in. Lassiter, Scarborough, Dowtin (3). Shore (3), Hord, Eatman (2). Two base hits: Shore, Hargrove. Home runs: Dowtin, Hord. Stolen bases: Albright, Foust. Sacrifice: Lanning. Left on bases: Wake Forest, 5: State, 10. Base on balls: off Lanning, 5. Struck out: by Allgood, 2: by Shore, 9: by Lanning, 5. Hit by pitcher: Freeman. Wild pitches: Allgood. Balk: Lanning. Umpires: Kearney and Walker. Time: 2:05.

The dance received similar notice in the local media during the following years. However, it is noteworthy in the April 1, 1929, article that the venue had changed:

> The Frank Thompson gymnasium of North Carolina State College was the scene of one of the most brilliant social events of the college year last evening when Pi Kappa Alpha fraternity entertained at its annual Easter dance 9 until 1 o'clock. The gymnasium was profusely decorated with long leaf pine and evergreens forming a basis for the color arrangement of garnet and gold, colors of the fraternity. From a center chandelier streamers of garnet and gold were hung that extended to the side balconies and fell to the floor. At one end of the hall a large fraternity insignia constructed of wood was electrically lighted and the fraternity banner hung at the opposite end of the hall. The orchestra pit was banked in pine and shrubbery and the fraternity shield formed a colorful background for Maynard's Southland Serenaders of Nashville, Tenn., who played during the evening ... two thousand invitations have been issued in the city and elsewhere in the state to men and women of the younger set.... Prior to intermission the fraternity figure was led by Mr. John Dunn, president of the fraternity....

The decade closed with a pitcher's duel that featured another fine performance by Lanning, Wake Forest's Asheville native, and State's right-hander, Bill Averette, a native of Oxford, North Carolina. McKevlin begins his account with an "all the world's a stage" analogy and continues in this excerpt with the flamboyance and tone of his other recent articles.

> TECHS WIN OVER WAKE FOREST IN EASTER CLASSIC
> Averette Gets 3–0 Decision Over Lanning in Battle of Pitchers
> THREE THOUSAND FANS SEE OLD RIVALS CLASH
> Double Steal Gives State Unearned Run in Opening Inning and Techs Clinch

Win with Two Earned Tallies in Eighth; Jit Benton Stars Abat
by ANTHONY J. McKEVLIN

A right-hander and a southpaw were the main actors yesterday as N.C. State and Wake Forest offered the 1930 performance of an Easter Monday baseball rivalry dating back to the early days of the century. The two rivals on the firing line were just about the whole show — and it was a good show — for the three thousand fans, and victory went to the right-hander, Bill Averette.

Wake Forest's lefthanded captain Tom Lanning outpitched State's Averette for the first seven innings. But State with the assistance of two errors, produced a run in their half of the first inning. This was the lone run of the game till the bottom of the eighth, when State, continuing their dominance of the small ball game, added two more runs on two singles, a walk, and a successful squeeze play. Furtado, Plonk, and Hargrove were responsible for the State rally.

Double Steal Counts Run

State's score in the first inning came when Benton's error gave Turner life. He moved up on Furtado's bunt and reached third while Plonk was getting life on Mills' bobble of his roller. Plonk headed for second and Gillespie's throw was accurate. Shortstop Allen became engrossed in the unsuccessful business of trying to put out Plonk and the steal became a two-sided one with Turner counting at the plate. Lanning fanned Hargrove and Snipes rolled out to end the inning.

State's only hit prior to the eighth came in the second when Bill Brake hit to right with one away. Brake stole second and continued to third when Gillespie's peg went to centerfield, but Wilkie fanned and Averette rolled out.... Although the Deacons made numerous threats, Averette was able to put out the fire each time multiple runners reached base. Benton led Wake Forest at the plate with two doubles and a single.

The 1930 season was another "slow" year for the two teams. Wake Forest did manage to rise above .500 at the end of the season, finishing 11–10, but State finished a disappointing 8–10–1. Neither team was a serious conference or State title contender for the second consecutive year.

Box score for this game is unavailable.

And then this from a 1930 article which mentioned several other post–Easter activities for the Raleigh area:

The Easter Monday Baseball Game

Tomorrow evening the Pi Kappa Alpha fraternity of North Carolina State College will give the twenty-fourth annual Easter dance in the Frank Thompson Memorial Gymnasium. The dance will attract a throng of young men and women from over the entire state and neighboring universities and colleges.

Dancing will continue from 9 until 1 o'clock and during the evening members of the host chapter and their ladies will participate in the Pi K.A. figure which will be led by chapter president, Allie P. Baggett of Dunn, with Miss Florence Briggs of Raleigh. They will be assisted by three couples. Decoration of the memorial hall which will be the scene of the dance has been in progress since last week and is expected to surpass in color and lavish beauty the arrangement of any preceding year. Russ Bolin and his Ohio Cotton Pickers will play for dancing.

There were also four large photographs that were accompanied by lengthy captions.

DEPRESSION AND WAR

1931–1940

Even as the Great Depression worsened, the state's population crossed the three million mark for the first time. Bank closures and business failings caused an enormous number of people to lose their life savings, yet in the midst of all the misfortune, in Asheville, the Biltmore House, a symbol of wealth and power, was transformed into a public museum that would become one of the state's leading tourist destinations.

Despite the lack of ample funding, North Carolina continued to improve its educational efforts. During the decade of the '30s, for the first time, the state began to provide free textbooks for elementary school students. On the higher education level, the General Assembly voted to consolidate the University in Chapel Hill, State College in Raleigh, and the women's college in Greensboro into one educational entity, laying the foundation for what would become a strong state university system. A law school for African-American students was also established at North Carolina Central, and an experimental arts institution was established as Black Mountain College in Buncombe County.

In the business arena, North Carolina continued to grow its furniture and textile industries, with the latter becoming a hotbed for union activity. At one time, over 100 textile mills were on strike. Halfway through the decade, the 21st Amendment was passed, ending the prohibition of alcohol in the U.S. However, many mountain areas continued a legacy of bootlegging that would continue for decades hence.

During the '30s, WPA projects employed many of the displaced workers and helped build major projects like the Blue Ridge Parkway as well as many park trails, local baseball fields, and other smaller projects.

The Easter Monday Baseball Game

At the end of the decade, World War II began in Europe, and our country's inevitable participation loomed over the lives of the young men who played in the Easter Monday Baseball Classic.

The 1931 Easter Monday game was rained out, as this article dated April 7 notes. Though this short article has no byline, the sarcastic tone with which it opens would seem to identify it as McKevlin's work.

> Easter Monday Card Washed Out; Deacons-Techs to Play at Later Date
>
> The beautiful Easter weather, consisting of rain and more rain, completely washed out yesterday's collegiate baseball program. Among other things, the rain of Monday smeared the record of the State College–Wake Forest holiday meetings.
>
> The annual Easter Monday clash of Techs and Deacons has been reeled off year after year although sometimes played in mighty mean weather. But yesterday was the first time the affair was completely washed off the boards and only the second time the schools failed to get in a regulation game.
>
> Chick Doak, veteran coach at N.C. State recalled an afternoon eleven years ago when the Easter Monday event here was stopped by rain in the third inning. Dr. J. Richard Crozier, who coached at Wake Forest in the latter part of the first decade of this great century, recalled no postponements in earlier times.

After a second rainout, the game was finally played over a month later on May 13, a Wednesday. In this game, which featured a rare triple play, Wake Forest regained its winning ways.

> Deacons Win Over Techs; Victors Pull Triple Play
> Joyner Leads Wake Forest's Heavy Hitting for 10–4 Win Over N.C. State
>
> The Wake Forest Deacons batters manhandled the two N.C. State pitchers, registering eleven hits including three extra base hits. In a game that was a makeup for the twice rained out Easter Monday Classic, the Deacons infielders also executed a triple play to prevent the State team from mounting a comeback in the eighth inning.
>
> The triple play came with runners on second and first as a result of a walk to Fuller and single by Kirkman. Rudy Seitz, second State hurler, slashed a liner between third and short which looked good for a safety, but Captain Jit Benton speared the ball a few inches off the ground, tossed to Mills at second to double Fuller and Mills threw to Joyner at first to nail Kirkman and complete the three-ply putout.

Deacons Get Hot

The Deacons had their big inning in the fourth as they connected for five hits and scored the same number of runs off the State southpaw, John Lanning. This put Wake Forest ahead for good with a 6–2 lead, each team having tallied a run in the second inning while State had pulled ahead with a second run in the home half of the third.

In the fifth, the Deacons continued to pound Lanning, reaching him for three hits before he was relieved by Seitz. Seitz allowed two more singles to account for Wake's four run inning. For the remainder of the afternoon, however, he pitched hitless ball, but it was too late by then.

Lefty Barnes, Deacon chucker, had things much his own way until the seventh. With one run in and a runner on base, Barnes was relieved by Joe Meador. Joe fanned the next two hitters and gave only one hit the rest of the way. Barnes had been reached for seven hits but the Techs mixed their licks with walks and one error for their four singletons in the score column.

Joyner Leads Hitters

Monk Joyner, with a triple and double, led both teams at bat, while Earp, Bethune, Benton and Joyner also got two hits each for the winners. Willie Duke and Outen hit safely twice to lead State.

Earp missed another hit when he failed to touch first on a smack to left good ordinarily for three bases.

The 1931 season was another poor one for both teams. The author of the baseball season synopsis in Wake Forest's *Howler* called it the worst season in eighteen years. Wake finished 9–15 while State compiled a 6–9–1 record. During this school year, the new lighting at Riddick Field made it impossible to play baseball there, so the games were moved to the less capacious Freshman Field. The Easter Monday game was moved to League Park, the first off-campus game of the series.

Wake Forest	*AB*	*R*	*H*	*O*	*A*	*E*
Cobb, cf	4	0	1	3	0	0
Mills, 2b	4	0	0	2	7	1
Edwards, rf	5	1	0	0	0	0
Joyner, 1b	5	2	2	14	0	1
Earp, ss	4	3	2	1	3	0
Bethune, lf	4	2	2	0	0	0
Benton, 3b	3	2	2	1	3	0
Hicks, c	4	0	1	5	0	0
Barnes, p	2	0	1	0	0	0
	35	10	11	26	13	2

The Easter Monday Baseball Game

State	AB	R	H	O	A	E
Morris, 2b-3b	3	0	0	1	2	0
Wood, 2b	2	1	0	0	1	0
Ebey, ss	2	1	0	1	3	1
McLawhorn	1	0	1	0	0	0
Wilkie, ss	1	0	0	0	2	1
Jeffrey, rf	3	0	0	1	0	0
Brake, rf	1	0	0	0	0	0
Duke, 2b-lf	4	0	2	0	1	0
Goodman, cf, 1b	3	1	1	5	1	0
Nelms, lf	2	1	0	0	0	0
Furtado, lf-2b	0	0	0	0	1	0
Hargrove, ph	1	0	0	0	0	0
Turner, c	3	0	1	4	1	0
Fuller, c	0	0	0	0	0	0
Gerrock, 1b	1	0	2	14	0	0
Kirkman, ph	2	0	0	1	2	0
Lanning, p	2	0	0	0	1	0
Seitz, p	0	0	0	0	1	0
	31	4	7	27	16	2

```
Wake Forest   0 1 0   5 4 0   0 0 0   10
State         0 1 1   0 0 1   1 0 0    4
```

SUMMARY: Two base hits: Joyner, Bethune. Three base hits: Joyner. Stolen bases: Earp, 2, Ebey, Duke, Mills. Sacrifices: Bethune, Benton, Barnes, Cobb. Double plays: Ebey, Morris and Gerock: Earp, Mills, and Joyner. Triple play: Benton, Mills and Joyner. Left on bases: State, 6; Wake Forest, 6. Base on balls: off Lanning, 2; Barnes, 2, Seitz, 1, Meador, 1. Struck out: by Lanning, 1, Barnes, 2, Seitz, 2, Meador, 2. Wild pitch: Barnes. Umpire: Morgan. Time 2:00.

On the Friday before Easter Monday in 1931, this text ran below the photographs of five young ladies:

> The group of charming young women (above) who will be leaders of the fraternity figure in the annual Pi Kappa Alpha Easter Monday dance at the N.C. State College, April 6 include Miss Marion Dunn of Enfield, Miss Dorothy Yaeger of Hickory, Miss Margaret Henderson of Monroe, Miss Elizabeth Styron of Plymouth and Miss Lucille Flynn of Hendersonville, all of whom will be guests of the fraternity at a house party at their lodge on Hillsboro Street this weekend. At the anniversary dance Miss Henderson will lead out, escorted by Harry Lee of Monroe, President of Alpha Epsilon of Pi Kappa Alpha.

In a separate society column describing the Easter entertainment by Melissa N. Browne:

> The glory of Easter's entertainment program has not completely departed but is seriously diminished. Only a few short years ago, Easter week was entirely given over by society of all ages for social revelry, nearly every hour brought forth some elaborate entertainment, nearly every party had its distinguished guests and brilliant array of attendants. Under the stress of times the Easter season has given away noticeably and this year but one notable annual entertainment remains to claim glory for Easter week.

After describing the dissolution of the Sphinx Club and the Black Cat Club, the Nine O'Clock Cotillion Club and the Circle Club, Miss Browne continues:

> But there remains for younger society the annual Easter Pi Kappa Alpha Dance, more glorious than ever this year as the fraternity celebrates its silver anniversary tomorrow evening when the twenty-fifth Easter Monday dance will be given in Frank Thompson Memorial Gymnasium on the State College campus. Alpha Epsilon Chapter of Pi K.A. has over this long period of years, given the opening Easter entertainment in the Capital City. This year its Easter dance is both the opening and closing of Easter week cotillions and whereas it was once the forerunner of a long line of social activity, it is now the only survivor of that popular custom.

It is easy to see how important this event had become. The list of special guests for this event included the Governor and Mrs. O. Max Gardner, General and Mrs. Albert Cox, Secretary of State and Mrs. James A. Hartness, and many other civic and business leaders.

The 1932 game was once again canceled.

> Deacons and Techs Will Try Again Here Saturday
> Blocked yesterday, the baseball team of State and Wake Forest will meet Saturday afternoon at League Park in what used to be an Easter Monday classic but which promises to become a rivalry with a record for postponements.
> Last year the Easter Monday meeting had to be passed up because of rain. Yesterday, the contest was called off shortly after noon because of high winds still prevailing and the cause of damage done at League Park by winds of Sunday night and early Monday. Then, too, there was quite a bit of chill in the air....

The Sunday, April 3, *News and Observer* reported the results of the game.

The Easter Monday Baseball Game

DEACS SCORE WIN IN OPENING VERSE
Lanning Hurls in Good Style After Deacs Get Three Runs In First Inning

Wake Forest's Deacons put scored three runs in the first inning against N.C. State at League Park on Saturday afternoon, and that proved exactly enough runs to assure the victory although the Deacons added a couple more in subsequent innings.

The handicap his mates accorded him by their opening fireworks was enough margin for Junie Barnes, southpaw hurler from Lexington and helped the Deacon left-hander to register his third victory against State in as many opportunities during the past two seasons.

Barnes got the pitching verdict over John Lanning, big State righthander from Asheville. After a tough start, Lanning pitched in fine style.

A colorful crowd of around 1500 — with bright spring fashions of feminine fans lending a rainbow hue — saw the play off of the annual Easter Monday game between the Wake county colleges. The contest had been blocked by inclement weather. Save for recurring winds, this Saturday was splendid.

It was the first Big Five game for both teams, and for an early season battle it was well played. Barnes had fine control and walked none while Lanning issued only three passes. Lanning fanned three and Barnes whiffed five....

This makeup game was not only Junie Barnes's third win over his rivals at State but also his second in the Easter Monday series. In the longstanding series it was not that unusual for a pitcher's number to come up twice, but Barnes was to get yet another chance the following year. On the other hand, this game was the second Easter Monday game where Johnny Lanning lost to Barnes.

Four years later, Lanning, nicknamed "Tobacco Chewin' Johnny," would begin an eleven-year career as a National League pitcher with the Boston Bees. Lanning won 58 games and saved 13, pitching mostly as a reliever the second half of his career. Lanning's older brother Tom pitched the 1929 and '30 Easter Monday games for Wake, winning one and losing the other. He also played minor league ball extensively and had a brief stint with the Philadelphia Phillies (three games) in his early thirties.

The 1932 Wake Forest team was a big improvement over the year before, finishing with an 11–7 record and winning the Big Five competition. Of the State team, it was said that they were "better than their record." They broke even with the both the Big Five teams and the four professional teams that they began the season against. One of the highlights of the season was a pitchers' duel between Lanning and the nephew of Jack Coombs (legendary player and coach) at Duke.

Wake Forest	AB	R	H	O	A	E
Earp, ss	3	1	1	3	1	2
Hunting, 2b	5	1	1	1	1	1
White, rf	5	1	1	3	0	0
Joyner, 1b	4	1	2	7	0	0
Mulhern, lf	4	0	1	1	0	0
Johnson, cf	1	0	0	1	0	0
Brogman, 2b	3	1	2	1	1	0
Hicks, c	4	0	0	10	1	0
Barnes, p	4	0	0	0	2	0
	33	5	8	27	6	3

State	AB	R	H	O	A	E
Morris, 3b-2b	6	1	1	0	5	0
Gerock, 1b	5	0	2	17	0	0
Duke, cf-3b	5	0	1	0	0	0
Brown, ss	1	0	0	2	3	1
McQuage, rf-cf	4	0	0	2	0	0
Ebey, lf	2	0	0	1	0	0
Nelms, lf	1	0	0	0	0	0
Woods, 2b	2	0	0	1	4	0
Fuller, c	3	0	1	4	1	0
Farris, c	0	0	0	0	0	0
Lanning, p	4	0	3	0	1	1
Jeffrey, rf	2	1	1	0	0	0
Griffin, ph	1	0	0	0	0	0
McLawhorn, ph	1	0	0	0	0	0
	37	2	9	27	14	2

```
Wake Forest   3 0 0   0 0 1   1 0 0   5
N.C. State    1 0 0   0 0 1   0 0 0   2
```

SUMMARY: Two base hits: Bunting, White, Morris, Lanning. Three base hits: Brogaen. Sacrifice hits: Hicks. Bases on balls: off Barnes, 0; Lanning, 3. Struck out: by Lanning, 3; by Barnes, 5. Stolen Bases: Duke, Brown. Left on bases: State, 10; Wake Forest, 7. Time: 1:45. Umpires: Kearney and Lenox.

For the first time in three years, the 1933 game was played on Easter Monday.

Deacons Rout State;
BARNES FEATURES DEACONS' VICTORY

The Easter Monday Baseball Game

June Hurls Six-Hit Ball and Stars at Bat in Wake Forest's 12 to 1 Win
by ANTHONY J. McKEVLIN

McKevlin noted the lucky circumstance of the weather in his introduction, the game actually being played on Easter Monday, and added that despite the calendar saying that it was April 17, it was "right much of a June afternoon." His tongue-in-cheek reference was to the Wake Forest pitcher who also starred at the plate in this one-sided game. Junie Shoaf Barnes, a slight man even for that era at 5'11", 170, became one of the few pitchers to record three victories in the series. The next year Barnes would get a cup of coffee with the Cincinnati Reds, making two appearances in which he walked one and recorded one out, his star status at the college level not transferring well to the major leagues. He did, however, like many players of the era, have a relatively long, successful minor league career. Barnes won 110 games for teams all over the east coast from Toronto to Shreveport. He ended his career, like many players of the time, with three years in a Class D league in Western North Carolina playing for towns such as Statesville and Mooresville.

> June Barnes pitched for Wake Forest yesterday in the latest renewal of an Easter baseball rivalry which goes back to the beginning of the century—and June pitched splendidly. On top of that, he proved quite a handy man at bat-swinging and helped materially in the attack which brought his team a 12 to 1 victory.
>
> To resurrect an old baseball phrase, it may truly be said that State's main trouble yesterday was "Too Much Barnes." The clever southpaw flinger held the Techs to six hits and struck out nine. On attack he hit a double and two singles to score once and bat in three runs.
>
> ### Close for Six Innings
> The Weather Man did an about face yesterday from his Sunday tactics, and the fine afternoon produced a turnout of some 3,500 spectators for the meeting of the Techs and Deacons at Freshman Field. Despite the one-sided final score, it was a good ball game for six innings—a span during which a three-run Wake Forest splurge in the second inning had been the only scoring.

Wake Forest eventually broke the closely contested game wide open, scoring nine runs over the last three innings and sending many of the State faithful home early.

For the first six innings Rudy Seitz, the big State right-hander, had kept the Deacons in check. Their second inning runs had been unearned runs. The first two-thirds of the game saw Seitz holding Wake Forest to five hits while his team's total off Barnes was three. Willie Duke's single in the second, and singles by Farris and Roach with two outs in between in the sixth had been the only hits off Barnes.

"Seitz relinquished pitching duties after four hits, a wild pitch and an error had brought four Deacon runs in the seventh." Bill Lynn pitched the eighth inning for State, but five hits, a walk and a couple of errors resulted in four runs. Joel Morris took over mound duties in the ninth and two walks, hits by Hicks and Barnes and an error netted the last two runs for the Deacons.

Deacons Win in Second

The Deacons got enough runs in the second inning to win. Joyner opened with a grounder to short but was safe on Lambeth's bad throw. Joe Mulhern tripled to left center to score Joyner. Johnson drew life at first on Lambeth's high throw, Brogden's fly to center scored Mulhern and put Johnson on second from where he tallied when Barnes rapped a double to center....

Wake Forest began 1933 with four victories, including this one, looking to repeat as champions of the Big Five. But shortly after the Easter Monday game, Barnes, Hicks, and Joyner were all injured in an automobile accident. Hicks and Barnes returned to play, but Barnes never regained effectiveness because of an injured shoulder. Joyner was out for the season. Without the services of their slugging first baseman, Wake struggled to a .500 season. Led by Captain "Snoozy" Morris, State roared to a 5–1 start in 1933, but their inability to beat Wake's lefty Barnes, and a late season loss to Carolina, cost them a shot at the Big Five Championship.

Wake Forest	*AB*	*R*	*H*	*O*	*A*	*E*
Earp, ss	6	1	2	4	1	0
Bunting, 2b	6	1	2	2	1	0
White, rf	5	2	2	2	1	0
Joyner, 1b	5	1	1	5	0	0
Mulhern, lf	4	1	2	1	1	0
Johnson, cf	5	1	0	3	1	0
Brogden, 2b	4	1	1	2	2	0
Hicks, c	3	3	2	9	1	0

The Easter Monday Baseball Game

Wake Forest	AB	R	H	O	A	E
Barnes, p	5	1	3	0	0	0
	43	12	19	28	8	0

N.C. State	AB	R	H	O	A	E
Wood, 2b	3	0	0	2	5	0
Griffin, 3b	1	0	0	0	0	1
Roach, 3b-2b	4	1	2	1	2	0
McQuage, lf-1b	2	0	1	4	0	0
Duke, cf	1	0	1	4	0	0
Bailey, 1b	2	0	0	11	0	0
Smith, lf	2	0	1	0	0	0
Nelms, rf	2	0	0	0	0	0
Jeffrey, rf	2	0	0	0	0	1
Lambeth, ss	2	0	0	1	4	2
Farris, c	3	0	1	2	1	0
Fuller, c	0	0	0	1	0	1
Seitz, p	2	0	0	0	3	1
Lynn, p	0	0	0	0	0	1
Morris, p	0	0	0	0	0	0
Oakden, ph	1	0	0	0	0	0
	29	1	6	26	15	7

```
Wake Forest   0 2 0   0 0 0   3 4 2   12
State         0 0 0   0 0 0   0 1 0    1
```

SUMMARY: Two base hits: Barnes, Hicks, Roach, McQuage. Three base hits: Mulhern. Stolen bases: Earp 2, Joyner. Left on bases: Wake Forest, 9; State, 5. Base on balls: off Seitz 2, Barnes, 3, Lynn, 1, Morris, 2. Struck out: by Seitz 2, Barnes 9, Lynn 1. Wild pitches: Seitz 2. Umpires: Kearney and Lennox. Time: 2:12.

By 1934, the Easter Monday baseball classic had become a staple in the Raleigh area as Anthony McKevlin announced in his preview article in the Sunday, April 1, *News and Observer*:

> Varied are the holiday features of Easter Monday, but for sports fans of this section, the main attraction is the annual meeting of baseball teams of State and Wake Forest.
>
> The old rivals clash at State tomorrow in a renewal of an Easter Monday series extending back beyond the turn of the century. The game is set to start at 3 o'clock and will be played at Freshman Field.

McKevlin followed this article with a Tuesday, April 3, article summarizing the game.

HERRING PITCHES WIN FOR DEACONS
Hurler Also Features Three-Run Splurge in Second.
3,500 See Game Here

Wake Forest defeated State 4–2 in a good ball game here yesterday afternoon and Bill Herring, right-hander from Williamston, was the big star for the Deacons as they made it for in a row over the Techs in the Easter Monday series dating back to the 90's.

Just as Junie Barnes had played a dominant role for Wake Forest in the past three years, their pitcher, Bill Herring did the same in this game both on the mound and at the plate.

For the past three years, the southpaw, June Barnes had pitched Wake Forest to victory over State in the annual holiday meeting. Yesterday Herring picked up where Barnes left off. In addition, the Williamston native, grabbed further laurels, by smacking a single to center in the second inning to send two runs across the plate. A bit later he tallied on Baldy Slayton single what proved to be the winning run.

3,500 See Game

Twas a fine afternoon for baseball and some 3,500 fans were on hand for the holiday engagement on Freshman Field at State. Fair fans provided more than a third of the crowd and their Easter finery made the occasion somewhat of a fashion show in addition to a baseball game. Old Sol shone on high and shone with the power at full.

Stewart Fletcher from Conway was Herring's pitching opponent. The Tech hurler was stingy enough with base hits, but he was very generous in other ways. He walked five, hit two and uncorked a pair of wild pitches and made two bad throws. His kindness figured in all but two of the Deacon runs....

Though Bill Herring never made it to the major leagues, more so than most of the Easter Monday participants, he had a career in baseball. First he pitched minor league ball for sixteen seasons in every level from Double A to Class D, winning 190 games and losing 103. He was also a threat at the plate where he collected sixteen home runs and hit for a very respectable .249 average. When his playing career ended at the age of 39, he remained involved first as a general manager and then as a coach, manager, and a finally as a professional scout. Herring chose the game he loved for a career despite having obtained a law degree from Wake Forest.

Stu Flythe, a native of Conway, North Carolina, the slender State right hander and loser in this game got a brief shot with the Philadelphia Athletics several years later.

Wake Forest	AB	R	H	O	A	E
Slayton, rf	5	0	1	1	0	0
Gold, 2b	5	0	0	3	0	1
Mitchell, ss	4	0	0	0	5	0
Wall, cf	3	0	0	2	1	0
Clark, 2b	5	1	0	2	0	0
Mulhern, lf	4	0	2	0	1	0
Patton, 1b	4	1	1	10	0	0
Myers, c	3	1	1	8	2	0
Herring, p	2	1	1	0	2	0
	35	4	6	26	11	1

State	AB	R	H	O	A	E
C.C. Cox, cf	1	0	0	0	0	0
Bailey, cf	3	0	0	1	0	0
Lambeth, 1b, ss	4	1	2	1	2	0
McQuage, 1b	3	1	1	12	0	1
Roach, 3b	4	0	1	2	0	1
Rex, lf	4	0	1	4	0	0
Johnson, 2b	3	0	0	1	6	0
Farris, c	3	0	1	5	0	0
Flythe, p	3	0	0	0	4	2
Kirkland, ph	1	0	0	0	0	0
	29	2	6	26	12	4

```
Wake Forest    0 3 0    0 1 0    0 0 0    4
State          0 0 0    1 0 1    0 0 0    2
```

Summary: Two base hit: Rex. Three base hit: McQuage. Stolen bases: Slayton, Gold 2. Sacrifice: Herring. Double play: Johnson, Lambeth and McQuage. Left on bases: Wake Forest 12, State, 5. Base on balls: off Flythe 5. Struck out: by Herring 7, Flythe 5. Hit by pitch: Wall, Mitchell. Wild pitches: Flythe 2. Passed balls: Farris 2. Umpires: Kearney and Fields. Time 2:00.

Wake Forest continued its dominance of the series in the 1935 edition of the Easter Monday classic. In the preview of the game, the reader finds the first newspaper reference to the state team as the "Red Terrors," although it had been used for several years in *Agromeck* articles.

DEACONS GET WIN IN SLUGGING FEST
Wall's Homer Tops Five-Run Third Inning; Scales Hits Homer for Tech
by ANTHONY J. MCKEVLIN

The bottom of the Wake Forest lineup carried the load in yet another victory over their rivals. In what began as a tightly contested "see-saw" battle for the first four innings, the Deacons took control and held on for an 11–6 victory.

The Techs held the momentum for the first couple of innings, and their fans were optimistic that they might be able to secure their first Easter Monday victory since 1930. However, in the third inning, the Deacons employed various methods, including a long homer by Dwight Wall, to score five times.

The bottom boys in the batting order started the big doings in the third. Pitcher Doug Johnson, who relieved Braxton Rhodes after the Techs' third inning, singled to start a three-run splurge in the fifth, and that inning's business sewed up the game. In the next inning Catcher Sheppard, who hits eighth, started things with a single to set the table for a rally.

Scales Hits Homer

Fans didn't know about this bad habit of the bottom trio of Deacons, and so it looked as if Lefty Freeman of State was going places when he retired the Deacons in order in the first two innings. In the meantime he was given a working margin of three runs. A triple by Williams, Chappell's error on Lambeth's bounder, a stolen base, and Norwood's single counted two in the first. Fairley Scales, Raleigh youth, opened the second by hitting a homer which landed beyond the top of the left field bank and rolled to the gymnasium.

The Deacons' third inning was set in motion when Walton Kitchin drew a walk. Sheppard singled. Pitcher Rhodes was the next batter, and most onlookers expected him to sacrifice. Rhodes banged a clean single to center, and Kitchin scored. Dallas Morris sacrificed the two runners, and Sheppard journeyed across the plate when Williams errored on Freeman's slightly high throw. Morris and Rhodes put on a double steal. Morris being retired and Rhodes scoring. Gold then singled to center, Mitchell flied to center, and Wall drove the ball to the far reaches of center field for a round trip.

Fat Man Steals Show

As usual, McKevlin had a way of selecting details about the crowd that closed the aesthetic distance for the readers:

The Easter Monday Baseball Game

The Deacons were in front and their supporters were making merry. And a slightly saddened fellow, although still very talkative, was the very fat and very cheerful gentleman in the "left field" standees, who insisted on standing outside the ropes and yelling, "Come on, State." Before the game was over, he was a cynosure for all the onlookers, and many small boys had passed up the game to gather around and listen to his observations on baseball and whatnot....

After a fast start, the 1935 State team hovered around .500 all year. Wake Forest, led by outfielder Milky Gold, had an excellent season though they fell just short, finishing second in the Big Five.

Box score for this game is unavailable.

The following article appeared in the 1935 *News and Observer* dated April 21. Note that the author, Betsy McKevlin, shares the same last name with the gentleman who was writing the baseball article at the time.

PiKA Ball, Country Club Easter Dance and Other Dances Fill Week-end

Easter week-end in Raleigh is proving a gala period for dancing contingents, with the series of holiday dances opening on Good Friday night and closing with the annual Easter Ball of the Pi Kappa Alpha fraternity and the Easter dance of the Country Club tomorrow (Monday) night.

The calendar for the week-end is giving also many other forms of entertainment including tea dances and bridge tournaments, banquets and theatre parties, most of which are affairs attendant upon the PiKA Ball.

The PiKA Ball, given each year by Alpha Epsilon Chapter of the fraternity at State College, will be held tomorrow night in the Frank Thompson gymnasium on the college campus. Elaborate decorations of garnet and gold will be featured by an illuminated fraternity pin, and the highlight of the evening will be the dance figure to be led by Miss Louise McLeod of Lillington with J.F. Scales, Miss Eleanor Doster of Monroe, with D.A. Brannon and Miss Jean Gray Scott of Graham and G.A. Holt. Music for the ball will be furnished by Jack Stern and his orchestra.... During the weekend the PiKAs are entertaining at a house party at their home on Hillsboro Street, their guests having arrived Friday, attending the White Spades Dance that night and the Tri-Fraternity Spring Festival Dances yesterday. The fraternity will entertain at a theatre party this afternoon and tonight....

As one might expect, the State team was given the role of the underdog the following year, as Fred Dixon noted in his preview article of

With a double and a home run, Eddie Yount led the Wake Forest nine in a losing effort in 1936. Yount had a brief major league career and then became a mainstay as a player and manager in the Class D minor leagues of western North Carolina (courtesy Chris Holaday).

Monday, April 13, 1936. "Wake Forest is the favored team," he admits, but he goes on to prognosticate that State, "because of its fine exhibition Saturday" against legendary Jack Coombs's Duke team, "is thought to have a fine chance of upsetting the Deacons." He added that the promise of good weather gives "every indication that the game will attract one of the largest crowds of the series which dates back more than a quarter of a century."

> Williams' Home Run in Ninth Gives State 8–7 Win Over Deacs
> TECHS PUT CHECK ON DEACONS' WINS
> Farrar and Yount Also Hit Homers: Over 3,000 See Holiday Game Here
> by FRED DIXON
>
> Captain Dorous Williams, first batter in the home half of the ninth inning hit the first pitch for a home run to give State an 8–7 win over Wake Forest here yesterday in their annual Easter Monday baseball game.

Williams's homer brought to an end a five-year winning streak for the Deacons in the Easter Monday series. The winning shot landed against the Frank Thompson Gymnasium beyond left field.

Dixon called the crowd "One of the largest ... ever to see the annual game." In this case, there was apparently an attempt to get a more exact attendance figure with the official announcement of attendance as 3,243, "but this total did not include those who 'slipped in,' the couple of hundred who viewed the game from the railroad, and a similar number who looked on from free parking places just outside the field."

Dixon described the game as an exciting one that offered outstanding performance in every phase of the game, whether pitching, hitting, or fielding.

Both Gaddy for Wake and Blount for State started out strong and turned in excellent performances for the first three innings: "Gaddy pitched to only nine men in those three frames—he fanned three in the first inning and two in the third. Blount pitched to but one extra batter in the three innings. He issued one base on balls in the first. In the second he set the Deacons down on strikes. A double play—Fairley Scales to Walter Rabb to Vince Farrar—helped Blount in the third."

The Big Parade

The game changed completely in the fourth inning as eleven runners crossed home plate, four for the Wake club and seven in the bottom half for State.

This was all the scoring State would do until the ninth. Meanwhile Wake Forest managed two more runs in the sixth and added the tying run in the seventh:

> Blount, State's starting hurler, retired with one away in the seventh, after the Deacons had tied the score. Jerry Davidson, southpaw, pitched the rest of the way for State and hurled hitless ball while fanning three in his $2\frac{2}{3}$ innings of duty.
>
> **Yount, Farrar Hit Homers**
> Home runs featured the big scoring parties of the teams in the fourth. The Deacons got the first run of the game when Preston Chappell tripled to left center and continued on home when shortstop Rabb threw low in an effort to get him at third. Dwight Wall walked. Doigt Morris fanned, and Patton walked. Eddie Yount then hit to deep center field for a homer.
>
> Singles by Williams and Dalrymple opened State's party in its half of the fourth. Gadd fanned; but Bugg singled to fill the bases. Up stepped Vince Farrar, best known as a football star and Farrar cleared the sacks with a homer which landed close to the spot where Yount's round-tripper landed.
>
> But the Techs didn't stop there. Fairley Scales singled to left and moved to third on a couple of wild pitches. Rabb fanned, Jake Mahoney walked, and Pitcher Blount singled to score Scales. Blount went to second on the throw-in. A balk by Pitcher Gaddy sent Mahoney home, and Carl Byrd replaced Gaddy on the hill for the Deacons. Byrd issued a pass to Williams, but Dalrymple made his second single of the inning — and Blount scored. Byrd fanned Gadd to end the inning; it was the second whiff for Gadd in the inning.
>
> The Deacons' two runs in the sixth were scored on a single by Patton, a double by Yount, an wild pitch and a single by Porter Sheppard. The tying run, in the seventh came as a result of a walk to Chappell, a single by Wall, and a long outfield fly hit by Doigt Morris. It was at this point that Davidson replaced Blount.

Farrar, playing first base, turned in good defensive work for the Techs. Captain Williams was switched to the outfield.

The Easter Monday Baseball Game

Shortstop Chapell was the outstanding defensive player for Wake.

Eddie Yount, who led the Deacons in this game with a double and a homer, would go on to play a short stint in the major leagues in 1937 and 1939. His minor league career continued to 1951, including four years as a manager for the Newton-Conover Twins and the Hickory Rebels in Class D leagues, where his teams won two league championships. In his last full season as a player for Newton-Conover, he batted an astounding .428.

Although Wake Forest lost this Easter Monday battle and had in fact not won a game to this point in 1936, the Deacons quickly turned things around and ended up winning the Big Five championship for the first time in four years. Outstanding hitting was the key feature of this team, which finished with six players hitting above .300, and with Chappel and Morris among the top five in the conference.

Wake Forest	AB	R	H	O	A	E
Dallas Morris, 3b	4	0	1	1	0	0
Chappell, ss	4	2	2	3	2	0
Wall, cf	2	1	1	3	0	0
Doight Morris, lf	5	0	0	1	0	0
Patton, 1b	3	2	1	5	0	0
Yount, rf	4	2	2	0	0	0
Payne, 2b	3	0	0	1	1	0
Shepherd, c	4	0	1	10	1	0
Gaddy, p	2	0	0	0	0	0
Byrd, p	2	0	0	0	2	0
	33	7	8	24	6	0

N.C. State	AB	R	H	O	A	E
Williams, lf	4	2	2	5	0	0
Dalrymple, 3b	4	1	2	2	4	1
Gadd, cf	4	0	1	2	0	0
Farrar, 1b	4	1	1	7	0	0
Scales, 2b	4	1	1	0	1	0
Rabb, ss	4	0	0	2	3	1
Wynn, c	1	0	0	6	0	0
Mahoney, c	2	1	1	3	1	0
Blount, p	3	1	1	0	0	0
Davidson, p	1	0	0	0	0	0
Bugg, rf	4	1	2	0	0	0
	35	8	11	27	9	2

```
Wake Forest   0 0 0   4 0 2   1 0 0   7
State         0 0 0   7 0 0   0 0 1   8
```

SUMMARY: Two base hits: Yount, Gadd. Three base hits: Mahoney, Chappell. Home runs: Yount, Farrar, Williams. Stolen bases: Dallas Morris, Wall 2, Payne. Double plays: Scales, Rabb to Farrar, Dalrymple to Farrar. Left on bases: Wake Forest 7: State 5. Base on balls: off Gaddy 1, Byrd 1, Blount 6, Davidson 2. Struck out: by Gaddy 7, by Byrd 4, by Blount 6, by Davidson 3. Wild pitches: Gaddy 2, Blount. Balk: Gaddy.

When Fred Dixon previewed the 1937 game, he could not have known to expect one of the wildest affairs on record in the series, but that is the bargain that the fans received.

FANS GET BARGAIN AT HOLIDAY GAME
Deacons Take 19–17 Verdict in Game of 42 Safeties; Over 4,000 on Hand
by FRED DIXON

If anyone should challenge the old saying that "Anything can happen in baseball," just refer the challenger to any of the more than 4,000 fans who yesterday afternoon turned out for the annual Easter Monday diamond meeting of State and Wake Forest.

Many of the 4,000 fans left during the latter stages of the game, particularly when Wake Forest seemed to have an insurmountable lead. The wild game eventually resembled more a football score than a diamond contest, passing the regulation with the teams locked in a 17–17 tie. Wake Forest finally scored a pair of runs in the top of the 12th, enough to secure the win.

The game included more hitting than had been seen in the series, though the Deacons made a little more with theirs, scoring their nineteen runs on "just" seventeen hits. State had twenty-five hits, making the total for the game forty-two, certainly a record for the classic, though not that unusual for an early spring college game.

See-Saw, See-Saw

Most of the fans enjoyed it. It was that kind of a game. Things see-sawed, and at more than one stage it looked as if one of the teams had sewed up victory. The run-making began at the very start — Wake scored three times in the first stanza. State scored twice. State tallied in the next two innings to take a 9–3 advantage; the Deacons made three in the fourth and a similar number in the fifth to make it 9–9.

Wake Forest went in front with a pair of tallies in the sixth, but State put over three in the seventh to make the count 12–11. Fans began departing after the Deacons scored six times in the eighth to take the apparently insurmountable lead of 17–12. The fans were wrong — State could, and did catch up. The Techs pushed over five in their half of the eighth to knot things at 17–17.

The reader will find in Dixon's writing more of the cliché rather than the colorful descriptions seen in his predecessor's prose styling. "It was no day for pitchers. The batters were having heap much fun. Base hits were a dime a dozen."

How Deacons Won

Surprising as it was, the teams went scoreless through three innings. Then the Deacons got busy in the 12th to win — with the help of a couple of State miscues. Hal Warren singled to start the inning. Porter Sheppard drew a pass. An outfield fly by Pitcher Forrest Glass advanced Warren to third. A wild pitch by Mac Berry, State's third flinger of the afternoon, let in Warren with what proved to be the winning run. Irvin Dickens grounded out. Sheppard advancing to third. Sheppard tallied when Catcher Julian Richardson couldn't handle one of Berry's slightly wide pitches. Berry whiffed Dallas Morris to end the inning.

There was no particular reason to venture a guess on what might happen in State's half. Albert Sandfoss led off with a triple, and it looked as if the game might go on and on. But Pitcher Glass and his mates weren't letting this latest lead get away from them — Dalrymple and Gadd popped out to Third-Baseman Dallas Morris, and Uriah Norwood flied out to Centerfielder Doigt Morris.

Unless someone can bob up with records to the contrary, we'll devote this paragraph to saying that yesterday's game set a record scoring in an intercollegiate game in this State. If you know of any to beat that, drop us a line.

Wake's 1937 team was one of Coach Caddell's finest. They finished with a 20–5 record and soundly defeated most of their competition.

This was the first of two years that Morrie Aderholt played second base for Wake Forest in the spring classic. A native of Mount Olive, North Carolina, he would later have a twelve-year minor league career in which he hit .304. During that time, he got called up to the majors for five seasons, playing in a total of 106 games for the Senators, Dodgers, and

Braves. Aderholt managed minor league teams for the Senators for six years and then worked as a scout until his death. He died of a heart attack at age 39 while on a scouting trip in Florida.

The official "opening of the game found Dr. R.P. Noble of Raleigh pitching to A.F. Bowen, treasurer of State College. Dr. Noble umpired the State–Wake Forest game played on Easter Monday of 1907 — and on that date Treasurer Bowen handed Umpire Noble a check for the big sum of $3.00 as remuneration for his services."

Wake Forest	AB	R	H	O	A	E
Dickens, ss	8	2	3	2	2	0
Dallas Morris, 3b	7	2	2	3	7	0
Chappell, lf	4	2	2	1	1	0
Doight Morris, cf	7	2	2	7	0	0
Mauney, 1b	5	3	1	11	1	0
Aderholt, 2b	6	1	2	2	2	0
Warren, rf	7	3	4	2	0	1
Sheppard, c	3	3	1	8	0	0
Byrd, p	1	0	0	0	4	0
Glass, p	5	1	0	0	4	0
	53	19	17	36	21	1

N.C. State	AB	R	H	O	A	E
Sandfoss, 2b	8	4	6	4	3	2
Dalrymple, 3b	5	3	1	3	5	0
Gadd, lf	5	4	3	3	0	0
Norwood, cf	7	3	5	4	0	3
Mann, 1b	6	0	3	10	1	1
Rabb, ss	5	0	2	3	4	2
Hines, rf	3	0	1	1	0	0
Wicker, rf	4	0	0	2	0	0
Berlinski, c	4	0	1	3	2	0
Richardson, c	3	1	2	3	0	0
Griffin, p	2	1	0	0	0	0
Green, p	1	0	0	0	1	0
Berry, p	2	1	1	0	2	0
	55	17	25	36	18	8

```
Wake Forest   3 0 0   3 3 2   0 6 0   0 0 2   19
State         2 5 2   0 0 0   3 5 0   0 0 0   17
```

SUMMARY: Two base hits: Sandfoss, Gadd, Rabb, Berry, Norwood. Three base hits: Sandfoss, Norwood 2, Dickens. Home run: Dallas Morris. Stolen bases: Dickens, Dallas Morris, Aderholt, Warren, Sheppard, Hines. Sacrifices: Mauney, Glass, Dalrymple, Gadd, Mann, Rabb, Berry. Left on bases: Wake Forest 9; State 14. Base on balls: off Byrd 3, Glass 2, Griffin 2, Green 3, Berry 5. Struck out: by Byrd 2, Glass 4,

Green 2, Berry 3. Hit by pitcher: Rabb. Wild pitches: Green, Berry. Passed ball: Richardson. Umpires: Kearney and Stephenson. Time 3:20.

Bad weather returned for the mid–April 1938 Easter Monday game, with the action finally halted in a tie.

RAIN AND HOMERS, HOMERS AND RAIN!
Wicker and Aderholt Bat in Runs; Only Losers in Game Are the Fans
by ANTHONY J. McKEVLIN

The only losers at yesterday's State–Wake Forest baseball game here were the 3,500 folks who came out to watch the collegians in baseball battle.

The diamond doings ended in a 2–2 stalemate; the fans wound up all wet.

The potential for bad weather was apparent all day. Some of the fans brought raincoats, which proved to be useful as play was halted first in the top of the third, then in the top of the fourth, and finally for good in the bottom of the sixth when, as McKevlin says, "The heavens really opened."

The Homers

Bob Wicker, Sandford's gift to the Techs, produced the first homer of the day. Charlie Beam opened State's second by slashing a hit past Third Baseman Tallie Dupree. Wicker's arrival at the plate brought cheers from State fans. His three-run homer put the Techs out in front in the first inning of Saturday's game with Duke here. The Tech fans wanted nothing less than a home run. Wicker tied into one of Jake Danning's offerings, and the ball headed towards the gym — but it swerved to the left, kept swerving, and was foul by a couple of first downs. The next pitch, well, that was different. Bob tied into that one too, and the result was a drive which cleared the hedge on the bank in left field — an "over the fence" homer.

There almost was another home run with two away in the Deacons' third — and just after rain made its first appearance — Irving Dickens hit far out in right-center. It was a safe triple and a probable homer. He gambled. The play in reached the plate well ahead of Dickens, and Catcher Larry Smith crouched — ready to tag the sliding Dickens. The Deacon didn't slide — he dove over Smith. Umpire Rasty Walters ruled that Dickens had been tagged and was out. The Deacons argued otherwise. Many fans figured Dickens had outsmarted Smith and had not been tagged. But Rasty stuck to his decision although he was willing to swap places, when such a change was requested by the Deacons, with Base Umpire Flora. Mr. Flora, evidently feeling that life was much easier on the bases, declined to accept such generosity. Rasty stayed on the plate job.

The rival hurlers fared nicely despite the very damp afternoon. Denning, Angier boy, yielded only three hits to State. Only State safety other than those of the scoring inning was Eddie Berlinski's infield rap in the third. Allen Green — he's from Zebulon — yielded five hits to the Deacons but stayed out of trouble except for that home-run ball thrown to Aderholdt. Green fanned six, walked only one. Denning fanned four, walked three....

McKevlin's comments on the weather and how the fans and the press handled it are humorous:

Those fair fans who put on their Easter finery for the occasion had a right to shed tears. A little more water wouldn't have hurt anything. And here's something those who were there won't believe — the Weather Man's official figure for rainfall during the 24 hours ending at eight o'clock last night was 18–100 of one inch. Eighteen times that much water went down the collar of each and every fellow at the press table.

The fans could take it. The first visit of rain cleared the field so quickly that it looked as if the customers might have been holding fire drills at some time or other. The rain stopped, the fans returned. The rain came again and the fans scattered again. Fans returned, and after a while rain came again. At least 162 persons broke the world's 100-yard record for a wet track in getting to the gym. Stock in Raleigh dry-cleaning firms should go up today.

There would be no playoff for the tie unless it was determined that the outcome would affect the championship for the Big Five.

For State's Coach Doak in his fourteenth year at the helm, it was another mediocre season, with the ball club finishing at 7-8-2.

Wake Forest	*AB*	*R*	*H*	*O*	*A*	*E*
Dickens, ss	3	0	1	1	2	0
Fuller, 1b	3	0	1	5	0	1
Payne, cf	2	1	0	0	0	0
Aderholt, 2b	3	1	1	3	3	0
Dupree, 3b	2	0	0	0	1	0
Eutsler, rf	2	0	1	0	0	0
F. Hoyle, lf	2	0	0	3	0	0
Sweet, c	2	0	1	4	0	0

The Easter Monday Baseball Game

Wake Forest	AB	R	H	O	A	E
Denning, p	2	0	0	0	1	0
	21	2	5	16	7	1

N.C. State	AB	R	H	O	A	E
Kearns, ss	2	0	0	1	2	0
Berlinski, cf	3	0	1	0	0	0
Smith, c	3	0	0	7	2	0
Beam, rf	2	1	1	0	1	0
Wicker, 3b	1	1	1	0	0	0
Peatross, lf	2	0	0	2	0	0
W. Hoyle, 2b	2	0	0	0	3	0
Harris, 1b	1	0	0	8	0	0
Green, p	2	0	0	0	2	0
	18	2	3	18	10	0

Summary: Three base hits: Eutsler, Dickens. Home runs: Wicker, Aderholt. Stolen bases: Peatross, Berlinski. Double plays: Dupree, Aderholt and Fuller: Aderholt, Dickens and Fuller. Left on bases: Wake Forest 2, N.C. State 3. Base on balls: Denning 3, Green 1. Strikeouts: Denning 4, Green 6. Umpires: Walters and Flora. Time 1:29.

Of course, the PiKAs publicized this now traditional weekend. The following is an excerpt from their 1938 newsletter, *The PiKA Post*:

> Continuing a custom which has been carried on for the last thirty-two years, the A-E chapter gave its annual PiKA Ball in the Frank Thompson Gym on Easter Monday, April 18.
>
> New faces and customs replaced the old at this year's ball. From eight until twelve the music was furnished by Johnny Long and his orchestra, who came from the Arcadia in Philadelphia and who has been broadcasting regularly over the Columbia Broadcasting System.
>
> The chapter gave a house party over the week end for the guests at our home on Hillsboro. On Saturday evening the members entertained their guests at a buffet supper. A theatre party was given on Sunday afternoon, followed by a banquet in the main dining room of the Sir Walter Hotel, honoring the alumni of the chapter. On Monday afternoon golf, tennis, and horseback riding were enjoyed.
>
> This year's guests of the dance were requested to wear black formal. The local brothers wore white dinner coats.
>
> As usual the gym was elaborately decorated in the fraternity colors. The electrically lighted pin was over the band stand. New decorations started last year, and continued this year were the printed balloons and the bags

Alpha Epsilon

of

Pi Kappa Alpha

requests the honor of your presence

at the Thirty-ninth Annual Pi. K. A. Ball

April seventh, Nineteen hundred forty-seven

Black Formal   Frank Thompson Gymnasium

Please Present   Eight 'til Twelve

Invitation to the 1947 black formal, similar to those received by thousands of attendees during the years of this iconic social event (courtesy R.G. Utley and Jean Utley).

of confetti. The dance went on the air for thirty minutes over WDNC, Durham.

Each year the PiKA Ball has increased in popularity until it is now surpassed by the final dances only.

The 1939 Easter Monday game featured the excellent pitching of Ray Scarborough, who would go on to pitch for ten seasons for three different major league teams. Scarborough won 80 games in a career that was interrupted by World War II. Scarborough's name also appears in records as a pitcher for the Hickory Rebels of the Carolina Independent (outlaw) League in 1937. During his college days, his first name is recorded as Rae. His professional records use the more conventional Ray.

The Easter Monday Baseball Game

Easter Monday stands, 1939. This was the 32nd meeting between the rivals, a game dominated by Wake Forest pitcher, Ray Scarborough, who pitched a two-hit, 2–0 shutout. About 3,500 fans attended the game (courtesy R.G. Utley).

This game would be remembered as one of the finest pitching performances in the entire series.

DEACON ACE GETS ANOTHER VICTORY
Rae Scarborough Comes Close to No-Hitter but Gives Up Two Singles
by BILLY ANDERSON

Rae Scarborough of Mount Gilead, senior righthander, struck out 11 and pitched two-hit ball as Wake Forest blanked State, 2–0, on Freshman Field here yesterday in the 32nd annual Easter Monday contest between the schools.

More than 3,500 fans turned out for the renewal of the oldest intercollegiate baseball rivalry on the State. And they were given one of the greatest college pitching performances that has been turned in here in many years.

Rae came very close to crashing into the hall of fame with a no-hitter. However, two singles by two Raleigh boys—Adolph Honeycutt in the eighth and Pinch Hitter O.F. (Pig) Peatross in the ninth — denied him that enviable position.

This was Scarborough's fifth straight victory of the season. He had already recorded victories over Springfield (Mass.) College, Colby College of Maine, Michigan State, Cornell, and State. For Coach John Caddell's Demon Deacs, it was the sixth win of the early season — they had also defeated Cornell twice with Tommy Byrne handling the duties on the mound.

Rae's Strikeout Record

At this point in the season, Scarborough had already struck out fifty batters in just 33 innings. It was his second straight shutout and complete game. The week before, Wake had defeated Cornell 1–0.

Scarborough was not the only hurler to turn in a nifty pitching performance. Allen (Pea) Green, a diminutive righthander, pitched well for State, giving up seven hits and fanning five. Green walked six; Scarborough, five.

Wake Forest bunched two hits for one run tallies in each of the eighth and ninth innings. Jack Williams started off the eighth-inning doings by singling after one out. He advanced on a passed ball, and Dick Hoyle drew a free ticket to first. Fred Eason singled sharply through shortstop and Williams came home.

It's Williams Again

Williams also figured in the ninth inning score. Bill Sweel set the stage for the tally by hitting a single through the box, and he moved up on Scarborough's sacrifice. Captain Irvin Dickens walked, and Williams lashed a single into deep center, bringing in Sweel with the final run.

State offered its most serious threat in the seventh inning. Captain Bob Wicker popped out to second, but Wade Brown walked. Cader Harris fanned, and then Scarborough gave walks to Fred Broyhill and Bill Ritter. Green had a chance to win his own ball game, but he grounded out, second to first.

With one out in the eighth — Honeycutt singled to deep center, but Winstead rolled out, third to first, and Bob Wicker popped up to rightfield. In the ninth, Brown fanned, and Pinch-hitter Hendrin fanned. Peatross in for Broyhill, singled, but Ritter rolled to Scarborough, who easily tossed him out at first.

The Easter Monday Baseball Game

This Wake Forest team included two of the most successful Major League pitchers ever produced by the Wake Forest baseball program: Ray Scarborough and Tommy Byrne. First row, left to right: Jack Williams, Tony Gallovich, Dick Hoyle, Pete Nelson, Fred Eason. Second row, left to right: Paul Wivers, Tallie Dupree, Bill Sweel, John Caddell (coach), Irvin Dickens, Bill Eutsler, Tony Balionis. Third row, left to right: Ray Scarborough, John Pendergast, Tommy Byrne, Jim Denning, Billy Weathers, Dave Fuller (courtesy Wake Forest University).

Wake Forest was led by Williams and Easton, each with two hits. Fielding honors went to State's Clinton Winstead, sophomore from Roxboro. He made a brilliant running shoe-string catch of Dave Fuller's liner in the eighth inning, preventing two runs from scoring.

Behind the pitching of Tommy Byrne and Rae Scarborough, Wake had a fine season in what proved to be Coach Caddell's last one, finishing 12–5.

Wake Forest	AB	R	H	O	A	E
Dickens, ss	4	0	1	2	1	1
Williams, cf	4	1	2	0	0	1
D. Hoyle, lf	3	0	1	0	0	0
Eason, rf	5	0	2	1	0	0
Nelson, 2b	4	0	0	2	7	0
Dupree, 3b	3	0	0	0	3	0
Fuller, 1b	4	0	0	11	0	1
Sweet, c	2	1	1	11	2	0

Wake Forest	AB	R	H	O	A	E
Scarborough, p	3	0	0	0	1	0
	32	2	7	27	14	3

State	AB	R	H	O	A	E
B. Hoyle, 2b	3	0	0	2	3	0
Honeycutt, lf	4	0	1	2	0	0
Winstead, cf	4	0	0	1	0	0
Wicker, 3b	4	0	0	0	4	0
Brown, rf	3	0	0	1	0	0
Harris, 1b	2	0	0	14	0	0
Broyhill, ss	2	0	0	1	7	1
Ritter, c	2	0	0	6	0	1
Green, p	3	0	0	0	2	0
Hendrin, ph	1	0	0	0	0	0
Peatross, ph	1	0	1	0	0	0
Roberts, ph	1	0	0	0	0	0
	30	0	2	27	16	2

```
Wake Forest   0 0 0   0 0 0   0 1 1   2
State         0 0 0   0 0 0   0 0 0   0
```

Summary: Stolen bases: D. Hoyle, Dickens, Eason, Broyhill, Fuller. Sacrifices: Scarborough. Double plays: B. Hoyle and Harris. Left on bases: Wake Forest 9, State 7. Bases on balls: off Green 6; Scarborough 5. Struck out: by Green 5; Scarborough 11. Umpires: Mitchell and Walters. Time: 2:12.

The March 1, 1939, edition of the *PiKA POST* sheds more light on the history of the fraternity dance:

> This dance was inaugurated in 1906, after just two years at North Carolina State College. It has gained in popularity and prominence through the years until today it is heralded far and wide by the younger members of society in several states.
>
> Alumni who have observed our recent dance have stated that there is very little resemblance between the PiKA ball of today and the first dance of 1906. The idea for the ball originated in a committee composed of Brothers Clarence Stedman, St. Julian Springs, and John Park. These were the three men who actually engineered the first PiKA ball, and to them should go the credit for establishing a custom that brought much credit to their chapter.
>
> At the time of the first PiKA ball there were five active fraternities on the campus. The college had allowed these fraternities only three dances a year, of which one was the PiKA ball. The other four fraternities had combined

their resources and had given the other two dances. There had been a great conflict over which of the fraternities would be given Easter Monday for their dance. The only reason in favor of our fraternity was the fact that we had given our first dance on the previous Easter Monday. The final decision of the faculty council was in favor of our fraternity. Thus for the following thirty-two years the PiKA ball has been given on Easter Monday night.

The 1940 season proved to be another odd year in this long-running series. It marked the debut of State coach Doc Newton, who had succeeded longtime Tech coach, Chick Doak. Easter came very early that year as well, with the game slated for March 25 at Freshman Field in Raleigh. Snow, however, forced a makeup date, and because of scheduling problems, the only Easter Monday game to be played outside of Raleigh, this one taking place at Grove Field at Wake Forest on Tuesday, April 9.

As mentioned earlier, State was not the only team with a coaching change. This is from the *Wake Forest Howler*:

> Baseball at Wake Forest has become one of the school's most widely recognized masteries. For nearly a score of years, the "Grand Old Man" of baseball to Wake Forest has been Coach John Caddell, but this year condition of his health forced him to the bench. At his resignation, athletic officials looked in the direction of Murray Greason, backfield coach of the football team and head basketball instructor, for Coach Murray was the logical man to give the Deacons another winning team.

> Deacs Get 7–6 Victory over State;
> FLETCHER BRINGS CONTEST TO END
> Soph Triples in Ninth and Tallies Winning Run in First Big Five Game
>   by BILLY ANDERSON
> [Note: This article also included the Big Five Standings.]

When the makeup game was played, because of the cold day and the distance from the Raleigh offices and businesses, only 1,100 fans attended. Sophomore John Fletcher of Charlotte proved to be the hero as Wake Forest edged N.C. State 7–6.

The contest was the beginning of play for the Big Five and was Wake Forest's first Southern Conference game for the season. For State, it was their second loss in their first three games.

Anderson began his game narrative at the conclusion and then worked his way back from the beginning:

> Fletcher, first up in the ninth and with the score tied at 6–all, slammed one of Pitcher Sammy Kaufman's fast balls to the far reaches of right field for a triple. Rightfielder Nixon and Centerfielder Constant scampered after the fast-traveling ball. However, his peg to home was wild, and Fletcher coasted in with the game-winning run.
>
> Coach Murray Greason's boys overcame State's four-run blast in the first inning in order to win. The Techs mixed four hits with an error, and a wild pitch in getting their first inning runs.
>
> Wake Forest pushed over singletons in the first and fourth and took the lead for the first time, with a three-run blast in the fifth by mixing five hits with two errors. Feature of the fifth inning was Bill (Bud) Sweel's double to leftfield, scoring Billy Eutsler.
>
> Curtis Ramsey, the Techs' big righthander, started the game but was knocked out in the sixth inning when he gave up nine hits and three walks for five runs. He also had two strikeouts. Lefty Sam Kaufman replaced Ramsey, yielding two hits and two walks for one run in the eighth, and gave up the game-winning hit in the ninth.
>
> The Techs drove Jim Denning to the showers with a four-run blast in the first. Dave (Slick) Fuller, former Raleigh high school athlete, took over and shut out the Techs on five hits until the ninth. Slick retired the first two batters in the ninth, but Kaufman's single and Constant's triple brought a run, and Lefty Tommy Byrne took over the pitching job. Tom was wild; he walked Chick Doak, first up, and a wild pitch allowed Constant to score. Tom Settled down and fanned Pat Fehley for the final out.
>
> Bob Read of Asheville, sophomore first baseman, led Wake Forest's 11-hit attack, with three singles for four tries. Runner-up honors went to Jack Williams and Byrne, with two for three. State's Cader Harris and Kaufman batted 1,000 with two singles. They were the only Techs to make more than one hit.

The top fielders for the two teams were State's Pat Fehley, who caught a line drive and began a double play in the eighth, and Wake's Polanski and Williams, both of whom made run-saving catches.

Tommy Byrne, a Baltimore native, who played four positions for Wake Forest in this game, also added two hits. Byrne would go on to become one of the most successful major league pitchers to emerge from the Easter Classic. He won 85 games in a thirteen-year career. He was a two-time world champion and pitched well in three World Series. His nickname was "Wildman" because of the control problems he experienced early in his career. For the first four years, he averaged six walks per nine innings pitched, a record eventually surpassed by the young Nolan Ryan. After his professional career, Byrne returned to Wake Forest, where he worked as both a pro scout and coach. He was the mayor of the city of Wake Forest from 1973 to 1987.

State	*AB*	*R*	*H*	*O*	*A*	*E*
Constant, cf	4	2	1	3	0	1
C. Doak, c	4	1	1	3	1	1
Fehley, 2b	5	0	1	4	4	0
Harris, 1b	2	1	2	7	0	0
Brown, lf	4	1	1	0	0	1
Ritter, ss	3	0	0	2	1	1
Henderson	1	0	0	0	0	0
Broyhill, ss	0	0	0	1	0	0
Absher, cf	3	0	1	3	0	0
R. Doak, ph	1	0	0	0	0	0
Nixon, rf	0	0	0	0	0	0
Morrison, 3b	3	0	0	1	2	0
Jones, ph	1	0	0	0	0	0
McAuley, lf	0	0	0	0	0	0
Ramsey, p	2	0	1	0	2	0
Kaufman, p	2	1	2	0	0	0
	35	6	10	24	10	4
Wake Forest	*AB*	*R*	*H*	*O*	*A*	*E*
Fletcher, 2b	5	1	0	4	1	0
Hoyle, ss	3	1	1	1	1	0
Eutsler, lf	1	2	0	2	0	0
Easog, rf	1	0	0	0	0	0
Reid, 1b	4	1	3	12	0	0
Byrne, cf-rf-lf-p	3	0	2	0	0	0
McCall, rf	1	0	0	0	2	0
Williams, cf	3	0	2	0	0	0
Polanski, 3b	3	0	0	1	3	1
Swell, c	4	1	1	7	2	0
Denning, p	0	0	0	0	0	0
Fuller, p-rf	3	1	1	0	5	0
	31	7	10	27	14	1

```
State         4 0 0   0 0 0   0 0 2   6
Wake Forest   1 0 0   1 3 0   0 1 1   7
```

Depression and War

SUMMARY: Two base hits: Constant, Swell. Three base hits: Constant, Fletcher. Stolen bases: Brown, Absher, Fehley, Reid, C. Doak. Sacrifices: Harris, Constant. Double plays: Doak, Morrison and Ritter; Williams and Reid; Fehley and Ritter. Left on bases: State 6, Wake Forest 7. Base on balls: off Ramsey 2, Fuller 1, Kauffman 1, Byrne 1. Struck out: by Ramsey 1, Fuller 5, Kauffman 1, Byrne 1. Wild pitches: Denning, Byrne. Passed ball: Doak. Umpires: Mitchell and Powell. Time 2:30.

The PiKA ball continued on as an important social event in the college's and state's youth culture. Through the '40s and '50s the local media continued to cover the event with a kind of journalistic template whose purpose was to recognize the fraternity leaders and the civic and business leaders who attended as special guests of the chapter. Much of the coverage during this time included elaborate pictorial spreads of the young women and men in attendance. As the personal accounts in this book would indicate, the PiKA ball was still the event of the season during the late '40s, one capable of stirring vivid memories more than fifty years later. However, the changing culture and growth of the college and of the area dictated that the ball would become marginalized and finally abandoned, just like the Easter Monday baseball classic.

Notes from the written histories of Alpha Epsilon indicate that the 1961 ball was held for the first time on a date other than Easter Monday. The tradition continued sporadically through the '60s, and in 1980, a Pi Ball (not PiKA Ball) was labeled the 72nd annual Pi Ball. It was a formal dance that was held at the Ramada Inn in Apex, N.C.

As historian R.G. Utley has noted, "The Easter Monday baseball game and the Easter Monday PiKA Ball were gradual victims of social and cultural changes at not only N.C. State but all the surrounding universities. Like the rest of America, the games, romance and revelry of a post–Easter Mardi Gras at N.C. State faded away."

1941–1950

Much of the activity in this decade centered around the buildup to and then the execution of the war. Three new military bases were established in North Carolina: Seymour Johnson Air Base in Goldsboro; a

Marine base in Cherry Point; and another large Marine training camp, Camp Lejeune, near Jacksonville. The shipyard in Wilmington was completed and would be responsible for the completion of 273 ships during the war effort. More than 360,000 North Carolinians would serve during World War II, and more than 7,000 would lose their lives. The Battle of Torpedo Junction off the coast of Dare County, North Carolina, would bring the war the closest to the U.S. mainland. During this struggle, German submarines sank over 100 ships. The USS *North Carolina* was commissioned just before the beginning of the war and served the Pacific effort. It would be decommissioned in 1947 and eventually be set up as a monument to North Carolina's war effort on the Cape Fear River near Wilmington.

The war effort created a more self-sufficient population. It is estimated that over 28 million quarts of food were canned while enormous amounts of cured meat and fresh garden vegetables were consumed. Despite all the hardships and tragic losses, the Soviet takeover of Eastern Europe and the Chinese communist revolution, the postwar mindset of North Carolinians was generally positive. The first TV stations began operations in Charlotte and Greensboro, signaling the advent of a new communications and entertainment age. The conversion of the war economy would create a booming economy and unprecedented growth in the construction business.

In 1941, with the arrival of a new decade, the venue for the Easter Monday game was changed from Freshman Field to the city-owned Devereaux Park, which increased the actual seated capacity from 1,500 to 4,500. For the first time, the preview article for the game included pictures of the star players for each team, Dick Hoyle, the third baseman for Wake Forest, and Ray Hardee, the scheduled starting pitcher for State. Unfortunately for State, Hardee was not as effective as hoped.

> Ray Fans 19 as Deacons Triumph, 19–0;
> DEACON GIVES UP ONLY THREE HITS
> Baptists Comb Three Tech Hurlers for 25 Hits for Easter Monday Win
>   by BILLY ANDERSON

It seems that the new downtown venue brought the crowd back out in the '40s. And this time they were treated to perhaps the most dominant pitching and hitting performance of the series. "Carl Grady Ray, Jr. of Walnut Cove, senior righthander, yesterday struck out 19 batters and pitched three-hit ball as Wake Forest romped to a 19–0 victory over N.C. State here before an Easter Monday crowd of more than 4,000 fans in Devereaux Meadow Park."

Ray had originally signed to play with State, but left to play at the small mountain school of Mars Hill. The State officials had to be a little more than upset when he returned to the area to pitch for their rivals.

Ray, who only allowed three hits, had a no-hitter until the sixth inning when Renfrow Doak broke through for State's first hit.

Other State Hits

The other State hits, both singles, came in the seventh and ninth innings. Jim Carney of Bethel, last man up in the seventh, bounced one into right field. For a moment that blow appeared to have assured State of a tally — Craig and Fahley, on base via walks, madly circled the bases and headed for home.

Fred Eason of Princeton, Deacon rightfielder, decided otherwise — his great peg home beat Craig by a step at the plate.

Craig opened State's ninth with a single to rightfield. He died at first as Ray proceeded to strike out the next three Techs in order.

State came close to scoring in the sixth inning. After Doak singled, he went to second on a sacrifice by Glass, and then stole third. That was as far as he could go. Constant grounded out, and Morrison fanned.

Ray is a slightly built hurler. He stands only eight inches over five feet, and weighs 160 pounds. Yet he manages to get a surprising amount of speed from his small frame. His curve ball repeatedly fooled the Techs — most of his victims, however, came as a result of his tantalizing change of pace.

Only Five Walks

Pitcher Carl Ray issued only five passes to first — he walked the first two batters to face him in the first, but he immediately retired the Techs in one-two-three order on strikes. He repeated this strikeout performance in the fourth, fifth, and ninth innings.

Just for the record all but five — Techs Cutie Carter, Leonard Constant, Jack Singer, Craig, and Doak — were victims at least one time of Ray's strike-out artistry.

Although Ray offered a fine exhibition, he was by no means the whole show. His teammates staged a 25-hit batting practice at the expense of three

Depression and War

State pitchers—Ray Hardee, Renfrow Doak, and Cutie Carter—for their runs.

The slugging parade started with a four-run explosion in the first inning. It came before many of the fans had reached the park, for the game started six minutes ahead of the scheduled time.

Four-Run First

The Deacons put together three singles by John (Rabbit) Fletcher, Art Vivian, and Fred Eason—with a double by Tony Gallovich, a passed ball, a wild pitch, and three errors for their runs.

George Edwards, subbing for Art Vivian in the left garden, led the Baptist attack with three singles for as many turns. Captain Dick (Rooster) Hoyle of Zebulon was runner-up with a triple, a double, and a brace of singles for four. Hoyle and Pitcher Ray each batted in three runs. The Deac mound ace did his turn at the bat, with three singles for six.

Fielding honors went to State on a fourth-inning double-play—Hardee, Singer, and Fahley.

Dr. Hubert A. Royster, well-known local surgeon and former Wake Forest athlete, was an enthusiastic spectator at yesterday's triumph was the golden anniversary of another historic Wake Forest conquest on the diamond.

Back in 1891 the Baptists gained a 10–7 victory over Carolina in an 11-inning battle here at Old Brookside Park—the diamond being where Fallon's Greenhouse now stands near Oakwood Cemetery. Dr. Royster played centerfield for the Baptists in that game.

Ray was the son of legendary Walnut Cove pitcher Carl Grady Ray, who made it briefly to the Philadelphia Athletics ball club, where he became close friends with Earl Mack, Connie's son. At the height of his fame, it was not uncommon for Stokes County natives to name their sons after him. Neither the young Ray nor the opposing pitcher, Ray Hardee, made it to the majors, but Hardee had his finest minor league season pitching for the Raleigh Capitals at Devereaux Meadows, winning 18 games.

The 1941 State nine only won a hand full of games while with a quick

Opposite: Devereaux Meadows ballpark was home to the Raleigh Capitals. The Easter Monday game was moved there after World War II. This is an overhead shot from 1952 that shows Capitol Boulevard and downtown Raleigh (courtesy the *News and Observer*).

start, the Deacons established themselves as a team to beat in the Southern Conference. Interestingly, from a standpoint of strategy, Wake's Coach Greason platooned his entire outfield against right- or left-handed pitchers.

Wake Forest	AB	R	H	O	A	E
Fletcher, 2b	6	3	3	1	0	0
Vivian, lf	4	1	3	0	0	0
Edwards, lf	3	1	3	0	0	0
Gallovich, ss	6	1	3	1	1	0
Reid, 1b	6	3	1	7	0	0
Eason, rf	3	2	2	0	1	0
Primm, cf	2	0	0	0	0	0
Hoyle, 3b	5	2	4	0	2	0
Polanski, cf	5	3	2	0	0	0
Lougett, rf	1	0	0	0	0	0
Sparrow, rf	0	0	0	0	0	0
Everly, c	3	2	1	10	2	0
Cross, c	1	0	0	8	0	0
Ray, p	6	1	3	0	1	0
	51	19	25	27	7	0

N.C. State	AB	R	H	O	A	E
Singer, ss	1	0	0	3	3	1
Glass, ph	1	0	0	0	0	0
Constant, cf	2	0	0	0	0	1
Gilbert, 3b	2	0	0	2	0	0
Morrison, 3b	2	0	0	1	2	0
Brown, cf	2	0	0	2	0	1
Craig, lf	1	0	1	2	0	0
C. Doak, c	2	0	0	4	1	1
Fleming, c	1	0	0	3	0	1
Suggs, ph	1	0	0	0	0	0
Fehley, 1b	3	0	0	8	0	0
Bailey, rf	4	0	0	1	0	0
Wheeler, 2b	2	0	0	0	2	0
Carney, 2b	1	0	1	1	1	0
Hardee, p	1	0	0	0	1	0
R. Doak, p	1	0	1	0	0	0
Carter, p	1	0	0	0	1	0
	28	0	3	27	11	5

```
Wake Forest   4 0 0   0 4 5   3 1 2   19
N.C. State    0 0 0   0 0 0   0 0 0    0
```

SUMMARY: Two base hits: Gallovich, Polanski, Hoyle, Edwards. Three base hits: Gallovich, Hoyle, Eason. Stolen bases: Everly, Fletcher, Polanski 2, R. Doak, Hoyle, Gallovich. Sacrifice: Glass. Double plays:

Hardee, Singer and Fehley. Left on bases: Wake Forest 13, State 7. Bases on balls: off Ray 5, Hardee 2, R. Doak, Carter 1. Struck out: by Hardee 4, Ray 19, Carter 3. Wild pitch: Hardee. Passed ball: C. Doak 2, Fleming. Umpires: Brandon and Porter. Time: 2:20.

IN THEIR OWN WORDS

For many years the Easter Monday Classic and PiKA Dance were a celebration that created enduring memories for the participants. Long after the tradition's conclusion, it is recalled with great fondness by some of those who witnessed it firsthand. The following interspersed narratives are first-person accounts of Easter Monday experiences.

In Her Own Words: Cora (Babe) Hoover — interviewed August 29, 2001 — widow of D. Ray McEachern, who was a member of the Alpha Epsilon Chapter of Pi Kappa Alpha 1937–39. Mrs. McEachern attended two PiKA Balls, 1937 and 1939.

When I was down at the PiKA House, they had a pet duck. I don't remember the name of that duck, but anyway, it was quite some duck, and he also had a fondness for beer, and every afternoon at a certain time, he waddled out of the house and down the street to the drug store where he was given his special bowl with his favorite drink. Now when he waddled back to the PiKA House, his quacks became much louder and faster. When he got home, he flopped down and took his nap, before supper.

During Dave's senior year at State, he had the job of planning the meals for the PiKA fraternity house. He usually did a pretty good job, but one time he heard a lot of

Miss Cora Elizabeth "Babe" Hoover of Concord, North Carolina, was escorted to the 1939 PiKA Ball by D. Ray McEachern, also of Concord, whom she later married (courtesy R.G. Utley).

The Easter Monday Baseball Game

talk about a certain meal, and it got next to him. So that night he gave them five different kinds of beans. You can believe he never heard any more complaints. They didn't want a repeat.

Nineteen thirty-nine was our last PiKA Ball. At that time, I was a student at the Pennsylvania Academy of Fine Art in Philadelphia, and I wanted a special dress for that Ball. At the residence house where I lived were two girls who were studying fashion design. They had just made a beautiful white dress for a student making her debut. So I had them design and make me a pink tulle with layers and layers in the skirt. The bodice was sheered and had small puffed sleeves and a round neck. The skirt floated fluffy like as I swirled around the dance floor. I had to lug it home in a big old box, and that was some job getting that thing home.

Now when you went to the PiKA Ball, you stayed at the PiKA House. The boys moved out. I don't remember where they stayed. You stayed in your date's room and used his iron bunk bed, and thank goodness that Dave had a lower bunk because I would never have gotten to the top bunk. I wonder how many lost articles they found when they cleaned up for us to come. We had all our meals at the PiKA House as well.

We were well-chaperoned. The boys had their favorite professor and his wife, who did a good job of not hanging around too much, but we knew they were there. It was really a nice weekend, and no one got out of line. There was not a lot of hanky-panky going on, but we had a good time enjoying it all. They had a good cook as well.

The ball was always a thrill. It was in the Frank Thompson Memorial Gymnasium on the State College campus. The PiKA boys had decorated it in the PiKA colors of garnet and gold. Around the edges of the room, they had banks of greenery. There was a great big crystal ball in the middle of the room, rotating and reflecting all the colors. It was really a pretty affair. Of course, they always had a big band — one of the big name bands to play — one of them was Gene Krupa. It was sad for us when we knew it was our last PiKA Ball.

State's coach, Doc Newton again entrusted the mound duties to Ray Hardee for the 1942 game with an improved yet disappointing result. As had become tradition by now, just a short number of miles away in Durham, the Duke team also opened what had become known as Big Five play as well as the Southern Conference schedule with a doubleheader.

Wake Forest Beats State, 5–4
DEACS WIN GAME ON STOLEN BASES
Seven Base Thefts Provide Winning Margin — 3,000 Fans Watch Game
by HERMAN BLACKMAN

A crowd of 3,000 witnessed a closely contested Wake Forest victory at Devereux Meadows. The Deacons took advantage of their superior speed on the base paths, amassing seven stolen bases, many of them in critical situations, in their 5–4 win.

State's Coach Newton used four different catchers in an attempt to slow down the athletic Deacons, finally achieving some success with Tom Turner, who had been just a batting practice catcher.

Wake Forest broke into the scoring column in the fourth inning. Red Cochran, the football star, drew one of the two passes that Ray Hardee issued during the game. He stole second and scored from that bag when Earl Stewart, second baseman, made a boot of Whitner's grounder.

State came back to tie the score at 1-1 in its half of the inning. Jakie Pearce, the Wake Forest hurler, hit Jack Singer with a pitch. Constant's sacrifice moved Singer to second. Stewart then delivered the first of two doubles that he got during the contest.

Wheeler Hits Homer

State took the lead temporarily when they scored again in the fifth. Grady Wheeler, the Techs' third baseman connected on a line drive that cleared the left field fence for a home run.

The Deacs staged a three-run party in the sixth on two hits, two stolen bases, a passed ball, and an error. Vivian drew a pass, stole second, advanced on an infield out, and scored on Cochran's single to right. Red promptly stole second. He scored when Wheeler made a bad throw to first after fielding Whitner's grounder: Whitner got to second on the play. An infield out moved him to third, and a single by Connelly drove him home with the third tally of the inning.

Rally Falls Short

Trailing 5–2 entering the bottom of the ninth, the State nine staged a rally that fell just short, providing another exciting finish for the holiday crowd.

The rally started with Hoot Gibson's single to left center. Wood forced him at second on a grounder to short. Wheeler connected for a double which scored Wood. Ralph Heath, batting for Turner, grounded to Primm. Primm booted the ball for a two-base error which scored Wheeler. At this point, Coach Murray Greason of the Deacs decided that Pearce was getting tired. He was replaced by Lefty Ripple who fanned Carney and forced Doak to ground out to second for the final out.

State won the battle for most hits, leading the Deacons 9–8, and both pitchers were successful at striking out opposing hitters with Hardee ringing up nine, and Pearce registering 9 as well. In the year's series State managed only one win over the Deacons and but six for the entire season. Perhaps the low point for them was a 17–8 drubbing by Wake in a game that had been slated as entertainment during State's commencement weekend.

Wake Forest	AB	R	H	O	A	E
Fletcher, ss	5	0	2	1	3	0
Primm, 2b	4	1	1	2	2	0
Vivian, lf	4	1	0	1	0	0
Reid, lf	4	0	1	8	1	0
Cochran, cf	3	2	1	2	1	0
Whitner, rf	4	1	2	2	0	2
Horchak, 3b	4	0	0	0	1	0
Connelly, c	4	0	1	10	1	0
Hawkins, c	0	0	0	1	0	0
Pearce, p	4	0	0	0	0	0
Ripple, p	1	0	0	0	0	0
	37	5	8	27	9	2
State	AB	R	H	O	A	E
Singer, ss	1	1	0	0	3	0
Newborn, ss	2	0	0	2	0	0
Doak, ph	1	0	0	0	0	0
Constant, cf	3	0	0	2	0	0
Stewart, 2b	4	0	3	1	2	1
Bailey, rf	4	0	2	2	0	1
Gibson, 1b	3	0	1	12	0	0
Craig, lf	3	0	0	1	0	0
Wood, ph	1	1	0	0	0	0
Wheeler, 3b	4	2	3	0	3	1
Devault, c	1	0	0	5	1	0
Fleming, c	1	0	0	0	0	0
Council, c	1	0	0	0	0	0
Turner, c	1	0	0	2	1	0

Depression and War

Jean Ritchie and Hank Utley, pictured here, attended the 1948 PiKA Ball. R.G. "Hank" Utley, who played third base in three Easter Monday games, has in retirement become a baseball historian and one of North Carolina's most avid advocates of the history of mill and outlaw baseball during the Depression era (courtesy R.G. Utley).

State	*AB*	*R*	*H*	*O*	*A*	*E*
Heath, ph	1	0	0	0	0	0
Hardee, p	3	0	0	0	1	0
Carney, ph	1	0	0	0	0	0
	35	4	9	27	11	3

Wake Forest	0 0 0	1 0 3	1 0 0	5
N.C. State	0 0 0	1 1 0	0 0 2	4

SUMMARY: Two base hits: Stewart 2, Wheeler. Home run: Wheeler. Stolen bases: Whitner 2, Fletcher, Cochran 2, Vivian. Sacrifice: Constant. Left on bases: Wake Forest 7, State 6. Base on balls: off Hardee 2, Pearce 1. Struck out: by Hardee 9, Pearce 9, Ripple 1. Passed balls: Council. Umpire: Kearney. Time: 2:10.

In His Own Words — Hank Utley — Easter Monday, April 22, 1946

I received my discharge from the U.S. Army Air Corp as 2nd Lt. Bombardier on a B-29 in October 1945. I entered NC State for the second semester in January 1946.

The Easter Monday Baseball Game

On Saturday before Easter, Coach Sorrell, in his first year, told us that we would be playing Wake Forest in the professional uptown ball park [Devereaux Meadow] Monday instead of on campus. After dressing in the old Thompson Gym, we took a bus to the uptown ball park. Within a very short time after we arrived, hundreds of girls dressed in their Easter hats, corsages and beautiful dresses started filling up the grandstand.

We looked at the coach and asked, "What's going on?" He replied that the girls were from Peace, St. Mary's, and Meredith College and that the legislators and their wives would be coming soon. And they did. The wives were dressed like they were going to church. It turned out to be a "see and be seen" social event.

The girls could not get home for Easter and back to college very easily in those days, so they celebrated Easter Monday at a social and cultural college baseball game. Over 3200 people attended the game.

The game continued to bring in large crowds for the next few years until the game ceased after 1956 when Wake Forest moved to Winston-Salem.

Never will I forget seeing so many dressed up girls and ladies at a ball park.

The 1943 game saw another change in the series, this time one related to the war effort. Wake Forest had eliminated most of its sports teams, including baseball, and State spent the year competing in the Ration League, so the 1943 version of the classic was played between the Techs and the Navy Pre-Flight team.

> State Wipes Out Nine-Run Deficit to Defeat Pre-Flight, 10–9
> by FRED DIXON

State managed to score all ten of its runs in the final three innings to defeat the Navy Pre-Flight team in the Easter Monday game played back on the State campus at Freshman Field.

The Techs hadn't scored a run in the first six innings. In fact, they had got only one man to third, and he got there on a wild pitch.

But, the seventh saw State push across four runs. A like number of runs were scored in the eighth and then in the ninth with one man away and two men on bases, R. C. Bryan slashed a double down the leftfield foul line and State had the game.

Second Win

This was State's second win of the season, but the Techs remained on the bottom of the Ration League. Their other win was also over the Pre-Flight team. The loss was their fourth against three wins and dropped the Pre-Flight team from a second-place tie with Duke.

Ivan Fleser, a fast ball righthander, held the Techs at bay through the first six innings, setting them down with just three hits—a single in the second by Johnson and singles in the fourth by Leo Katkaveck and Jimmy Wilson. In fact just four extra batters faced Fleser in those six innings.

Dayvault Starts

Dayvault opened the seventh for State with a hard triple to right and scored when Marousek errored Johnson's grounder at first. Bryan moved Johnson to third on a single to right. Ravashiere made a bad throw to third on Bryan's single, and Johnson scored, Bryan going to second.

Charlie Godwin hit a slow grounder to Second Baseman Hagstrom who miscued and Godwin was safe. Bryan moving to third. J.A. (Lefty) Warren, who had relieved Herman Vernon on the mound for State to start the seventh, beat out a single to right, Bryan scoring. Godwin tried to go all the way to third but was thrown out. Ravashiere to Conlin. McLaughlin flied out to the second baseman, and Wood was walked, but Silson singled to score Warren, and Katkaveck, the ninth man up, ended the inning by striking out.

Dayvault Again

Dayvault started things in the eighth when he was issued a ticket to first. Johnson and Bryan singled, and Godwin laced a triple deep to centerfield, scoring all three. Warren was hit by Pitcher Simms who had come in to replace Fleser after Godwin's triple. McLaughlin was safe at first on a fielder's choice, Godwin scoring and Warren being thrown out at second. Wood popped out, and Wilson struck out.

Kavkaveck opened the ninth with a single, and Dayvault was safe on a fielder's choice. Johnson popped out and then came Bryan's double down the third-base line that scored the winning runs. Bryan is a lefthanded batter and his blow caught the leftfielder far to the right.

Pre-Flight scored in the fourth on singles by Marchand and Ravashiere, a stolen base by Marchand, a walk, and error. Ravashiere's single drove in Marchand and the error resulted in the second run. Ravashiere scoring.

The Easter Monday Baseball Game

No Hit, Three Runs

The three runs scored by the visitors in the fifth were unearned and attained without a hit. The runs scored on a walk, a fielder's choice, a sacrifice and two costly State errors.

Navy's three runs in the sixth came with two men out and no one on. The third man up walked, a triple by Bonifant, who then scored on another error.

The visitors' final run came in the seventh on a single by Neverdausky, who stole second and came home on Conlin's single to center field.

Pre-Flight	AB	R	H	O	A	E
Hagstrom, 2b	4	2	1	3	2	2
Bonifant, ss	5	2	2	1	0	0
Marchand, cf	4	1	1	1	0	0
Raveshlere, rf	5	2	1	0	1	1
Northington, lf	2	0	0	2	0	0
Neverdausky, lf	2	1	1	0	0	0
Marousek, 1b	4	0	1	5	0	1
Conlin, 3b	4	0	1	3	1	0
Kettle, c	3	0	0	7	1	1
Eastman, c	1	0	0	3	0	0
Fieser, p	3	1	0	3	0	0
Sims, p	0	0	0	0	0	0
	37	9	8	28	5	5
State	**AB**	**R**	**H**	**O**	**A**	**E**
Watson, ss	3	0	0	3	2	2
McLaughlin, ss	2	0	0	1	0	0
Wood, cf	4	0	1	2	0	0
Wilson, 2b	5	0	1	4	0	2
Katkaveck, 3b	5	1	2	3	1	0
Dayvault, rf	3	3	1	1	0	0
Johnson, lf	5	2	2	1	0	0
Bryan, 1b	5	2	3	7	0	1
Godwin, c	3	1	1	5	1	0
Vernon, p	2	0	0	0	1	0
Warren, p	1	1	1	0	0	0
	38	10	12	27	5	5

Pre-Flight	0 0 0	2 3 3	1 0 0	9
State	0 0 0	0 0 0	4 4 2	10

SUMMARY: Two base hit: Bryan. Three base hits: Dayvault, Bonifant, Godwin. Stolen bases: Johnson, Marchand, Neverdausky, McLaughlin. Sacrifice: Marchand. Double play: Watson and Bryan. Left on bases: Pre-Flight 8, State 8. Base on balls: off Vernon 4, Warren 2,

Fieser 2, Sims 1. Struck out: by Vernon 2, Warren 2, Fieser 7, Sims 2. Wild pitch: Fieser. Umpires: Kearney and Bledsoe. Time: 2:22. No attendance given for this game.

In Her Own Words — Jean Ritchie Utley — PiKA Ball 1948

I was a senior in high school. My sorority was planning a spring dance for the same weekend as the PiKA Ball.

I tried to talk Hank into coming home for my dance, but he wanted to stay in Raleigh, and also he had a ball game on Easter Monday.

In February, my sorority decided to postpone our dance because too many people were going out of town. I wrote Hank to tell him, and he replied that he had already asked another date.

My mother decided we were going to Raleigh to visit her brother and his family. She asked Norman Alston, a family friend and PiKA, to go with us to Raleigh and to take me to the dance.

We went on Friday afternoon, visited with my uncle and aunt — then Normie and I hit the PiKA house for all the festivities.

Needless to say, it was quite sticky when Hank showed up with his date.

The PiKA Ball was crowded and fun. Hank and I ignored each other until the last dance. He came over and asked me to dance. I went back to Concord the next day.

I got even with Hank two years later. I married him.

The 1944 and 1945 versions of the Easter Monday classic were again played as Ration League games and garnered much less publicity. As the results suggest, the State team was very depleted, and as in the past year, Wake Forest did not field a team.

Pre-Flight Defeats State, 9–2 in Opener of Ration League
NINE ERRORS HURT STATE BALL CLUB
Cloudbusters Use Four on Mound — Techs Are Limited to Three Hits

Carolina Pre-Flight opened the Ration League season by defeating State, 9–2, at Doak Field yesterday before a large crowd.

State's inexperienced team had the opening-day jitters, committing nine errors which helped the Cloudbusters in their victory.

The Navy team scored two runs in the first inning on a single, error, fielder's choice, and a passed ball. It held the lead the rest of the way.

Pre-Flight used four pitchers in gaining the decision. Farley, who pitched the last six innings, giving up two hits and fanning seven, received credit for the victory.

Depression and War

Gaither, Pre-Flight leftfielder was batting star of the game. He hit a home run with one on in the fifth and also had a single. The Cloudbusters made nine hits off the three State pitchers who worked. Wilson hit a home run for State in the second inning.

The following short article about the 1945 game is from the *Raleigh Times*, as the *News and Observer* did not have an article available on microfilm.

Wolfpack Nine Wins Ration League Opener

Behind the effective hurling of Bill Riggan, State College's baseball team opened the Ration League schedule here Wednesday [not played on Easter Monday] by downing Carolina Pre-Flight's Cloudbusters, 9–7.

Riggan yielded seven hits, pitched airtight ball in the clutches, walked two and struck out six.

State collected ten hits off a half dozen Pre-Flight pitchers. Seven errors by the Navy cadets kept the visiting pitchers continually in hot water. State was guilty of eight miscues.

The Red Terrors scored three runs in the third, added one in the fourth, three in the sixth and two in the seventh.

Pre-Flight rallied for five runs in the seventh and scored two more in the eighth before Riggan quelled the uprising.

Batting leaders for State were Catcher John Evans and Centerfielder Jimmy Wilson, each with two for five. No Pre-Flight batsman got more than one hit.

Pre-Flight	AB	R	H	O	A	E
Gaulin, 2b	6	3	2	2	2	0
Barnes, ss	4	0	1	3	2	1
Hoos, c	3	0	0	6	0	0
Pierozzi, cf	2	0	0	0	0	0
Kollnige, 1b	5	1	1	8	0	1
Crampsey, rf	4	3	1	0	0	0
Gaither, lf	5	2	2	1	1	0
Falk, 3b	5	0	1	1	1	1
Schneider, cf	2	0	0	1	0	0
Mills, c	2	0	0	5	0	0

Opposite: The 40th annual PiKA Ball on Easter Monday 1948. Among those in attendance were Donald Lampke, president; Oscar Miller, vice-president; Lewis Perry, secretary; Atwood Skinner, treasurer; Reid Farrell and R.G. Utley (courtesy Lamont Whitley).

The Easter Monday Baseball Game

Pre-Flight	AB	R	H	O	A	E
Somerville, p	1	0	0	0	0	0
Shankwilder	1	0	0	0	0	0
Burkewtiz, p	0	0	0	0	1	0
Waywald, p	0	0	0	0	0	0
Farley, p	3	0	1	0	1	0
	43	9	9	27	8	3

State	AB	R	H	O	A	E
Evans, 2b	4	0	0	2	2	3
Clark, 1b	1	0	0	8	1	0
Grandy, 1b	2	1	0	2	0	0
Wiggs, lf	3	0	1	3	0	0
Wilson, rf	3	1	1	1	1	2
Wood, 3b	3	0	1	2	2	2
Allen, cf	1	0	0	0	0	0
Purvis, cf	3	0	0	1	0	0
Lamb, ss	1	0	0	1	1	0
Edwards, p	1	0	0	1	1	0
Page, p	0	0	0	0	1	0
Humphrey, p	0	0	0	0	1	0
Baker, c	2	0	0	1	0	0
Alford, c	1	0	0	2	0	0
	30	2	3	27	10	9

```
Pre-Flight   2 1 1   0 2 1   1 1 0   9
State        0 1 0   1 0 0   0 0 0   2
```

SUMMARY: Home runs: Wilson, Gaither. Stolen bases: Kollnige, Crampsey, Gaither 2, Gaulin. Double plays: Barnes, Gaulin, Kollnige. Left on bases: Pre-Flight 8, State 4. Passed balls: Baker 4, Alford 3. Umpires: Hicks and Porter. Time: 2:15.

The 1945 box score is unavailable.

In Their Own Words—Reid D. Farrell, Class of 1949

PiKA Ball weekends were, without a doubt, THE most fun weekends we ever had at N.C. State! Don't remember many details about the one we had our Freshman year, but sure do remember the last 3 Balls our group enjoyed when we got back from being in the service in 1947, '48 and '49.

Always thought having the Ball on Easter Monday was so great, Thanks to N.C. having declared that day a state holiday, just for the PiKA Ball!! (Only N.C. and the Virgin Islands had that day as a holiday.)

The parties at the "House," the trips to the beach, the picnic, then the Ball on Monday night, seeing our dates off Tuesday morning, made for a great long weekend, unsurpassed by all other festive events put on at State.

Most of our dates had to take double or triple cuts from their schools to be there (Adelaide did), so it had to be an important weekend to them also. Remember how some of our guys went to early classes Tuesday, still dressed in their tuxedos. A great time was had by all!

Adelaide and I have told all four of children (who all went to Florida, which has the reputation as being a party school) about PiKA Ball at N.C. State, and they said they never had any party at UF that compared to it.

In 1946, the teams renewed their rivalry with quite a bit of anticipation and fanfare. Once again the game was played at Devereux Meadows before a large and enthusiastic crowd.

State's Techs Beat Deacons, 6–3, before 3,200 at Devereux
RAMSEY PITCHES LEAGUE TRIUMPH
Big Righthander Holds Deacs to Six Hits — Strikes Out 10 Batters
by HERMAN BLACKMAN

Curt Ramsey, State's husky righthanded pitcher and also the captain of the football team, was the star of the first postwar game. He scattered six hits and six walks over the nine innings and gave State its second win of the season over Big Four rival, Wake Forest.

The Deacons held their only lead in the fourth inning. "David Sams walked, went to second on a balk by Ramsey, and scored on a two hit to right field by Clyde Whitener. Ramsey worked himself out of a hole soon after Whitener's hit. George Edwards singled, and Hank Lougee walked." Ramsey stopped the rally by fanning Red Cochran and Dane Lane, and getting Art Williams to ground to second.

The Techs got back the run in their half of the frame, and one for good measure. Charlie Richkus opened with a walk, was sacrificed to second by Jimmy Edwards, and then scored on Jimmy Wilson's line drive double over Lane's head in leftfield. Courts popped out, but Josh Mewborn scratched a hit to second, moving Wilson to third. Pinky Gardner hit to third and beat the toss to first, driving home Wilson.

Stanton Homers

The Techs picked up two more runs in the sixth. After Wilson had popped to second, Bobby Courts, Newborn, Gardner, and Stanton delivered consecutive singles. The outburst was halted when Ramsey rolled into a double

play. In the seventh, Richkus lined a double into left, and then scored on Jimmy Edwards' drive past short.

Bill Stanton, a veteran of the Battle of the Bulge, sent a drive 345 feet over the left center field fence to complete the State's scoring for the afternoon.

Murray Greason's club added its second run in the seventh on a hit to second by Cochran, a walk to Lane, and a hit through short by Catcher Williams. The Techs pulled a double play to halt further run-making. With one gone in the eighth Whitener drew a walk, went to second on G. Edwards' blow to left, took third after Gardner hauled in Lougee's fly to right, and then scored when Red Cochran smashed a single through the pitcher's box. McCall fanned to end the inning.

Ramsey pitched a good game, and was backed up in the field with excellent support. He fanned 10 batters, seven of them coming in three innings. He passed six. The husky mound ace had the Deacon batters biting at bad pitches throughout the contest.

This season marked the successful beginning to Vic Sorrell's twenty-one year coaching career at State. Sorrell, a former Wake Forest star who had himself played in several Easter Monday contests, had a ten-year major league career, winning 92 games for the Detroit Tigers. The Morrisville, North Carolina, native was on two World Series teams, though he did not see action in the 1934–35 fall classics. He had previously man-

Opposite: 1947 PiKA N.C. State Ball, November 1947. First row, left to right: Lamont Whitley, Levy Bridger, Buddy Farrell, Sid Jennette, Park White, "Duby" Merritt, Dick Underwood, Louis Cramer, Harry Cramer, Dan Horning. Second row, left to right: Norman Alston, Steve Conrad, Don Freeman, Ed Moran, Dick Wilkins, W.C. Winn, Bruce Beamon, "Zeb" Jones, "Hank" Milligan, Jack Tate, Bobby Helms, Pitt Beam, Bill English. Third row, left to right: Jimmy Brown, Lawrence Watts, "Speed" Noell, Kelly Batson, Bob Hicks, Louis Perry, A. Skinner, Oscar Miller, Don Lampke (president), Perton Holloman, Johnny Boyter, C.G. Bigenheimer, Joe Smart, Sidney Allen. Fourth row, left to right: Don Stadler, Bobby Bird, unknown, unknown, unknown, W.W. Gayle, Hall Wingfield, Don Spencer, Ken Winston, Bill Corbitt, "Bo" White, H.K. Witherspoon, "Hank" Utley, "Burt" Steen, Ben Ivey, "Rusty" Lovin, Bob Vanstory, Johnny Jones, Freddie Stafford. Fifth row, left to right: A.G. Brady, Bill Simpson, Tom Winston, Larry Sanford, Jimmie Randle, Bill Lynn, Preston Andrews, Sam Butler, H.F. Sutton, Johnny Moore, Charles Wolhar, Jimmie Jones, Sam Moore, Bynam Neal, Gilbert Smith, Lester Gross, C.H. Farris. Not pictured: T.A. McAdams, Beverly Ross, Pete Kelly, Bill Kelly, Bob Saunders, Pete McDowell, Bonnie Moffitt, Jim Johnson, Bob Wooten (courtesy Lamont Whitley and R.G. Utley).

aged the Bluefield, West Virginia, minor league team for two years at the end of his professional career.

The game also marked the Easter Monday debut of baseball historian, R.G. "Hank" Utley, who had just returned along with many of his teammates from service in World War II. Utley was the leadoff hitter and third baseman for the "Red Terrors."

At the beginning of the spring, when forty potential players showed up, many of them returning veterans, Sorrell had declared that State might have a "fair team." As it turned out, they were much more than that, as they managed to win what had now become the Big Four competition. For Wake's Coach Greason, the 1946 comeback season was a rare weak one. The Deacons finished 6–14 and were swept by State in their three games.

Wake Forest	AB	R	H	O	A	E
Fleet, ss	3	0	0	1	3	0
Martin, ph	1	0	0	0	0	0
Sams, 2b	3	1	0	5	3	0
Whitener, rf	3	1	1	1	0	0
G. Edwards, 1b	4	0	2	11	0	0
Lougee, 3b	3	0	0	1	2	0
Cochran, cf	4	1	2	1	0	0
Lane, lf	2	0	0	0	0	0
McCall, lf	1	0	0	0	0	0
Williams, c	4	0	1	4	1	0
Pearce, p	3	0	0	0	3	0
Auld, ph	1	0	0	0	0	0
	32	3	6	24	12	0
State	AB	R	H	O	A	E
Utley, 3b	4	0	1	1	3	0
Richkus, ss	3	2	1	0	3	0
J. Edwards, c	3	0	1	10	0	0
Wilson, cf	4	1	1	0	0	0
Courts, lf	4	1	1	0	0	0
Newborn, 2b	3	1	2	1	0	0
Gardner, rf	4	0	3	3	0	0
Stanton, 1b	3	1	2	12	0	0
Ramsey, p	4	0	0	0	6	0
	32	6	12	27	12	0

Opposite: 1949 PiKAs pictured in front of house on Hillsborough Street.

Wake Forest	0 0 0	1 0 0	1 1 0	3
State	0 0 0	2 0 2	1 1	6

SUMMARY: Two base hits: Whitener, Wilson, Richkus. Home run: Stanton. Stolen bases: Sams, Newborn. Sacrifice: J. Edwards. Double plays: Pearce, Sams, and G. Edwards; Utley and Stanton. Left on bases: Wake Forest 7, State 6. Base on balls: Ramsey 5, Pearce 3. Struck out: Ramsey 10, Pearce 4. Balk: Ramsey. Umpires: Matthews and Milaker. Time: 2:03.

In Their Own Words—W.G. Smith, 1949

They were really great weekends and the memories still linger, if you still "dig back" that far. One or two additional things come to mind—one year we had our Sat. night banquet at the S.& W. downtown and the entertainment was Andy Griffith doing "What it was was Football." Andy was still at Chapel Hill and just getting started and would perform any where he could get an audience. Also, many of the girls from out of town would stay at Mrs Kirby's [rooming house] on Hillsboro Street and/or the Yellow Gables, a small motel on Wake Forest Rd., run by Mrs. Johnson who was usually "3 sheets in the wind"—but lots of "fun." Many stories can be told!!!!

As for lasting relations, several brothers that are in that group picture later married their dates. To name a few: Reid Farrell, Gil Smith, Jack Tate, Pete McDowell, Bill Corbitt, Bob Hicks (he was already married), Burt Steen, Levi Bridger, H.K. Witherspoon—I'm sure there were others. Anyway, those were great times—too bad they had to come to an end, but I'm sure they were replaced with others just as meaningful.

In 1947, Ramsey was unable to duplicate the effort of the year before and was in fact pummeled by the Wake Forest batters.

HOCK [sic], BAUER PACE DEACONS' VICTORY
3,000 Spectators Watch Wake Forest Youngsters Trounce State Club

Reports that Wake Forest had the baseball talent necessary to make a strong bid for the Big Four League championship in 1947 were confirmed for the 3,000 fans who attended the traditional game at Devereux

Opposite: The 41st annual PiKA Ball on Easter Monday 1949. Among those in attendance were William F. Kelly, president; L.V. Perry, vice-president; F.R. Hicks, secretary; and R.E. Merritt, treasurer (courtesy Lamont Whitley).

Meadows. Wake Forest delivered one of the most decisive victories in recent contests between the two rivals.

> Though the outcome had no bearing on the Big Four standings, Coach Murray Greason's freshman-packed Deacons gave notice with an authoritative ring that they have an eye on the crown, putting on an awesome display of hitting and fielding prowess to win in a walk from State's Big Four defending Champions. The Baptist boys combed a trio of State moundsmen for a total of 14 hits in their relentless attack, while their own Lefty "Mo" Bauer, one of Greason's several freshmen discoveries went the distance and looked like a winner all the way in doling out seven safeties.
>
> ### Hoch Stars
> Art Hoch, a slender shortstopping frosh from Pennsylvania was the big noise in the Deacon victory. Hoch covered the shortfield like a blanket, and grabbed the hitting laurels in a walk by clubbing the Tech hurlers for three hits in five attempts, a feat which he climaxed in the eighth inning by scaling one of Ernest Johnson's slants over Devereux's leftfield, with two mates aboard.
>
> Bauer, a southpaw elbower from Hertford, spun his mastery around the Tech batsmen all afternoon, and in only two innings was he ever in difficulty. Of the seven hits collected by the West Raleigh boys, six of the blows came in bunches of three in the sixth and eighth frames.
>
> The Deacons, with six freshmen in their lineup, stirred up trouble for big Curt Ramsey, who started on the mound for State, in the first inning. Charley Teague led off with a walk and came all the way home when Clyde Whitener's double to right-center was booted momentarily by Tech Centerfielder Willie Evans. Whitener made it to third on the throw-in and scored as Hoch grounded out, short to first.
>
> ### Techs Score
> State managed a run in the second when Gordon Lea opened with a line double to rightfield, advanced to third when Billy Fowler grounded out, and crossed the plate as Leo Katkaveck's bounder got by Gene Hooks at third.

Opposite: The 42nd annual PiKA Ball on Easter Monday 1950. Among those in attendance were Lawrence Sanford, president; B. Ross, vice-president; J.T. Lowremore, secretary; and J.R. Wilkins, treasurer. The Alpha Epsilon chapter was chartered in October 1904 (courtesy Lamont Whitley).

Depression and War

The Deacons began to warm up to Ramsey's offerings in the fourth and chased the big righthander in a two-run spurt. Hoch started it with a single. On the hit and run, First Baseman George Edwards pumped a single into left and Hoch reached third. Cochran's fly to deep left, which Lea caught on the bank in a nice play, enabled Hoch to score after the catch. Fulghum rifled a two-bagger to right-center, and Hooks dropped a lazy single to center, scoring Edwards from third and sending Ramsey to the shower. Ernest Johnson went to the mound for the Techs and ended the rally.

A three-run uprising in the fifth iced the game for the Deacons. Whitener's single, and a booming triple by Hoch to deep centerfield began the damage. Edwards' fly to left brought Hoch home after the catch. With two out, Cochran landed on second when Shortstop Charlie Richkus overthrew first. Cochran went to third on a wild pitch by Johnson and tallied on a single by Hooks.

The Techs added a run in the sixth on two freak singles and a Wake Forest error. Jim Edwards hit one off the handle of his bat to short and beat it out. Lea got a solid one-timer to left, and then Fowler rolled one toward Hoch which eluded the shortstop on a crazy hop. Edwards rounded third for home and made it as Hoch recovered in time, but threw low, hitting a bat in front of the plate....

It is amazing to see that a game which included 20 hits and 16 runs could be played in just over two hours. Today's conventions, with the constant string of timeouts lengthening the time between pitches, would have certainly pushed this contest over the three-hour mark. While this article had no byline, the descriptive flair would seem like a throwback to McKevlin's work during the previous decade.

State was unable to repeat as Big Four Champion, finishing second mostly because of the difficulty they experienced against the last place Deacons. Greason had brought in twelve freshmen pitchers and hired former Major League star Garland Braxton to work with them, so their future appeared to be bright.

Opposite: The house parties that began early during the Easter weekend celebration were popular events. This photograph shares a rare glimpse into one of the 1950 parties (courtesy Lamont Whitley).

Red Terrors

'46 baseball team lives up to nickname in winning Big Four title.

They were last of the Techs and bridged a new sports era for N.C. State

By TIM STEVENS
Times sports writer

They call themselves the last of the Red Terrors and they were ... but they also were pioneers of a new era in N.C. State athletics.

When the 1946 State College baseball team won the Big Four crown, it was the first baseball title won by a State team in 18 years and one of the school's first athletic championships. The Red Terrors, or Techs as they were sometimes called, formed the bridge to a new era in sports competition at the school.

Red Terrors

First row (l to r): Clint Hege, Roy Nesbit, Hank Utley, Coach Vic Sorrell, Jim Wilson, John Evans, Charles Richlux. Second row, Curt Ramsey, Ernie Johnson, Stan Kohler, Don "Pinky" Gardner, Hal Owens, Chick Doak, Ralph Barksdale, Bob Courts. Third row: Josh Morrison, Bill Stanton, Paul Gibson, J.S. Edwards, Manager Paul Jordan, Manager M.E. Barnhill

They were part of the beginning, because they were the first team coached by Vic Sorrell, a former Detroit Tiger pitcher lured to the campus to build a baseball program.

But they also were at the end of a simpler age. There were no scholarship baseball players in '46, although by some standards many of the players were already professionals because of the money they earned in the summer playing in small Eastern North Carolina towns.

THEY WERE the last State College team to be called the Red Terrors. In the fall of '46, the school adopted the nickname "Wolfpack" for all its athletic teams. It was the Wolfpack that football coach Beattie Feathers carried to a berth against Oklahoma in the Gator Bowl the following winter and the Wolfpack that a former Indiana high school basketball coach by the name of Everett Case greeted at his first practice.

Wake Forest	AB	R	H	O	A	E
Teague, 2b	3	2	1	3	2	0
Whitener, lf	4	3	2	2	0	0
Hoch, ss	5	3	3	1	5	1
G. Edwards, 1b	5	1	1	12	0	0
Cochran, cf	5	2	1	3	0	0
Fulghum, rf	4	1	2	0	0	0
Hooks, 3b	5	1	3	2	2	2
Batchelor, c	5	0	1	4	1	0
Bauer, p	3	0	0	0	2	0
	39	13	14	27	12	3

State	AB	R	H	O	A	E
Evans, cf	5	0	0	2	0	1
Barden, 2b	3	1	1	1	3	0
J. Edwards, c	4	1	2	1	2	1
Lew, lf	4	1	2	4	0	0
Fowler, rf	4	0	1	4	1	0
Katkavek, 3b	4	0	1	3	0	0
Stanton, 1b	4	0	0	11	0	0
Richkus, ss	2	0	0	1	4	1
Mussack, ph	1	0	0	0	0	0
Ramsey, p	1	0	0	0	0	0
Johnson, p	2	0	0	0	0	0
F. Edwards, p	0	0	0	0	0	0
J. Evans, ph	1	0	0	0	0	0
	35	3	7	27	10	3

```
Wake Forest   2 0 0   2 3 0   0 5 1   13
State         0 1 0   0 1 0   0 1 0    3
```

SUMMARY: Two base hits: Teague, Fulghum, Whitener. Three base hits: Hoch, Cochran. Home run: Hoch. Sacrifices: Bauer. Double plays: Fowler, Richkus, and Katkaveck. Left on base: Wake Forest 4; State 7. Bases on balls: off Bauer 2, Ramsey 1, Johnson 3. Struck out: by Bauer 4, Johnson 1. Wild pitch: Johnson. Passed balls: J. Edwards. Umpires: Fields and Bledsoe. Time: 2:10.

A crowd of 3,500 fans showed up for 1948's chilly version of the Easter Monday classic.

Blackwell and Bauer Shut Out Wolfpack, 5-0
EACH TEAM GETS LIGHT OPPOSITION

Opposite: The 1946 "Red Terrors," featuring many returning war veterans surprised the league by winning the Big Four Championship. This was the first of 21 seasons that former Wake Forest star and major league pitcher, Vic Sorrell would coach the cross-town rival (courtesy R.G. Utley).

The Easter Monday Baseball Game

Despite their best efforts, this State team was shut out in the Easter Monday Classic by Wake Forest's crafty lefthander, Moe Bauer (courtesy R.G. Utley).

Wake Forest's young players continued to dominate Sorrell's Red Terrors. Once again the game was played at the minor league home of the Raleigh Capitals. "Dale (Blackie) Blackwell, a husky freshman from Lawrenceville, Va., and Lefty Raymond (Moe) Bauer, a slim sophomore from Norfolk yesterday fashioned a shutout for Wake Forest as the Deacons stopped State, 5-0, at Devereux Meadow in the traditional Easter Monday game between the Wake County rivals."

About 3,500 people attended on a chilly late March afternoon the game in which the Wake Forest hurlers limited State to five hits and never allowed a runner to pass second base.

Blackwell, who started for the Deacons, only allowed two hits in his five innings while Bauer picked up where he left off for Frank Novosel's young team, allowing three hits in his four innings.

> Wake Forest took the lead in the second inning with a walk to Vic Matney, a hit batsman, an infield out, and Catcher Russ Batchelor's clean single to left chased two runs across the plate. In the third inning, Centerfielder Kent Rogers reached second on First Baseman Don Cheek's error, and he scored from there when Second Baseman Charlie Teague dropped a double into leftfield. Single runs were added in the eighth and ninth frames. The run in the ninth resulted from Teague's second extra-base hit of the day — a triple to the fence in centerfield.

Ernie Johnson, veteran righthander from Mt. Gilead, went the route on the mound for the Wolfpack and gave up eight hits. All but one of the State blows came after two were out, and the Wolfpack was able to work the Deacon hurlers for only one base on balls.

Although not very happy about their inability to score a run, the Wolfpack had the satisfaction of knowing the game does not count in the Big Four standings. The remaining four contests between the Wake rivals are league contests.

Each team turned in good defensive play for so early in the season. Two errors were charged against each club, but for the most part they grabbed everything in sight.

Blackwell got behind on a number of batters but he always managed to locate the plate after that and did not issue a base on balls. He turned in hitless pitching until two were out in the fourth, when big Bill Fowler drilled a double down the leftfield foul line that was fair by inches. The other hit made off Blackwell was a scratch single by Second Baseman John Holland which started the fifth inning for State, but that threat was erased quickly as Shortstop Tom McLaughlin grounded to Teague, who started a double play. Holland's hit in the fifth was the only one made by the Wolfpack which came when two men were not out.

Wake Forest	AB	R	H	O	A	E
Hoch, ss	5	0	0	2	3	0
Rogers, cf	4	2	1	1	0	0
Teague, 2b	5	0	2	1	3	0
Fulghum, lf	5	0	0	3	0	0
Matny, rf	3	1	0	1	0	0
Hooks, 3b	2	2	1	1	2	2
Warren, 1b	4	0	1	11	1	0
Batchelor, c	3	0	1	5	1	0
Blackwell, p	2	0	1	1	0	0
Bauer, p	2	0	1	1	2	0
	35	5	8	27	12	2

State	AB	R	H	O	A	E
Utley, 3b	2	0	0	0	3	0
Council, 3b	1	0	0	1	1	0
Lee, lf	4	0	1	3	0	1
W. Evans, cf	4	0	0	3	0	0
Fowler, rf	4	0	1	2	0	0
Cheek, 1b	2	0	0	8	0	1
Norrell, 1b	2	0	1	3	0	0
Holland, 2b	4	0	2	0	1	0

The Easter Monday Baseball Game

State	AB	R	H	O	A	E
McLaughlin, ss	3	0	0	0	3	0
J. Evans, c	3	0	0	7	1	0
Johnson, p	3	0	0	0	2	0
	32	0	5	27	11	2

Wake Forest	0 2 1	0 0 0	0 1 1	5
State	0 0 0	0 0 0	0 0 0	0

SUMMARY: Two base hits: Blackwell, Teague, Fowler, Lee. Three base hit: Teague. Stolen bases: Batchelor, Rogers. Double play: Teague, Hoch, and Warren. Left on base: Wake Forest 8, State 6. Base on balls: off Bauer 1, Johnson 3. Strikeouts: Blackwell 2, Bauer 2, Johnson 6. Umpires: Fields and Bledsoe. Time: 2:10.

The Wake Forest team entered the 1949 Easter Monday classic with a fourteen-game winning streak and were favored in what was expected to be a pitchers' duel.

Deacons Defeat State
Bauer Hurls 3–1 Triumph
Ninth-Inning Homers by Livick, Hooks Give Deacs Big Four Victory
by BOB BROOKS

Those who had expected a pitchers' duel were not disappointed as Wake's Ray "Moe" Bauer and State's knuckleballer Ernie Johnson battled before a large crowd. This was Johnson's second appearance in the series and the middle game of what would be three appearances for Bauer.

After an eight-year minor league career in the Chicago Cubs organization, Dr. Raymond Bauer would start the highly successful baseball program at North Carolina Wesleyan, where he served for thirty-three years as a professor, coach, and then athletic director. The field in Rocky Mount bears his name.

The game was a "first rate pitchers' duel," with Bauer holding the upper hand this time, only allowing one hit. Wake Forest finally broke through with a pair of solo home runs in the ninth inning to secure the victory before a crowd of 3,000 at Devereux Meadows.

With eight fast innings gone and the scoreboard tender rapidly running out of zeros, Paul Livick and Gene Hooks blasted successive four-baggers over the leftfield fence, the latter's coming with Charlie Teague on base, to

Depression and War

For the second year in a row, this State team was shut down in a pitchers' duel between Moe Bauer and State's knuckleballer, Ernie Johnson (courtesy R.G. Utley).

bring the powerful Baptists their second Big Four League triumph and their 12th straight of the season.

Pack Gets One Hit

The explosion climaxed the tightest kind of pitchers' battle between Wake Forest's Raymond (Moe) Bauer and State's Ernie Johnson, with Bauer's performance coming within one hit and an attack of wildness of a classic. The slender Deacon southpaw held the Wolfpack to one hit, a solid double by Bill Fowler in the seventh inning, but he had to be replaced with one man out in the ninth when State loaded the bases on three walks.

Harry Nicholas, Wake Forest's righthanded sophomore star came to Bauer's rescue and choked off the Wolfpack's last-stand threat, but not until State had saved itself of a shutout. One of Nicholas's fast balls eluded Catcher Russ Batchelor, who was charged with a passed ball, and Fowler scored from third base.

Johnson in Fine Form

Wake Forest's fame-winning home run punch was introduced with startling suddenness. In the eight preceding scoreless innings, Johnson, the Wolfpack's veteran knuckleballer, had held up his end of the mound argument with an effectiveness only slightly less impressive than Bauer's. The

Deacons had reached him for only four hits when Teague, last year's Big Four League batting champion, got his second knock of the day, a ground single to centerfield after Charlie Kersh fanned to open the ninth.

Johnson retired Joe Fulghum on a liner into short centerfield, and up came Livick. The Deacon rightfielder connected as Teague broke for second on the hit-and-run, and the ball sailed well out of the park over the left-centerfield sector, some 360 feet distant.

Hooks, the Wake Forest third baseman, stepped to the plate and followed suit. He lifted a drive over the 320-foot leftfield barrier, and the Deacs thus extended their winning streak to 12 in a row. But not without a scare in the home half of the ninth....

A lead story for this game credited Wake Forest with a fourteen-game winning streak entering the game. The game article stated that this was their twelfth consecutive win.

Before this season was over, Wake would run the streak to twenty games, win the Southern Conference and make an astounding run in the NCAA playoffs which only ended in the championship against the powerful University of Texas team. Ex–major leaguer Lee Gooch left a twenty-year retirement to coach the team, which returned all but two starters from 1948's second-place team. Wake's final record stood at 31–4, a great accomplishment for their program.

Wake Forest	AB	R	H	O	A	E
Hoch, ss	4	0	1	0	2	0
Kersh, cf	4	0	1	3	0	0
Teague, 2b	4	1	2	3	1	0
Fulghum, lf	4	0	0	3	0	0
Livick, rf	3	1	2	1	0	0
Hooks, 3b	4	1	1	1	1	0
Warren, 1b	4	0	0	9	1	0
Batchelor, c	3	0	0	6	1	0
Bauer, p	2	0	0	1	2	0
Nicholas, p	0	0	0	0	0	0
	32	3	7	27	8	0
State	AB	R	H	O	A	E
Evans, cf	3	0	0	2	0	0
Utley, 3b	3	0	0	2	2	0
Fowler, c	3	1	1	5	1	0
McComas, ss	2	0	0	0	9	0
Cheek, rf	3	0	0	2	0	0

State	AB	R	H	O	A	E
B. Livingston, 2b	3	0	0	3	2	0
Council, 1b	4	0	0	12	0	0
Mussack, lf	2	0	0	1	1	0
H. Livingston, ph	1	0	0	0	0	0
Johnson, p	2	0	0	0	0	1
	26	1	1	27	15	1

Wake Forest	0 0 0	0 0 0	0 0 3	3
State	0 0 0	0 0 0	0 0 1	1

SUMMARY: Two base hit: Fowler. Home runs; Livick, Hooks. Sacrifices: Utley, Johnson. Left on base: Wake Forest 4, State 7. Double play: Mussack, Utley and B. Livingston. Base on balls: Bauer 7, Johnson 2. Struck out: Bauer 4, Nicholas 1, Johnson 5. Passed ball: Batchelor. Umpires: Weaver and Murray. Time: 1:55.

Wake Forest closed out the decade in 1950 with another fine performance by lefthander Ray Bauer. Bauer's third quality performance would certainly rate him high all-time among pitchers who took the mound in the Easter Classic.

Deacs Beat Pack, 8–3
Bauer Halts State Nine; Fulghum Hits

by FRANK O'BRIEN

Led by Bauer, Wake Forest appeared to be on the verge of another powerhouse season in this game which opened the conference season for both teams.

Wake Forest's skinny Ray (Moe) Bauer, who was a nemesis to the State Wolfpack all last season, picked up the role again yesterday in their first Big Four clash of the year, puzzling the Pack, 8–3.

The tall lefthander limited Coach Vic Sorrell's improved Pack to seven safeties, three of them by Second Baseman, John Norrell, while his Deacon mates squared off against Starter Irv Page and Reliever Smith for 10.

Bauer struck out eight and held the Wolfpack to one hit for the first four innings, before State managed to solve the lefthander's slants.

Bauer's effectiveness and a combination of Deacon hitting and alertness, despite four errors, furnished Wake Forest with an early lead which they maintained throughout the traditional Easter Monday meeting of these two Big Four cousins.

The Deacs, who hogged the Big Four last year, started the same familiar

The Easter Monday Baseball Game

routine again yesterday which made them a power in national collegiate baseball competition in 1949.

They took a 3–1 lead against the Pack in the first inning when they jumped on Irv Page for hits by Art Hoch, Charlie Teague and Joe Fulghum, and a walk to Paul Harris. Teague's blow sent in Hoch, and Wake Forest's peppery second baseman crossed the plate on Fulghum's safety after Gene Hooks' infield out had scored Harris.

John Norrell, who led State at the plate with three for four, scored the Wolfpack's first run. He crossed the plate after Charlie Westbrook's singled, Welch walked, and Bill Smith lined into a double play.

Leads Deacs

Fulghum, Wake Forest's strapping leftfielder, topped the hitting for the Deacs. He tagged Page for two singles, and added a third off Bob Smith in five trips.

The victory gave Wake Forest two wins and no losses in the southern division of the Southern Conference....

It would seem that Wake Forest had gained the upper hand in terms of quality recruits during the last era of the Easter Monday game. During the '40s and '50s they had seven players to reach the major leagues while State had none.

Playing for a second year under Lee Gooch, the 1950 Wake Forest team went 24–4, won the Big Four and Southern Conference, and were runner-ups in the District III of the NCAA playoffs, losing out to the University of Alabama. During the season, they defeated five minor league teams, including three from the tough Carolina League. State had an outstanding season as well, finishing 16–9, the best mark in several years.

Wake Forest	*AB*	*R*	*H*	*O*	*A*	*E*
Hoch, ss	5	1	2	3	4	2
Harris, rf	3	1	0	3	0	0
Teague, 2b	5	2	2	2	1	0
Hooks, 3b	4	1	1	1	1	1
Fulghum, lf	5	0	3	0	0	0
Kersh, cf	3	1	0	2	0	1
Wrenn, c	5	2	2	10	0	0
Warren, 1b	4	0	0	5	1	0
Bauer, p	2	0	0	1	0	0
	36	8	10	27	7	4

State	AB	R	H	O	A	E
Norrell, 2b	4	2	3	3	5	0
Dinan, 2b	0	0	0	0	0	0
Westbrook, rf-cf	5	1	2	4	0	0
Fowler, cf	0	0	0	0	0	0
Lewis, ph	0	0	0	0	0	0
Welch, rf	4	0	0	1	0	0
W. Smith, 1b	3	0	0	12	1	1
Wilhelm, c	4	0	0	2	0	1
Cheek, lf	4	0	1	4	0	0
Council, 3b	4	0	0	0	2	0
Brinson, ss	4	0	1	0	5	0
Page, p	0	0	0	0	0	0
Martin, ph	1	0	0	0	0	0
R. Smith, p	3	0	0	1	0	0
	36	3	7	27	13	2

```
Wake Forest   3 0 2   0 0 1   1 0 1   8
State         1 0 0   0 0 2   0 0 0   3
```

Summary: Two base hit: Cheek. Three base hit: Wrenn. Stolen bases: Hoch, Hooks, Wreen, and Kersh. Double plays: Teague, Hoch, and Warren; Norrell and Smith. Left on base: Wake Forest 9, State 9. Base on balls: Page 4, Smith 3, Bauer 4. Strikeouts: Page 1, R. Smith 1, Bauer 8. Umpires: Veazey and Stallings. Time: 2:23.

Attendance: 3,000 (est.).

END GAMES

1951–1956

For the first time, North Carolina's population exceeded four million as the "Eisenhower Decade" began. These years would prove to be a time of great social change in the country as well as in the state. In 1951, a court order forced the state's universities to accept African-American students into graduate and professional programs. In 1954, the Supreme Court's ruling on *Brown vs. Board of Education of Topeka* set into motion the process that would integrate the state's public schools during the following decade. The immediate effect of this ruling was a state amendment, known as the Pearsall Plan, which allowed the state to pay for students to attend private schools and to proceed slowly with the process of integration. In 1955, the University of North Carolina at Chapel Hill enrolled its first African-American class, three young men from the nearby city of Durham.

In terms of education, the action that had the greatest effect on the Easter Monday Classic was the relocation of Wake Forest College to Winston-Salem. This move ended the long tradition of the Easter Monday game in Raleigh.

The Easter Monday classic began to wind down as the two schools entered the decade of the '50s. The best indicator of this in 1951 was the attendance of 1,200, a small crowd even for a cold March game.

> Deacs Open Title Defense by Whipping State, 6–2
> Stan Johnson Goes Distance as Wake Forest Takes Big Four Victory
> by HERMAN BLACKMAN
> Wake Forest's Demon Deacons opened defense of their Southern Conference and Big Four League baseball titles here yesterday afternoon by defeating State's Wolfpack at Devereux Meadow, 6–2.

A crowd of 1,200 braved cold weather to see the old rivals clash in their annual Easter Monday contest.

Eight State errors, coupled with eight bases on balls, enabled the Deacons to take an easy win from what had opened as a hotly-contested scrap. The Deacons were limited to five hits by a trio of State pitchers.

The victory was the third straight for Coach Taylor Sanford's Deacs. It was the second successive setback for Vic Sorrell's State nine.

Johnson Fans 12

Stan Johnson, a smooth-working righthander from Greensboro, twirled five-hit ball for the Deacons in notching the mound victory. En route to his win, he whiffed 12 Pack batters. Six walks kept Johnson in trouble. Johnson looked like just the ticket to take up some of the pitching slack left on the Deacon staff by the departure of such sturdies as Moe Bauer and Harry Nicholas.

Two runs in the seventh inning broke a 2–2 tie and provided Wake Forest with its margin of victory — and the Deacons got their tallies without the benefit of a base hit. Two more runs in the ninth inning, on one hit, clinched matters for good.

In the seventh, with one out, Bob Coluni walked and Jack Stallings fanned. Junie Floyd walked and Paul Ellis was hit by a pitched ball. Roland Brinson bobbled Murphrey's grounder and Coluni scored. The Deacons then pulled off a double steal, with Floyd coming home on an error by McGillis....

Although the 1951 State team managed an 11–10 record, they tied with Wake at the bottom of the Big Four with 5–7 records. Wake had lost many of its top players, and though they started their season with a successful appearance at the Pan-Am Games in Argentina, their season did not live up to the previous two.

Wake Forest	AB	R	H	O	A	E
Coluni, ss	4	1	1	0	1	0
Stallings, 2b	4	0	1	3	2	1
Floyd, lf	3	1	0	0	0	0
Ellis, rf	3	0	0	3	0	0
Brown, rf	1	1	0	0	0	0
Murphrey, 3b	2	2	0	0	0	0
Warren, 1b	2	1	1	7	2	0
Rogers, cf	5	0	1	0	0	0
Wrenn, c	4	0	0	13	2	1

Wake Forest	AB	R	H	O	A	E
Johnson, p	4	0	1	1	2	0
	32	6	5	27	9	2

State	AB	R	H	O	A	E
Brinson, 2b	2	0	0	2	2	1
Kolbacker, 2b	2	0	0	0	1	1
Thompson, lf	4	0	0	1	0	2
Horbett, rf	4	0	0	1	0	0
McGillis, c	3	1	1	10	0	1
Fuscoe, cf	4	0	3	1	0	0
Cheek, 1b	3	0	0	11	0	0
Sharpe, ph	0	0	0	0	0	0
Bryant, 3b	2	0	0	0	2	1
Uzzle, ss	3	1	0	1	1	1
Atwell, ph	0	0	0	0	0	0
Lewis, p	1	0	1	0	4	0
Smith, p	1	0	0	0	1	1
Beene, p	0	0	0	0	0	0
Bagonis, ph	1	0	0	0	0	0
	30	2	5	27	11	8

```
Wake Forest   0 0 0   2 0 0   2 0 2   6
State         0 0 0   1 1 0   0 0 0   2
```

SUMMARY: Two base hit: Fuscoe. Three base hit: McGillis. Stolen bases: Coluni, Floyd. Double plays: Coluni, Stallings, and Warren. Johnson, Wrenn and Warren. Lewis, Uzzle, and Cheek. Bryant, Brinson, and Cheek. Left on base: Wake Forest 10; State 8. Base on balls: Lewis 2, Smith 6, Johnson 6. Strikeouts: Lewis 4, Smith 3, Beene 4, Johnson 12. Passed ball: Wrenn. Umpires: Veasey and Stallings. Time: 2:33.

Having defeated Wake Forest once already in 1952, N.C. State brought a more confident team to the classic. Note that the coverage of this game makes no mention of attendance, another sign that the game had lost some its previous gravity.

Pack Edges Deacs, 3–2
State Scores Win in 11th

Opposite: A number of top players had left the Wake Forest program by 1951, making it impossible for them to defend their reign as two-time conference and Big Four champion. This team, however, began the season by representing the country well in the Pan-Am Games in Argentina. Playing with only 12 players and losing their catcher in the first game, they managed to win games over Argentina, Brazil, Colombia and Venezuela before losing to Nicaragua and Cuba and finishing in a second place tie with Mexico (courtesy Wake Forest University).

The Easter Monday Baseball Game

Lunsford Lewis Defeats Frosh Rudy Williams in Long Pitching Duel

by DICK HERBERT

Lunsford Lewis, a righthander with a reputation of being a hard luck pitcher, came out on the winning end of a close one for a change as State defeated Wake Forest, 3–2, in an 11-inning thriller at Devereux Meadow yesterday afternoon.

Lewis gave up only five hits and struck out nine as the Wolfpack gained its second straight victory over the Deacons and took over second place in the Big Four race.

Rudy Williams, a freshman righthander from Whiteville, pitched himself out of one tight spot after another, but the Wolfpack finally managed to get a clutch hit off him in the eleventh. Ed Horbelt, an outfielder who also is one of Coach Vic Sorrell's front line pitchers, sent a single into rightfield to score Ed Morris from second base with the winning run.

Morris got into scoring position when he worked Williams for a walk after Johnny Yvars, the batting star of the day had struck out. George Thompson, the hitting hero of State's first win over the Deacs, then got an infield hit which set the stage for Horbelt's poke which broke up the three-hour marathon.

The Wolfpack missed a lot of opportunities to win in regulation time. They left runners on base in the first six innings and a total of 16 for the game. In the ninth they had the bases loaded, but Williams slipped a third strike past Horbelt on a three-and-two pitch.

Horbelt, however, atoned for that with his game-winning single in the second extra inning.

Lewis was working on a no-hitter and a 2–0 lead when the spell was broken by the Deacons in the sixth inning when they tied the score. Jack Stallings, leadoff batter, got a walk. Johnny Alford sent a bounder over third base, and both runners were safe when Jack Turney made the throw to second. It was scored as a hit. John Liptak then sent a solid single through the box which brought in Stallings. Buddy Smith got a walk, and then Alford scored from third when Catcher Hugh Laughridge permitted a pitch to get by him. Junie Floyd and George Lefelar struck out, and the rally ended when Liptak tried to steal home and was retired.

That turned out to be the only scoring for the Deacons all afternoon. State left two on base in the first inning and couldn't score with the bases loaded and none out in the second. Yvars opened the third with a 340-foot drive over the left-centerfield fence, and another run came across in that inning on Horbelt's single, a walk to John Fuscoe, and an infield hit by Hugh Laughridge....

Wake Forest	AB	R	H	O	A	E
Stallings, 2b	4	1	0	3	3	0
Alford, cf	4	1	1	1	1	0
Tatum, 3b	1	0	0	0	0	0
Liptak, 3b	4	0	1	3	1	0
Smith, 1b	3	0	1	0	0	0
Floyd, lf	3	0	0	3	1	1
Lefever, rf	4	0	0	4	0	0
Brooks, c	2	0	0	7	0	0
Morris, ss	4	0	2	0	3	0
Williams, p	4	0	0	0	0	0
	33	2	5	21	9	1
State	AB	R	H	O	A	E
Brinson, 2b	4	0	3	3	4	2
Turney, 3b	1	0	0	0	1	0
Yvars, ss	4	1	3	3	6	0
Morris, 1b	4	1	1	13	1	0
Thompson, lf	4	0	2	2	0	0
Herbert, cf	3	1	2	0	0	0
Fuscoe, rf	4	0	1	2	0	0
Laughridge, c	4	0	1	10	1	0
Lewis, p	3	0	1	1	1	0
	31	3	14	34	14	2

```
Wake Forest  0 0 0   0 0 2   0 0 0   0 0 2
State        0 0 2   0 0 0   0 0 0   0 1 3
```

SUMMARY: Two base hits: Yvars, Brinson. Home run: Yvars. Stolen bases: Yvars. Sacrifice: Laughridge. Double plays: Yvars, Brinson, and Morris 2. Laughridge and Morris. Left on base: Wake Forest 6, State 14. Base on balls: Williams 6, Lewis 3. Strikeouts: Williams 6, Lewis 9. Passed ball: Laughridge. Umpires: Rubino and Allen. Time: 2:00.

The 1953 game, scheduled for Monday, April 7, was postponed because of rain. Clearly, by this date, the game was viewed as just another Big Four/Southern Conference game. It was finally played on May 12, with Wake Forest taking the Wolfpack by a 5–1 score. The attendance was listed as 1,100.

The 1954 season marked the beginning of play in the newly founded Atlantic Coast Conference. The game, which proved to be one of the most dramatic of the whole series, was played on the State campus because of road construction around Devereaux Meadows.

The Easter Monday Baseball Game

Deac Delivers in Last Frame
Catcher Connects with Two Out and Two On in Ninth Inning

by MAC McDUFFIE

With defeat only one strike away, sophomore Lynwood Holt blasted a three-run homer over the right field barrier to give Wake Forest's Demon Deacons a thrilling 4–2 victory over State in their annual Easter Monday classic at State College yesterday afternoon.

In a tense struggle which saw both teams unable to get hits with men on the bases, Holt collected the only extra-base blow of the battle. Each team left ten runners stranded.

Lowell (Lefty) Davis pitched for Wake Forest until he was lifted for a pinch-hitter in the ninth and kept the Wolfpack fairly subdued, but most of the 3,000 fans figured the slender Deacon southpaw was headed for defeat in the closing innings of the game. Davis had been trailing 2–1 since the fourth inning and Wake Forest was not making any serious scoring threats.

Yvars Hurts Back

Jack Yvars, big sophomore righthander who is considered the ace of the West Raleigh mound staff, started and gave up a run in the fourth inning. He called his older brother, captain and shortstop Johnny over for a conference during that frame and informed him that his back was beginning to hurt. Jack faced only four men in the fifth, walking one, and yielded a single to the first batter in the sixth. He then struck out Bob Waggoner for the third straight time and called for Coach Vic Sorrell to send in a relief pitcher.

Tommy Hargrove, a sophomore lefthander from Graham, came in and held the Deacons in check until the ninth. He walked pinch-hitter Bruce Hillenbrand to open the fatal inning, but Bruce was cut down at second on pinch-hitter Billy Lyles' grounder. Dickie Harris popped to first for the second out. Luther McKeel smashed a drive between first and second for a single to set the stage for Holt.

Hargrove got two strikes on Holt before the hustling young catcher caught the third one and sent it over the fence with plenty of room to spare. It was the second straight game he won for Wake Forest in the ninth. The Deacons rallied for four runs in the ninth last Saturday to win, 6–5. Holt's single drove in the deciding run....

1953 Makeup Game, Played May 11, 1953

Wake Forest	AB	R	H	O	A	E
Signore, 2b	3	2	1	3	4	0
McKeel, cf	4	0	0	2	0	0
Brown, lf	4	1	1	2	0	0
Liptak, c	4	2	3	5	0	0
Floyd, 3b	3	0	1	3	1	1
Smith, 1b	4	0	2	8	1	0
Harris, ss	3	0	1	4	4	0
Cole, rf	3	0	0	0	0	0
Walsh, p	0	0	0	0	0	0
Davis, p	4	0	0	0	0	0
	32	5	9	27	10	1

State	AB	R	H	O	A	E
Whitley, 3b	3	1	1	1	2	0
Turney, 2b	4	0	0	6	5	1
Yvars, ss	4	0	2	1	6	1
Morris, 1b	4	0	0	11	0	0
Fuscoe, cf	3	0	0	1	0	0
Wyles, c	3	0	0	4	2	0
Horbelt, rf	4	0	1	3	0	0
Santoli, lf	4	0	2	1	0	0
Hardison, p	2	0	0	0	1	0
Barringer, ph	1	0	0	0	0	0
	32	1	6	28	16	2

```
Wake Forest   2 0 3   0 0 0   0 0 0   5
State         1 0 0   0 0 0   0 0 0   1
```

SUMMARY: Two base hit: Liptak. Sacrifice: McKeel. Double plays: Yvars, Turney, Morris 3. Hardison, Yvars, Morris. Left on bases: State 8, Wake Forest 7. Base on balls: Walsh 3, Davis 1, Hargrove 1, Hardison 3. Struck out: Davis 4, Hardison 4. Umpires: Beck and Dee. Time: 2:10.
Attendance: 1,100.

1954 Game

Wake Forest	AB	R	H	O	A	E
Abbot, ss	3	0	1	0	1	1
Lyles, ss	1	1	0	0	1	0
Harris, 2b	5	0	2	2	0	0
McKeel, cf	4	1	2	1	0	0
Holt, c	5	1	2	7	0	0
Cole, rf	4	1	1	4	0	0
Waggoner, 1b	3	0	0	3	0	0
Warren, lf	0	0	0	1	0	0

The Easter Monday Baseball Game

Wake Forest	AB	R	H	O	A	E
Livengood, lf	1	0	0	5	0	0
Smith, ph	1	0	0	0	0	0
Honzagni, 1b	0	0	0	2	0	0
Tatum, 3b	4	0	1	2	2	1
Davis, p	3	0	0	0	0	0
Hillenbrand, ph	0	0	0	0	0	0
Walsh, p	0	0	0	0	0	0
	34	4	9	27	4	2

State	AB	R	H	O	A	E
Babyak, rf	2	1	0	1	0	1
Greene, rf	1	0	0	0	0	0
Turney, 2b	5	0	2	3	3	0
Wyles, c	4	0	1	8	1	0
John Yvars, ss	4	0	1	3	3	0
Peed, 1b	4	0	0	8	0	0
Santoli, cf	4	1	1	0	0	0
Barringer, 3b	4	0	0	1	2	0
Norris, lf	2	0	1	3	0	0
Jack Yvars, p	2	0	1	0	0	0
Hargrove, p	0	0	0	0	0	0
Hardison, p	1	0	0	0	0	0
	33	2	7	27	9	1

```
Wake Forest   0 0 0   1 0 0   0 0 3   4
State         1 0 0   1 0 0   0 0 0   2
```

SUMMARY: Home run: Holt. Stolen bases: Holt, Norris, Santoli, Peed. Left on bases: Wake Forest 10, State 10. Base on balls: Davis 4, Jack Yvars 4, Hargrave 1. Struck out: Davis 4, Walsh 2, Jack Yvars 4, Hargrove 3. Wild pitch: Davis. Umpires; Hall and Faircloth. Time 2:20. Attendance: 3,000 (est.).

In 1955, the Easter Monday classic was again rained out. Originally scheduled for Monday, April 11, the game was not made up until Monday, May 10. In a reversal of sorts from the year before, the Wolfpack staged a four-run rally in the ninth to defeat Wake Forest 9–8. The game was played before 1,200 fans. Appropriately, this, which turned out to be the last game in the longstanding series, turned out to be a rather contentious affair.

The game was delayed by ten minutes in the second inning when a long fly to left field was deflected by Wake's leftfielder, Frank McRae. The umpire only gave Norman Norris two bases despite the fact that he had rounded the bases before McRae could retrieve the ball.

The 1955 Wake Forest baseball team brought home the school's first national championship. Front row, left to right: Abbott, Moore, Anglin, Davis, McKeel, Barnes, Stokoe, Bonzagni Second row, left to right: Brewster, Koontz, Walsh, McGinley, Fichter, Waggoner, Cole, Bryant, Moore Third row, left to right: Muse, Miller, Adams, Holt, Sanford (coach), McRae, Warren, Horn, Adams (courtesy Wake Forest University).

Coach Sanford of Wake Forest entered an official protest in the fifth inning when McKeel was sent from third back to second after an overthrow at first by Barringer, the State third baseman. There is no mention of the result of Sanford's protest, but it was likely overruled in favor of the call on the field.

The Deacons lost the Easter Monday game, but 1955 turned out to be Wake Forest's year and the pinnacle of Coach Sanford's five-year stint at Wake. Led by outfielder Tommy Cole, future NFL champion (1960 Philadelphia) running back Billy Ray Barnes, top pitcher "Lefty" Davis, an All-ACC basketball player, and All-American senior catcher Lynwood Holt, the Deacons won the ACC championship with an 11–3 record. From there, they won nine more games, including two out of three over West Virginia and two of three from Western Michigan, capturing the College World Series for the school's first national championship. The Series included some controversy as Wake had to make a decision on whether to play or forfeit a Sunday game. Athletic Director Pat Preston chose to play the game, angering a minority of Wake supporters.

Wake Forest	AB	R	H	O	A	E
Moore, ss	5	1	2	5	1	2
McKell, cf	3	1	1	5	0	1

Wake Forest	AB	R	H	O	A	E
Miller, rf	5	0	0	1	0	0
Holt, c	3	1	2	3	0	0
Cole, 3b	5	1	2	2	2	1
McRae, lf	5	2	2	1	0	0
Barnes, 2b	4	1	1	3	3	0
Waggoner, 1b	0	1	0	2	1	0
Abbot, ph	1	0	0	0	0	0
Benzagal, 1b	1	0	0	1	0	0
Davis, p	5	0	4	4	0	0
Fichter, p	0	0	0	0	0	0
	39	8	14	27	6	4

State	AB	R	H	O	A	E
Whitley, ss	5	1	2	2	0	0
Stantoli, cf	5	1	1	1	1	0
Turney, 2b	5	2	1	6	3	0
Peed, 1b	4	1	2	7	0	0
Barringer, 3b	4	1	3	1	6	3
Casteen, rf	4	1	1	1	0	0
Morris, lf	4	0	1	5	0	0
West, c	4	1	1	4	1	1
Hargrove, p	2	0	0	0	1	0
Franklin, p	0	0	0	0	0	0
Meadlock, ph	1	0	0	0	0	0
Dickman, p	0	1	0	0	0	0
	38	9	12	27	12	4

```
Wake Forest   0 1 0   0 0 4   2 1 0   8
State         0 0 0   1 0 1   1 2 4   9
```

SUMMARY: Two base hits: Barringer, Norris, Moore. Three base hits: Moore, Peed, and West. Home run: Casteen. Double plays: Waggoner and Moore. Left on bases: State 6, Wake Forest 8. Base on balls: Hargrove 5, Davis 2. Strikeouts: Davis 4, Hargrove 2, Franklin 1. Wild pitches: Hargrove 2. Kickman. Umpires: Butler, McAfee and Dee. Time 2:25.
Attendance: 1,200.

The 1956 Easter Monday game was scheduled to be played in Raleigh on April 2. The *News and Observer* edition of that day ran the following on their editorial page: "In Raleigh there will be the traditional baseball game with [Wake Forest] at State College and at Winston-Salem there

Opposite: **Photograph from the November 1995 reunion in Raleigh of post–World War II PiKA members (courtesy Lamont Whitley).**

will be open house at the magnificent new plant which the college [Wake Forest] will occupy for its summer session."

On the sports page: "Charlie Teague, a star second baseman for Wake Forest not long ago, will be coaching the Deacons for the first time in a Big Four battle. Vic Sorrell, veteran State coach, is a former Deacon himself."

From the following day's sports page: "For the second straight year, rain washed out the annual Easter Monday baseball game between State and Wake Forest. Since the teams had three games scheduled, the game yesterday will not be made up."

This ended the traditional series of Easter Monday baseball games between N.C. State and Wake Forest. Wake Forest College would be located in Winston-Salem, North Carolina, by Easter Monday of 1957.

Another reason for ending the series was the beginning (in 1955) of an annual Dixie Baseball Classic, hosted by Duke University, where four teams outside of the North Carolina area would be invited to play Duke, the University of North Carolina, Wake Forest, and N.C. State.

Legendary N.C. State baseball coach Chick Doak died from a heart attack on April 21, 1956, and with his passing an era of tradition that affected life both on and off the field in North Carolina's state capital was gone.

Appendix A:
Major League Statistics — N.C. State Players

The remarkable number of Easter Monday baseball participants who made it to the major leagues is a testament to the quality of play in the series. Following are the big league records for players from the N.C. State program.

Jimmy Brown

Birth Name:	James Roberson Brown
Nickname:	Jim or Jimmy
Born On:	4-25-1910 (Taurus)
Born In:	Jamesville, North Carolina
Died On:	12-29-1977
Died In:	Bath, North Carolina
College:	North Carolina College of Agriculture and Engineering
Bats:	Both
Throws:	Right
Height:	5' 8½"
Weight:	165
First Game:	4-23-1937 (Age 26)
Last Game:	9-15-1946
Draft:	Not Applicable

Hitting Stats

Yr	Age	Team	G	AB	R	H	2B	3B	HR	RBI	BB	AVG	OBP	SLG
1937	27	Cardinals	138	525	86	145	20	9	2	53	27	.276	.313	.360
1938	28	Cardinals	108	382	50	115	12	6	0	38	27	.301	.350	.364
1939	29	Cardinals	147	645	88	192	31	8	3	51	32	.298	.335	.384
1940	30	Cardinals	107	454	56	127	17	4	0	30	24	.280	.317	.335
1941	31	Cardinals	132	549	81	168	28	9	3	56	48	.306	.363	.406
1942	32	Cardinals	145	606	75	155	28	4	1	71	52	.256	.315	.320
1943	33	Cardinals	34	110	6	20	4	2	0	8	6	.182	.224	.255
1946	36	Pirates	79	241	23	58	6	0	12	18	18	-.241	.293	.266

Appendix A: Major League Statistics—N.C. State Players

Career	G	AB	R	H	2B	3B	HR	RBI	BB	AVG	OBP	SLG
8 Years	890	3,512	465	980	146	42	9	319	231	.279	.326	.352

DICK BURRUS

Birth Name:	Maurice Lennon Burrus
Nickname:	Dick
Born On:	1-29-1898 (Aquarius)
Born In:	Hatteras, North Carolina
Died On:	2-02-1972
Died In:	Elizabeth City, North Carolina
College:	North Carolina College of Agriculture and Engineering
Bats:	Left
Throws:	Left
Height:	5'11"
Weight:	175
First Game:	6-23-1919 (Age 21)
Last Game:	8-21-1928
Draft:	Not Applicable

Hitting Stats

Yr	Age	Team	G	AB	R	H	2B	3B	HR	RBI	BB	AVG	OBP	SLG
1919	21	Athletics	70	194	17	50	3	4	0	8	9	.258	.294	.314
1920	22	Athletics	71	135	11	25	8	0	0	10	5	.185	.225	.244
1925	27	Braves	152	588	82	200	41	4	5	87	51	.340	.396	.449
1926	28	Braves	131	486	59	131	21	1	3	61	37	.270	.324	.335
1927	29	Braves	72	220	22	70	8	3	0	32	17	.318	.370	.382
1928	30	Braves	64	137	15	37	6	0	3	13	19	.270	.367	.380

Career	G	AB	R	H	2B	3B	HR	RBI	BB	AVG	OBP	SLG
6 Years	560	1,760	206	513	87	12	11	211	138	.291	.347	.373

JOE DEBERRY

Birth Name:	Joseph Gaddy DeBerry
Nickname:	Joe
Born On:	11-29-1896 (Sagittarius)
Born In:	Mount Gilead, North Carolina
Died On:	10-09-1944
Died In:	Southern Pines, North Carolina
College:	North Carolina College of Agriculture and Engineering
Bats:	Left
Throws:	Right
Height:	6'1"
Weight:	175
First Game:	8-24-1920 (Age 23)
Last Game:	9-03-1921
Draft:	Not Applicable

Pitching Stats

Year	Age	Team	G	GS	W	L	PCT	ERA	CG	SHO	SV	IP	H	BB	SO
1920	24	Browns	10	7	2	4	.333	4.94	3	1	0	54.2	65	20	12
1921	25	Browns	10	1	0	1	.000	6.57	0	0	0	12.1	15	10	1
Career			G	GS	W	L	PCT	ERA	CG	SHO	SV	IP	H	BB	SO
2 Years			20	8	2	5	.286	5.24	3	1	0	67.0	80	30	13

BILL EVANS

Birth Name:	William James Evans
Nickname:	Bill
Born On:	2-10-1893 (Aquarius)
Born In:	Reidsville, North Carolina
Died On:	12-21-1946
Died In:	Burlington, North Carolina
College:	Elon and North Carolina
Bats:	Right
Throws:	Right
Height:	6'
Weight:	175
First Game:	8-13-1916 (Age 23)
Last Game:	6-01-1919
Draft:	Not Applicable

Pitching Stats

Year	Age	Team	G	GS	W	L	PCT	ERA	CG	SHO	SV	IP	H	BB	SO
1916	23	Pirates	13	6	2	5	.286	3.00	3	0	0	63.0	57	16	21
1917	24	Pirates	8	2	0	4	.000	3.37	1	0	0	26.2	24	14	5
1919	26	Pirates	7	3	0	4	.000	5.65	2	0	0	36.2	41	18	15
Career			G	GS	W	L	PCT	ERA	CG	SHO	SV	IP	H	BB	SO
3 Years			28	11	2	13	.133	3.85	6	0	0	126.1	122	48	41

STU FLYTHE

Birth Name:	Stuart McGuire Flythe
Nickname:	Stu
Born On:	12-05-1911 (Sagittarius)
Born In:	Conway, North Carolina
Died On:	10-18-1963
Died In:	Durham, North Carolina
College:	North Carolina College of Agriculture and Engineering
Bats:	Right
Throws:	Right
Height:	6' 2"
Weight:	175
First Game:	5-31-1936 (Age 24)
Last Game:	9-06-1936
Draft:	Not Applicable

Appendix A: Major League Statistics—N.C. State Players

Pitching Stats

Year	Age	Team	G	GS	W	L	PCT	ERA	CG	SHO	SV	IP	H	BB	SO
1936	25	Athletics	17	3	0	0	.000	13.04	0	0	0	39.1	49	61	14
Career			G	GS	W	L	PCT	ERA	CG	SHO	SV	IP	H	BB	SO
1 Year			17	3	0	0	.000	13.04	0	0	0	39.1	49	61	14

DUTCH HOLLAND

Birth Name:	Robert Clyde Holland
Nickname:	Dutch
Born On:	10-12-1903 (Libra)
Born In:	Middlesex, North Carolina
Died On:	6-16-1967
Died In:	Lumberton, North Carolina
College:	North Carolina College of Agriculture and Engineering
Bats:	Right
Throws:	Right
Height:	6'1"
Weight:	190
First Game:	8-16-1932 (Age 28)
Last Game:	8-10-1934
Draft:	Not Applicable

Hitting Stats

Yr	Age	Team	G	AB	R	H	2B	3B	HR	RBI	BB	AVG	OBP	SLG
1932	29	Braves	39	156	15	46	11	1	1	18	12	.295	.345	.397
1933	30	Braves	13	31	3	8	3	0	0	3	3	.258	.324	.355
1934	31	Indians	50	128	19	32	12	1	2	13	13	.250	.319	.406
Career			G	AB	R	H	2B	3B	HR	RBI	BB	AVG	OBP	SLG
3 Years			102	315	37	86	26	2	3	34	28	.273	.332	.397

JOHNNY LANNING

Birth Name:	John Young Lanning
Nickname:	Tobacco Chewin' Johnny
Born On:	9-06-1910 (Virgo)
Born In:	Asheville, North Carolina
Died On:	11-08-1989
Died In:	Asheville, North Carolina
College:	North Carolina College of Agriculture and Engineering
Bats:	Right
Throws:	Right
Height:	6'1"
Weight:	185
First Game:	4-17-1936 (Age 25)
Last Game:	5-12-1947
Draft:	Not Applicable

Appendix A: Major League Statistics — N.C. State Players

Pitching Stats

Year	Age	Team	G	GS	W	L	PCT	ERA	CG	SHO	SV	IP	H	BB	SO
1936	26	Bees	28	20	7	11	.389	3.65	3	1	0	153.0	154	55	33
1937	27	Bees	32	11	5	7	.417	3.93	4	1	2	116.2	107	40	37
1938	28	Bees	32	18	8	7	.533	3.72	4	1	0	138.0	146	52	39
1939	29	Bees	37	6	5	6	.455	3.42	3	0	4	129.0	120	53	45
1940	30	Pirates	38	7	8	4	.667	4.05	2	0	2	115.2	119	39	42
1941	31	Pirates	34	23	11	11	.500	3.13	9	0	1	175.2	175	47	41
1942	32	Pirates	34	8	6	8	.429	3.32	2	1	1	119.1	125	26	31
1943	33	Pirates	12	2	4	1	.800	2.33	0	0	2	27.0	23	9	11
1945	35	Pirates	1	0	0	0	.000	36.00	0	0	0	2.0	8	0	0
1946	36	Pirates	27	9	4	5	.444	3.07	3	0	1	91.0	97	31	16
1947	37	Braves	3	0	0	0	.000	9.82	0	0	0	3.2	4	6	0
Career			G	GS	W	L	PCT	ERA	CG	SHO	SV	IP	H	BB	SO
11 Years			278	104	58	60	.492	3.58	30	4	13	1,071.0	1,078	358	295

GEORGE MURRAY

Birth Name:	George King Murray
Nickname:	Smiler
Born On:	9-23-1898 (Virgo)
Born In:	Charlotte, North Carolina
Died On:	10-18-1955
Died In:	Memphis, Tennessee
College:	North Carolina College of Agriculture and Engineering
Bats:	Right
Throws:	Right
Height:	6'2"
Weight:	200
First Game:	5-08-1922 (Age 23)
Last Game:	5-01-1933
Draft:	Not Applicable

Pitching Stats

Year	Age	Team	G	GS	W	L	PCT	ERA	CG	SHO	SV	IP	H	BB	SO
1922	24	Yankees	22	2	4	2	.667	3.97	0	0	0	56.2	53	26	14
1923	25	Red Sox	39	18	7	11	.389	4.91	5	0	0	177.2	190	87	40
1924	26	Red Sox	28	7	2	9	.182	6.72	0	0	0	80.1	97	32	27
1926	28	Senators	12	12	6	3	.667	5.64	5	0	0	81.1	89	37	28
1927	29	Senators	7	3	1	1	.500	7.00	0	0	0	18.0	18	15	5
1933	35	White Sox	2	0	0	0	.000	7.72	0	0	0	2.1	3	2	0
Career			G	GS	W	L	PCT	ERA	CG	SHO	SV	IP	H	BB	SO
6 Years			110	42	20	26	.435	5.38	10	0	0	416.1	450	199	114

CHINK OUTEN

Birth Name:	William Austin Outen
Nickname:	Bill or Chink
Born On:	6-7-1905 (Gemini)

Appendix A: Major League Statistics—N.C. State Players

Born In: Mount Holly, North Carolina
Died On: 9-11-1961
Died In: Durham, North Carolina
College: North Carolina College of Agriculture and Engineering
Bats: Left
Throws: Right
Height: 6'
Weight: 200
First Game: 4-16-1933 (Age 27)
Last Game: 10-01-1933
Draft: Not Applicable

Hitting Stats

Yr	Age	Team	G	AB	R	H	2B	3B	HR	RBI	BB	AVG	OBP	SLG
1933	28	Dodgers	93	153	20	38	10	0	4	17	20	.248	.335	.392
Career			G	AB	R	H	2B	3B	HR	RBI	BB	AVG	OBP	SLG
1 Year			93	153	20	38	10	0	4	17	20	.248	.335	.392

BUCK REDFEARN

Birth Name: George Howard Redfearn
Nickname: Buck
Born On: 4-07-1902 (Aries)
Born In: Asheville, North Carolina
Died On: 9-08-1964
Died In: Asheville, North Carolina
College: North Carolina College of Agriculture and Engineering
Bats: Right
Throws: Right
Height: 5'11"
Weight: 165
First Game: 4-11-1928 (Age 26)
Last Game: 10-06-1929
Draft: Not Applicable

Hitting Stats

Yr	Age	Team	G	AB	R	H	2B	3B	HR	RBI	BB	AVG	OBP	SLG
1928	26	White Sox	86	261	22	61	6	3	0	35	12	.234	.267	.280
1929	27	White Sox	21	46	0	6	0	0	0	3	3	.130	.184	.130
Career			G	AB	R	H	2B	3B	HR	RBI	BB	AVG	OBP	SLG
2 Years			107	307	22	67	6	3	0	38	15	.218	.255	.257

DAVE ROBERTSON

Birth Name: Davis Aydelotte Robertson
Nickname: Dave

Appendix A: Major League Statistics — N.C. State Players

Born On: 9-25-1889 (Libra)
Born In: Portsmouth, Virginia
Died On: 11-05-1970
Died In: Virginia Beach, Virginia
College: North Carolina College of Agriculture and Mechanical Arts
Bats: Left
Throws: Left
Height: 6'
Weight: 186
First Game: 6-05-1912 (Age 22)
Last Game: 9-27-1922
Draft: Not Applicable

Hitting Stats

Yr	Age	Team	G	AB	R	H	2B	3B	HR	RBI	BB	AVG	OBP	SLG
1912	23	Giants	3	2	0	1	0	0	0	1	0	.500	.500	.500
1914	25	Giants	82	256	25	68	12	3	2	32	10	.266	.299	.359
1915	26	Giants	141	544	72	160	17	10	3	58	22	.294	.326	.379
1916	27	Giants	150	587	88	180	18	8	12	69	14	.307	.326	.426
1917	28	Giants	142	532	64	138	16	9	12	54	10	.259	.276	.391
1919	30	Giants	1	0	0	0	0	0	0	0	0	.000	.000	.000
1919	30	Cubs	27	96	8	20	2	0	1	10	1	.208	.224	.260
1920	31	Cubs	134	500	68	150	29	11	10	75	40	.300	.353	.462
1921	32	Cubs	22	36	7	8	3	0	0	14	1	.222	.243	.306
1921	32	Pirates	60	230	29	74	18	3	6	48	12	.322	.361	.504
1922	33	Giants	42	47	5	13	2	0	1	3	3	.277	.320	.383
Career			**G**	**AB**	**R**	**H**	**2B**	**3B**	**HR**	**RBI**	**BB**	**AVG**	**OBP**	**SLG**
9 Years			804	2,830	366	812	117	44	47	364	113	.287	.318	.409

APPENDIX B:
MAJOR LEAGUE STATISTICS —
WAKE FOREST PLAYERS

MORRIE ADERHOLT

Birth Name:	Morris Woodroe Aderholt
Nickname:	Morrie
Born On:	9-13-1915 (Virgo)
Born In:	Mount Olive, North Carolina
Died On:	3-18-1955
Died In:	Sarasota, Florida
College:	Wake Forest College
Bats:	Left
Throws:	Right
Height:	6'1"
Weight:	188
First Game:	9-13-1939 (Age 24)
Last Game:	9-30-1945
Draft:	Not Applicable

Hitting Stats

Yr	Age	Team	G	AB	R	H	2B	3B	HR	RBI	BB	AVG	OBP	SLG
1939	24	Senators	7	25	5	5	0	0	1	4	2	.200	.259	.320
1940	25	Senators	1	2	0	0	0	0	0	0	0	.000	.000	.000
1941	26	Senators	11	14	3	2	0	0	0	1	1	.143	.200	.143
1944	29	Dodgers	17	59	9	16	2	3	0	10	4	.271	.317	.407
1945	30	Dodgers	39	60	4	13	1	0	0	6	3	.217	.254	.233
1945	30	Braves	31	102	15	34	4	0	2	11	9	.333	.387	.431

Career			G	AB	R	H	2B	3B	HR	RBI	BB	AVG	OBP	SLG
5 Years			106	262	36	70	7	3	3	32	19	.267	.317	.351

GAIR ALLIE

Birth Name:	Gair Roosevelt Allie
Nickname:	None
Born On:	10-28-1931 (Scorpio)

Born In: Statesville, North Carolina
Still Living
High School: Statesville High School (Statesville, N.C.)
College: Wake Forest College
Bats: Right
Throws: Right
Height: 6'1"
Weight: 190
First Game: 4-13-1954 (Age 22)
Last Game: 9-26-1954
Draft: Not Applicable

Hitting Stats

Yr	Age	Team	G	AB	R	H	2B	3B	HR	RBI	BB	AVG	OBP	SLG
1954	23	Pirates	121	418	38	83	8	6	3	30	56	.199	.294	.268

Career			G	AB	R	H	2B	3B	HR	RBI	BB	AVG	OBP	SLG
1 Year			121	418	38	83	8	6	3	30	56	.199	.294	.268

JUNIE BARNES

Birth Name: Junie Shoaf Barnes
Nickname: Lefty
Born On: 12-01-1911 (Sagittarius)
Born In: Linwood, North Carolina
Died On: 12-31-1963
Died In: Jacksonville, North Carolina
College: Wake Forest College
Bats: Left
Throws: Left
Height: 5'11½"
Weight: 170
First Game: 9-12-1934 (Age 22)
Last Game: 9-21-1934
Draft: Not Applicable

Pitching Stats

Year	Age	Team	G	GS	W	L	PCT	ERA	CG	SHO	SV	IP	H	BB	SO
1934	23	Reds	2	0	0	0	.000	0.00	0	0	0	0.1	0	1	0

Career			G	GS	W	L	PCT	ERA	CG	SHO	SV	IP	H	BB	SO
1 Year			2	0	0	0	.000	0.00	0	0	0	0.1	0	1	0

TOMMY BYRNE

Birth Name: Thomas Joseph Byrne
Nickname: The Wildman or Tommy
Born On: 12-31-1919 (Capricorn)
Born In: Baltimore, Maryland
Died On: 12-20-2007

Appendix B: Major League Statistics—Wake Forest Players

Died In: Wake Forest, North Carolina
College: Wake Forest College
Bats: Left
Throws: Left
Height: 6'1"
Weight: 182
First Game: 4-27-1943 (Age 23)
Last Game: 9-21-1957
Draft: Not Applicable

Pitching Stats

Year	Age	Team	G	GS	W	L	PCT	ERA	CG	SHO	SV	IP	H	BB	SO
1943	24	Yankees	11	2	2	1	.667	6.54	0	0	0	31.2	28	35	22
1946	27	Yankees	4	1	0	1	.000	5.79	0	0	0	9.1	7	8	5
1947	28	Yankees	4	1	0	0	.000	4.15	0	0	0	4.1	5	6	2
1948	29	Yankees	31	11	8	5	.615	3.30	5	1	2	133.2	79	101	93
1949	30	Yankees	32	30	15	7	.682	3.72	12	3	0	196.0	125	179	129
1950	31	Yankees	31	31	15	9	.625	4.74	10	2	0	203.1	188	160	118
1951	32	Yankees	9	3	2	1	.667	6.86	0	0	0	21.0	16	36	14
1951	32	Browns	19	17	4	10	.286	3.82	7	2	0	122.2	104	114	57
1952	33	Browns	29	24	7	14	.333	4.68	14	0	0	196.0	182	112	91
1953	34	White Sox	6	2	0	1.000	10.13	0	0	0	16.0	18	26	4
1953	34	Senators	6	5	0	5	.000	4.28	2	0	0	33.2	35	22	22
1954	35	Yankees	5	5	3	2	.600	2.70	4	1	0	40.0	36	19	24
1955	36	Yankees	27	22	16	5	.762	3.15	9	3	2	160.0	137	87	76
1956	37	Yankees	37	8	7	3	.700	3.36	1	0	6	109.2	108	72	52
1957	38	Yankees	30	4	4	6	.400	4.36	1	0	2	84.2	70	60	57

Career			G	GS	W	L	PCT	ERA	CG	SHO	SV	IP	H	BB	SO
13 Years			281	170	85	69	.552	4.11	65	12	12	1,362.0	1,138	1,037	766

RIP COLEMAN

Birth Name: Walter Gary Coleman
Nickname: Rip
Born On: 7-31-1931 (Leo)
Born In: Troy, New York
Died On: 5-14-2004
Died In: Wolfeboro, New Hampshire
College: Wake Forest & Syracuse (DNP)
Bats: Left
Throws: Left
Height: 6'2"
Weight: 185
First Game: 8-15-1955 (Age 24)
Last Game: 5-05-1960
Draft: Not Applicable

Pitching Stats

Year	Age	Team	G	GS	W	L	PCT	ERA	CG	SHO	SV	IP	H	BB	SO
1955	24	Yankees	10	6	2	1	.667	5.28	0	0	1	29.0	40	16	15

Year	Age	Team	G	GS	W	L	PCT	ERA	CG	SHO	SV	IP	H	BB	SO
1956	25	Yankees	29	9	3	5	.375	3.67	0	0	2	88.1	97	42	42
1957	26	Athletics	19	6	0	7	.000	5.93	1	1	0	41.0	53	25	15
1959	28	Athletics	29	11	2	10	.167	4.56	2	0	2	81.0	85	34	54
1959	28	Orioles	3	0	0	0	.000	0.00	0	0	0	4.0	4	2	4
1960	29	Orioles	5	1	0	2	.000	11.25	0	0	0	4.0	8	5	0
Career			G	GS	W	L	PCT	ERA	CG	SHO	SV	IP	H	BB	SO
5 Years			95	33	7	25	.219	4.58	3	1	5	247.1	287	124	130

JOHN GADDY

Birth Name:	John Wilson Gaddy
Nickname:	Sheriff
Born On:	2-05-1914 (Aquarius)
Born In:	Wadesboro, North Carolina
Died On:	5-03-1966
Died In:	Albemarle, North Carolina
College:	Wake Forest College
Bats:	Right
Throws:	Right
Height:	6'½"
Weight:	182
First Game:	9-27-1938 (Age 24)
Last Game:	10-02-1938
Draft:	Not Applicable

Pitching Stats

Year	Age	Team	G	GS	W	L	PCT	ERA	CG	SHO	SV	IP	H	BB	SO
1938	24	Dodgers	2	2	2	0	1.000	0.69	1	0	0	13.0	13	4	3
Career			G	GS	W	L	PCT	ERA	CG	SHO	SV	IP	H	BB	SO
1 Year			2	2	2	0	1.000	0.69	1	0	0	13.0	13	4	3

LEE GOOCH

Birth Name:	Lee Currin Gooch
Nickname:	None
Born On:	2-23-1890 (Pisces)
Born In:	Oxford, North Carolina
Died On:	5-18-1966
Died In:	Raleigh, North Carolina
College:	Wake Forest College
Bats:	Right
Throws:	Right
Height:	6'
Weight:	190
First Game:	8-17-1915 (Age 25)
Last Game:	6-28-1917
Draft:	Not Applicable

Appendix B: Major League Statistics—Wake Forest Players

Hitting Stats

Year	Age	Team	G	AB	R	H	2B	3B	HR	RBI	BB	AVG	OBP	SLG
1915	25	Indians	2	2	0	1	0	0	0	0	0	.500	.500	.500
1917	27	Athletics	17	59	4	17	2	0	1	8	4	.288	.333	.373

Career			G	AB	R	H	2B	3B	HR	RBI	BB	AVG	OBP	SLG
2 Years			19	61	4	18	2	0	1	8	4	.295	.338	.377

WILLARD HUNTER

Birth Name:	Willard Mitchell Hunter
Nickname:	None
Born On:	3-08-1934 (Pisces)
Born In:	Newark, New Jersey
	Still Living
College:	Wake Forest College
Bats:	Right
Throws:	Left
Height:	6'2"
Weight:	180
First Game:	4-16-1962 (Age 28)
Last Game:	10-04-1964
Draft:	Not Applicable

Pitching Stats

Year	Age	Team	G	GS	W	L	PCT	ERA	CG	SHO	SV	IP	H	BB	SO
1962	28	Dodgers	1	0	0	0	.000	40.50	0	0	0	2.0	6	4	1
1962	28	Mets	27	6	1	6	.143	5.57	1	0	0	63.0	67	34	40
1964	30	Mets	41	0	3	3	.500	4.41	0	0	5	49.0	54	9	22

Career			G	GS	W	L	PCT	ERA	CG	SHO	SV	IP	H	BB	SO
2 Years			69	6	4	9	.308	5.68	1	0	5	114.0	127	47	63

TOM LANNING

Birth Name:	Thomas Newton Lanning
Nickname:	Tom
Born On:	4-22-1907 (Taurus)
Born In:	Asheville, North Carolina
Died On:	11-04-1967
Died In:	Marietta, Georgia
College:	Wake Forest College
Bats:	Left
Throws:	Left
Height:	6'1"
Weight:	165
First Game:	9-14-1938 (Age 31)
Last Game:	10-02-1938
Draft:	Not Applicable

Appendix B: Major League Statistics — Wake Forest Players

Pitching Stats

Year	Age	Team	G	GS	W	L	PCT	ERA	CG	SHO	SV	IP	H	BB	SO
1938	31	Phillies	3	1	0	1	.000	6.43	0	0	0	7.0	9	2	2

Career			G	GS	W	L	PCT	ERA	CG	SHO	SV	IP	H	BB	SO
1 Year			3	1	0	1	.000	6.43	0	0	0	7.0	9	2	2

BUDDY LEWIS

Birth Name:	John Kelly Lewis
Nickname:	Buddy
Born On:	8-10-1916 (Leo)
Born In:	Gastonia, North Carolina
Died On:	2-18-2011
Died In:	Gastonia, North Carolina
College:	Wake Forest College
Bats:	Left
Throws:	Right
Height:	6'1"
Weight:	175
First Game:	9-16-1935 (Age 19)
Last Game:	9-30-1949
Draft:	Not Applicable

Hitting Stats

Year	Age	Team	G	AB	R	H	2B	3B	HR	RBI	BB	AVG	OBP	SLG
1935	19	Senators	8	28	0	3	0	0	0	2	0	.107	.107	.107
1936	20	Senators	143	601	100	175	21	13	6	67	47	.291	.347	.399
1937	21	Senators	156	668	107	210	32	6	10	79	52	.314	.367	.425
1938	22	Senators	151	656	122	194	35	9	12	91	58	.296	.354	.431
1939	23	Senators	140	536	87	171	23	16	10	75	72	.319	.402	.478
1940	24	Senators	148	600	101	190	38	10	6	63	74	.317	.393	.443
1941	25	Senators	149	569	97	169	29	11	9	72	82	.297	.386	.434
1945	29	Senators	69	258	42	86	14	7	2	37	37	.333	.423	.465
1946	30	Senators	150	582	82	170	28	13	7	45	59	.292	.359	.421
1947	31	Senators	140	506	67	132	15	4	6	48	51	.261	.330	.342
1949	33	Senators	95	257	25	63	14	4	3	28	41	.245	.355	.366

Career			G	AB	R	H	2B	3B	HR	RBI	BB	AVG	OBP	SLG
11 Years			1,349	5,261	830	1,563	249	93	71	607	573	.297	.368	.420

WILLARD MARSHALL

Birth Name:	Willard Warren Marshall
Nickname:	None
Born On:	2-08-1921 (Aquarius)
Born In:	Richmond, Virginia
Died On:	11-05-2000
Died In:	Norwood, New Jersey
College:	Wake Forest College

Bats: Left
Throws: Right
Height: 6'1"
Weight: 205
First Game: 4-14-1942 (Age 21)
Last Game: 6-15-1955
Draft: Not Applicable

Hitting Stats

Year	Age	Team	G	AB	R	H	2B	3B	HR	RBI	BB	AVG	OBP	SLG
1942	21	Giants	116	401	41	103	9	2	11	59	26	.257	.307	.372
1946	25	Giants	131	510	63	144	18	3	13	48	33	.282	.327	.406
1947	26	Giants	155	587	102	171	19	6	36	107	67	.291	.366	.528
1948	27	Giants	143	537	72	146	21	8	14	86	64	.272	.350	.419
1949	28	Giants	141	499	81	153	19	3	12	70	78	.307	.401	.429
1950	29	Braves	105	298	38	70	10	2	5	40	36	.235	.319	.332
1951	30	Braves	136	469	65	132	24	7	11	62	48	.281	.351	.433
1952	31	Braves	21	66	5	15	4	1	2	11	4	.227	.271	.409
1952	31	Reds	107	397	52	106	23	1	8	46	37	.267	.333	.390
1953	32	Redlegs	122	357	51	95	14	6	17	62	41	.266	.342	.482
1954	33	White Sox	47	71	7	18	2	0	1	7	11	.254	.349	.324
1955	34	White Sox	22	41	6	7	0	0	0	6	13	.171	.364	.171

Career			G	AB	R	H	2B	3B	HR	RBI	BB	AVG	OBP	SLG
11 Years			1,246	4,233	583	1,160	163	39	130	604	458	.274	.347	.423

JACK MEYER

Birth Name: John Robert Meyer
Nickname: Jack
Born On: 3-23-1932 (Aries)
Born In: Philadelphia, Pennsylvania
Died On: 3-09-1967
Died In: Philadelphia, Pennsylvania
College: Delaware (DNP) & Wake Forest
Bats: Right
Throws: Right
Height: 6'1"
Weight: 175
First Game: 4-16-1955 (Age 23)
Last Game: 4-30-1961
Draft: Not Applicable

Pitching Stats

Year	Age	Team	G	GS	W	L	PCT	ERA	CG	SHO	SV	IP	H	BB	SO
1955	23	Phillies	50	5	6	11	.353	3.43	0	0	16	110.1	75	66	97
1956	24	Phillies	41	7	7	11	.389	4.41	2	0	2	96.0	86	51	66
1957	25	Phillies	19	2	0	2	.000	5.73	0	0	0	37.2	44	28	34
1958	26	Phillies	37	5	3	6	.333	3.59	1	0	2	90.1	77	33	87
1959	27	Phillies	47	1	5	3	.625	3.36	1	0	1	93.2	76	53	71
1960	28	Phillies	7	4	3	1	.750	4.32	0	0	0	25.0	25	11	18
1961	29	Phillies	1	0	0	0	.000	9.00	0	0	0	2.0	2	2	2

Appendix B: Major League Statistics — Wake Forest Players

Career	G	GS	W	L	PCT	ERA	CG	SHO	SV	IP	H	BB	SO
7 Years	202	24	24	34	.414	3.92	4	0	21	455.0	385	244	375

DOYT MORRIS

Birth Name:	Doyt Theodore Morris
Nickname:	None
Born On:	7-15-1916 (Cancer)
Born In:	Stanley, North Carolina
Died On:	7-04-1984
Died In:	Gastonia, North Carolina
College:	Wake Forest College
Bats:	Right
Throws:	Right
Height:	6' 4"
Weight:	195
First Game:	6-06-1937 (Age 20)
Last Game:	9-22-1937
Draft:	Not Applicable

Hitting Stats

Yr	Age	Team	G	AB	R	H	2B	3B	HR	RBI	BB	AVG	OBP	SLG
1937	21	Athletics	6	13	0	2	0	0	0	0	0	.154	.154	.154

Career			G	AB	R	H	2B	3B	HR	RBI	BB	AVG	OBP	SLG
1 Year			6	13	0	2	0	0	0	0	0	.154	.154	.154

DICK NEWSOME

Birth Name:	Heber Hampton Newsome
Nickname:	Dick or Heber-Dick
Born On:	12-13-1909 (Sagittarius)
Born In:	Ahoskie, North Carolina
Died On:	12-15-1965
Died In:	Ahoskie, North Carolina
College:	Wake Forest College
Bats:	Right
Throws:	Right
Height:	6'
Weight:	185
First Game:	4-25-1941 (Age 31)
Last Game:	9-27-1943
Draft:	Not Applicable

Pitching Stats

Year	Age	Team	G	GS	W	L	PCT	ERA	CG	SHO	SV	IP	H	BB	SO
1941	32	Red Sox	36	29	19	10	.655	4.13	17	2	0	213.2	235	79	58
1942	33	Red Sox	24	23	8	10	.444	5.01	11	0	0	158.0	174	67	40
1943	34	Red Sox	25	22	8	13	.381	4.49	8	2	0	154.1	166	68	40

Appendix B: Major League Statistics — Wake Forest Players

	G	GS	W	L	PCT	ERA	CG	SHO	SV	IP	HR	BB	SO
Career													
3 Years	85	74	35	33	.515	4.50	36	4	0	526.0	32	214	138

CHARLIE RIPPLE

Birth Name: Charles Dawson Ripple
Nickname: Charlie
Born On: 12-01-1920 (Sagittarius)
Born In: Bolton, North Carolina
Died On: 5-06-1979
Died In: Wilmington, North Carolina
College: Wake Forest College
Bats: Left
Throws: Left
Height: 6'2"
Weight: 210
First Game: 9-25-1944 (Age 23)
Last Game: 6-28-1946
Draft: Not Applicable

Pitching Stats

Year	Age	Team	G	GS	W	L	PCT	ERA	CG	SHO	SV	IP	H	BB	SO
1944	24	Phillies	1	1	0	0	.000	15.43	0	0	0	2.1	6	4	2
1945	25	Phillies	4	0	0	1	.000	7.04	0	0	0	7.2	7	10	5
1946	26	Phillies	6	0	1	0	1.000	10.80	0	0	0	3.1	5	6	3
Career			G	GS	W	L	PCT	ERA	CG	SHO	SV	IP	H	BB	SO
3 Years			11	1	1	1	.500	9.45	0	0	0	13.1	18	20	10

RAY SCARBOROUGH

Birth Name: Rae Wilson Scarborough
Nickname: Ray
Born On: 7-23-1917 (Leo)
Born In: Mount Gilead, North Carolina
Died On: 7-01-1982
Died In: Mount Olive, North Carolina
College: Wake Forest College
Bats: Right
Throws: Right
Height: 6'
Weight: 185
First Game: 6-26-1942 (Age 24)
Last Game: 9-25-1953
Draft: Not Applicable

Pitching Stats

Year	Age	Team	G	GS	W	L	PCT	ERA	CG	SHO	SV	IP	H	BB	SO
1942	25	Senators	17	5	2	1	.667	4.12	1	1	0	63.1	68	32	16

Appendix B: Major League Statistics — Wake Forest Players

Year	Age	Team	G	GS	W	L	PCT	ERA	CG	SHO	SV	IP	H	BB	SO
1943	26	Senators	24	6	4	4	.500	2.83	2	0	3	86.0	93	46	43
1946	29	Senators	32	20	7	11	.389	4.05	6	1	1	155.2	176	74	46
1947	30	Senators	33	18	6	13	.316	3.41	8	2	0	161.0	165	67	63
1948	31	Senators	31	26	15	8	.652	2.82	9	0	1	185.1	166	72	76
1949	32	Senators	34	27	13	11	.542	4.60	11	1	0	199.2	204	88	81
1950	33	Senators	8	8	3	5	.375	4.01	4	2	0	58.1	62	22	24
1950	33	White Sox	27	23	10	13	.435	5.30	8	1	1	149.1	160	62	70
1951	34	Red Sox	37	22	12	9	.571	5.09	8	0	0	184.0	201	61	71
1952	35	Red Sox	28	8	1	5	.167	4.81	1	1	4	76.2	79	35	29
1952	35	Yankees	9	4	5	1	.833	2.91	1	0	0	34.0	27	15	13
1953	36	Yankees	25	1	2	2	.500	3.29	0	0	0	54.2	52	26	20
1953	36	Tigers	13	0	0	2	.000	8.27	0	0	2	20.2	34	11	12
Career			G	GS	W	L	PCT	ERA	CG	SHO	SV	IP	H	BB	SO
10 Years			318	168	80	85	.485	4.13	59	9	12	1,428.2	1,487	611	564

ELMER SEXAUER

Birth Name:	Elmer George Sexauer
Nickname:	None
Born On:	5-21-1926 (Taurus)
Born In:	St. Louis County, Missouri
Died On:	6-27-2011
Died In:	University Village, Florida
College:	Wake Forest College
Bats:	Right
Throws:	Right
Height:	6' 4"
Weight:	220
First Game:	9-06-1948 (Age 22)
Last Game:	9-12-1948
Draft:	Not Applicable

Pitching Stats

Year	Age	Team	G	GS	W	L	PCT	ERA	CG	SHO	SV	IP	H	BB	SO
1948	22	Dodgers	2	0	0	0	.000	13.49	0	0	0	0.2	0	2	0
Career			G	GS	W	L	PCT	ERA	CG	SHO	SV	IP	H	BB	SO
1 Year			2	0	0	0	.000	13.49	0	0	0	0.2	0	2	0

VIC SORRELL

Birth Name:	Victor Garland Sorrell
Nickname:	Lawyer or The Philosopher
Born On:	4-09-1901 (Aries)
Born In:	Morrisville, North Carolina
Died On:	5-04-1972
Died In:	Raleigh, North Carolina
College:	Wake Forest College
Bats:	Right

Appendix B: Major League Statistics—Wake Forest Players

Throws:	Right
Height:	5'10"
Weight:	180
First Game:	4-22-1928 (Age 27)
Last Game:	6-03-1937
Draft:	Not Applicable

Pitching Stats

Year	Age	Team	G	GS	W	L	PCT	ERA	CG	SHO	SV	IP	H	BB	SO
1928	27	Tigers	29	23	8	11	.421	4.79	8	0	0	171.0	182	83	67
1929	28	Tigers	36	31	14	15	.483	5.18	13	1	1	226.0	270	106	81
1930	29	Tigers	35	30	16	11	.593	3.86	14	2	1	233.1	245	106	97
1931	30	Tigers	35	32	13	14	.481	4.15	19	1	1	245.0	267	114	99
1932	31	Tigers	32	31	14	14	.500	4.03	13	1	0	234.1	234	77	84
1933	32	Tigers	36	28	11	15	.423	3.79	13	1	1	232.2	233	78	75
1934	33	Tigers	28	19	6	9	.400	4.79	6	1	2	129.2	146	45	46
1935	34	Tigers	12	6	4	3	.571	4.03	4	0	0	51.1	65	25	22
1936	35	Tigers	30	14	6	7	.462	5.28	5	1	3	131.1	153	64	37
1937	36	Tigers	7	2	0	2	.000	9.00	0	0	1	17.0	25	8	11
Career			*G*	*GS*	*W*	*L*	*PCT*	*ERA*	*CG*	*SHO*	*SV*	*IP*	*H*	*BB*	*SO*
10 Years			280	216	92	101	.477	4.43	95	8	10	1,671.2	1,820	706	619

LARRY WOODALL

Birth Name:	Charles Lawrence Woodall
Nickname:	Larry
Born On:	7-26-1894 (Leo)
Born In:	Staunton, Virginia
Died On:	5-16-1963
Died In:	Cambridge, Massachusetts
College:	Wake Forest and North Carolina
Bats:	Right
Throws:	Right
Height:	5'9"
Weight:	165
First Game:	5-20-1920 (Age 25)
Last Game:	5-09-1929
Draft:	Not Applicable

Hitting Stats

Yr	Age	Team	G	AB	R	H	2B	3B	HR	RBI	BB	AVG	OBP	SLG
1920	26	Tigers	18	49	4	12	1	0	0	5	2	.245	.275	.265
1921	27	Tigers	46	80	10	29	4	1	0	14	6	.363	.407	.438
1922	28	Tigers	50	125	19	43	2	2	0	18	8	.344	.388	.392
1923	29	Tigers	71	148	20	41	12	2	1	19	22	.277	.371	.405
1924	30	Tigers	67	165	23	51	9	2	0	25	21	.309	.387	.388
1925	31	Tigers	75	171	20	35	4	1	0	13	24	.205	.303	.240
1926	32	Tigers	67	146	18	34	5	0	0	15	15	.233	.304	.267
1927	33	Tigers	88	246	28	69	8	6	0	39	37	.280	.375	.362
1928	34	Tigers	65	186	19	39	7	1	0	13	24	.210	.300	.258
1929	35	Tigers	1	1	0	0	0	0	0	0	0	.000	.000	.000

Appendix B: Major League Statistics — Wake Forest Players

Career	*G*	*AB*	*R*	*H*	*2B*	*3B*	*HR*	*RBI*	*BB*	*AVG*	*OBP*	*SLG*
10 Years	548	1,317	161	353	52	15	1	161	159	.268	.347	.333

EDDIE YOUNT

Birth Name:	Floyd Edwin Yount
Nickname:	Eddie
Born On:	12-19-1915 (Sagittarius)
Born In:	Newton, North Carolina
Died On:	10-26-1973
Died In:	Newton, North Carolina
College:	Wake Forest College
Bats:	Right
Throws:	Right
Height:	6'1"
Weight:	185
First Game:	9-09-1937 (Age 21)
Last Game:	9-10-1939
Draft:	Not Applicable

Hitting Stats

Yr	Age	Team	G	AB	R	H	2B	3B	HR	RBI	BB	AVG	OBP	SLG
1937	22	Athletics	4	7	1	2	0	0	0	0	0	-	.286	.286
1939	24	Pirates	2	2	0	0	0	0	0	0	0	.000	.000	.000
Career			*G*	*AB*	*R*	*H*	*2B*	*3B*	*HR*	*RBI*	*BB*	*AVG*	*OBP*	*SLG*
2 Years			6	9	1	2	0	0	0	1	0	.222	.222	.222

BIBLIOGRAPHY

Periodicals

"A & M Defeated Wake Forest 8 to 2." *News and Observer* (Raleigh, NC), March 29, 1909.
"A & M Defeats Bingham by a Score of 5 to 4 in Eleven Inning Game." *News and Observer* (Raleigh, NC), April 4, 1899.
"A & M Takes Game from Foresters." *News and Observer* (Raleigh, NC), April 14, 1914.
"Again Defeat for the Cadets." *News and Observer* (Raleigh, NC), April 9, 1901.
"Allgood Heaves Clever Game to Defeat Deacons." *News and Observer* (Raleigh, NC), April 10, 1928.
"Bad for the Farmer Boys." *News and Observer* (Raleigh, NC), April 13, 1895.
"Baptists Clean Up Old Rivals." *News and Observer* (Raleigh, NC), April 6, 1920.
"Baptists Defeat Old Time Hoodoo." *News and Observer* (Raleigh, NC), March 25, 1913.
"Baseball Monday." *News and Observer* (Raleigh, NC), April 15, 1906.
"Baseball Train." *News and Observer* (Raleigh, NC), March 29, 1907.
"Beal and James Clash in Mound Duel in Classic." *News and Observer* (Raleigh, NC), April 19, 1927.
"Best Base Ball Game of Season: Wake Forest and A & M Play Tomorrow." *News and Observer* (Raleigh, NC), April 19, 1908.
"Blackwell and Bauer Shut Out Wolfpack, 5–0." *News and Observer* (Raleigh, NC), March 30, 1948.
"Dance Easter Monday." *News and Observer* (Raleigh, NC), March 21, 1913.
"Deac Delivers in Last Frame." *News and Observer* (Raleigh, NC), April 20, 1954.
"Deacon Ace Gets Another Victory." *News and Observer* (Raleigh, NC), April 21, 1939.
"Deacons and Techs Will Try Again Here Saturday." *News and Observer* (Raleigh, NC), March 29, 1932.
"Deacons Defeat State Bauer Hurls 3–1 Triumph." *News and Observer* (Raleigh, NC), April 19, 1949.
"Deacons Get Win in Slugging Fest." *News and Observer* (Raleigh, NC), April 23, 1935.
"Deacons Rout State." *News and Observer* (Raleigh, NC), April 13, 1933.
"Deacons Win Over Techs." *News and Observer* (Raleigh, NC), April 9, 1931.
"Deacs Beat Pack, 8–3 Bauer Halts State Nine." *News and Observer* (Raleigh, NC), April 11, 1950.
"Deacs Get 7–6 Victory Over State." *News and Observer* (Raleigh, NC), April 9, 1940.
"Deacs Open Title Defense by Whipping State, 6–2." *News and Observer* (Raleigh, NC), March 27, 1951.

Bibliography

"Deacs Score Win in Opening Verse." *News and Observer* (Raleigh, NC), April 3, 1932,

"Easter German Given by the Pi Kappa Alpha Fraternity of the A and M College." *News and Observer* (Raleigh, NC), March 29, 1907.

"Easter Monday Card Washed Out; Deacons-Techs to Play at Later Date." *News and Observer* (Raleigh, NC), April 7, 1931.

"Errors Cost Wake Forest the Game." *News and Observer* (Raleigh, NC), April 21, 1908.

"Fans Get Bargain at Holiday Game." *News and Observer* (Raleigh, NC), March 30, 1937.

"The Farmers Beat Baptists." *News and Observer* (Raleigh, NC), April 13, 1908.

"Farmers Show Wake Forest How." *News and Observer* (Raleigh, NC), April 18, 1911.

"The Farmers Win." *News and Observer* (Raleigh, NC), April 17, 1900.

"Fraternity Dance." *News and Observer* (Raleigh, NC), April 19, 1908.

"Fraternity Dance." *News and Observer* (Raleigh, NC), April 9, 1912.

"Herring Pitches Win for Deacons." *News and Observer* (Raleigh, NC), April 3, 1934.

"Hock, Bauer Pace Deacons' Victory." *News and Observer* (Raleigh, NC), April 8, 1947.

"Homer by Hord Proves Margin of Deacon Win." *News and Observer* (Raleigh, NC), April 2, 1929.

"Largest Throng Sees State Win Easter Monday Classic, 4–1." *News and Observer* (Raleigh, NC), April 22, 1924.

"N.C. State and Wake Forest Battle to Sixteen Inning Tie 6–6." *News and Observer* (Raleigh, NC), April 25, 1923.

"Pack Edges Deacs, 3–2." *News and Observer* (Raleigh, NC), April 15, 1952.

"Pre-Flight Defeats State, 9–2 in Opener of Ration League." *News and Observer* (Raleigh, NC), April 9, 1944.

"Rain and Homers, Homers and Rain!" *News and Observer* (Raleigh, NC), April 19, 1938.

"Rain Puts Speedy End to Ball Game." *News and Observer* (Raleigh, NC), March 29, 1921.

"Rain Stops Game: Horner and A & M Were Hard at It When Water Fell." *News and Observer* (Raleigh, NC), April 14, 1903.

"Ray Fans 19 as Deacons Triumph, 19–0." *News and Observer* (Raleigh, NC), April 15, 1941.

"Sitton's Spit Ball Scores a Shut Out." *News and Observer* (Raleigh, NC), April 25, 1905.

"Snowfall in the State Was Nearly a Billion Tons." *News and Observer* (Raleigh, NC), April 4, 1915.

"State College Is Victor in Annual Easter Game, 4–2." *News and Observer* (Raleigh, NC), April 17, 1922.

"State College Is Victorious Again." *News and Observer* (Raleigh, NC), April 22, 1919.

"State Wipes Out Nine-Run Deficit to Defeat Pre-Flight, 10–9." *News and Observer* (Raleigh, NC), April 27, 1943.

"State's Techs Beat Deacons, 6–3, Before 3,200 at Devereux." *News and Observer* (Raleigh, NC), April 23, 1946.

"Syracuse Beat A and M 12 to 11." *News and Observer* (Raleigh, NC), April 3, 1904.

"Techs Lose Their Annual Classic to Wake Forest Team." *News and Observer* (Raleigh, NC), April 10, 1917.

"Techs Win Over Wake Forest in Easter Classic." *News and Observer* (Raleigh, NC), April 22, 1930.

"To the Easter Game." *News and Observer* (Raleigh, NC), March 30, 1907.

Bibliography

"Too Much Jaynes for Wake Forest." *News and Observer* (Raleigh, NC), April 6, 1915.
"Trinity Trims Boys in Gray." *News and Observer* (Raleigh, NC), April 17, 1906.
Untitled. *News and Observer* (Raleigh, NC), April 24, 1916.
Untitled. *News and Observer* (Raleigh, NC), May 10, 1955.
"Visitors from Durham." *News and Observer* (Raleigh, NC), April 18, 1906.
"Wake Forest Beats State, 5–4." *News and Observer* (Raleigh, NC), April 7, 1942.
"Wake Forest Beats State in Eleventh." *News and Observer* (Raleigh, NC), April 6, 1921.
"Wake Forest Trims A & M." *News and Observer* (Raleigh, NC), April 2, 1907.
"Wake Forest vs. A & M." *News and Observer* (Raleigh, NC), April 16, 1911.
"Wake Forest Wallops State in Easter Monday Classic, 10 to 3." *News and Observer* (Raleigh, NC), April 6, 1926.
"Wake Forest Were the Losers." *News and Observer* (Raleigh, NC), April 8, 1912.
"Wake Forest Wins Big Easter Game." *News and Observer* (Raleigh, NC), April 2, 1918.
"Wake Forest Won." *News and Observer* (Raleigh, NC), April 2, 1902.
"Williams' Home Run in Ninth Gives State 8–7 Win." *News and Observer* (Raleigh, NC), April 15, 1936.

Personal Interviews

Reid D. Farrell, August 15, 2010.
Cora Hoover, August 29, 2001.
W.G. Smith, August 12, 2010.
Jean Ritchie Utley, August 20, 2001.
R.G. Utley, August 20, 2001.

Online

Baseball-Reference.com. Web.
"City of Raleigh." *North Carolina History Project*. 2012. Web.
"History of the Chapter." *Notes from the Written Histories of Alpha Epsilon Chapters*. 1980.
Ncmuseumofhistory.org. Web.
North Carolina State Agromeck. www.e-yearbook.com. Web.
Wake Forest University Howler. www.e-yearbook.com. Web.
Suarez, Leo. "Baseball in Downtown, Devereux Meadow Meets Progress in Raleigh." *The Raleigh Connoisseur*. Web site, March 11, 2010 (accessed August 15, 2012).
Utley, R.G., and Gary Freeze. "Easter Monday at NC State." *Baseball Outlaws*. Web site, August 12, 2010. Web.

INDEX

Abbot (WF; SS) 191, 193, 195
Abernethy (ST; 1907) 35, 36
Absher (ST; CF) 144, 145
Aderholt, Morrie 132, 133, 134, 135, 204
Agromeck (NC State) 97, 124
Albright (ST; 2B) 108, 109, 110
Albritton (WF; LF) 89, 90, 91
Alford (Bingham; SS) 12
Alford (ST; C) 162
Alford, Johnny 188, 189
Allen (ST; CF) 162
Allen (ST; SS) 16
Allen (Umpire) 189
Allen, Jimmy 93, 94, 95, 96, 97
Allen, Sydney 165
Allgood, Larry 104, 105, 106, 107, 109, 110
Allie, Gair 204
Alpha Epsilon 6, 31, 32, 52, 58, 116, 117, 126, 137, 151
Alston, Norman 159, 165
Anderson, Billy 138, 142, 146
Anderson, Fred 53, 59
Andrews, Preston 165
Anglin (WF; 1955) 193
Armstrong (WF: 1B) 85, 90, 91, 96, 97, 98
Arnette (WF; 2B) 91, 93, 96, 97
Asbury (ST; 3B) 16, 19, 20, 21, 25
Atlantic Coast Conference 189
Atwell (ST; PH) 187
Austin (WF; P) 68, 69, 76, 77, 83, 101, 102, 104
Averette, Bill 109, 111

B.F.U 22, 24, 26
Babyak (ST; RF) 192
Baggett. Allie P. 111
Bagonis (ST; PH) 187
Bailey (ST; 1B) 122, 124
Bailey (ST; RF) 150, 154
Baker (ST; C) 162

Baker (ST; P) 67, 69
Baker (Syracuse; 1904) 19, 21
Balionis, Tony 140
Ball (WF; 1927) 102
Baltimore Orioles 65
Barden (ST; 2B) 175
Barnes, Billy Ray 193, 195
Barnes, Junie 115, 116, 118, 119, 120, 121, 122, 205
Barnes, Saxe 75, 76, 77, 79, 80, 84, 85, 86, 89, 91
Barringer (ST; PH) 191, 192, 195
Batchelor, Russ 176, 177, 179, 180
Bauer, Raymond "Mo" 176, 178, 179, 180, 181, 182, 183, 185
Beam, Charlie 134, 136
Beam, Pitt 165
Beamon, Bruce 165
Bean (WF; RF) 51, 52
Beene (ST; P) 187
Benton (WF; 1909) 35, 37, 38
Benton, Jit 108, 109, 111, 115
Benzagal (WF; 1B) 195
Berlinski, Eddie 133, 135, 136
Berry, Mac 132, 133, 134
Bethune (WF; LF) 115
Betts (WF; 2B) 49
Bigenheimer, C.G. 165
Billings (WF; SS) 51, 52, 54, 55, 56, 57, 58, 59, 60, 63, 66, 68
Bird, Bobby 165
Black (ST; 1907) 35, 36, 38, 40, 41, 42, 43, 44
Black (ST; 2B) 75, 76, 77, 79, 80
Black Mountain College 113
Blackman, Herman 153, 163, 184
Blackwell, Dale 176
Blanchard (WF; C) 72, 73, 74, 75, 77
Bledsoe (Umpire) 159, 176
Blount (ST; P) 128, 129, 130, 131

Index

Blue (ST; 2B) 85, 86, 91
Bolin, Russ 111
Bonifant (Pre-Flight; SS) 158
Bonitz, F.W. 11, 12, 16
Boone (Bingham; CF) 12
Bost (ST; 1910) 37, 41, 43
Boston Bees 118
Boston Red Sox 73
Bowen, A.F. 133
Bowen, Mrs. A.F. 32
Boylan, James 53
Boylin (WF; C) 80, 93
Boyter, Johnny 165
Brady, A.G. 165
Brake (ST; RF) 116
Bramham (Minor League President) 87
Brandon (Umpire) 151
Brannon, D.A. 126
Bratt (WF; 1B) 40, 42, 43
Braxton, Garland 173
Brewer (WF; RF) 71, 73
Brewster (WF; 1955) 193
Bridger, Levy 165, 169
Briggs, Florence 111
Brinson (ST; SS) 183, 187, 189
Brittain (ST; 1B) 66
Britton (ST; 3B) 55, 57, 58
Brockwell (ST; C) 19, 20
Brogden (WF; 2B) 121
Brogman (WF; 2B) 119
Brooks (WF; C) 189
Brooks, Bob 178
Brown (ST; RF) 37, 38, 40, 41, 42, 43, 44, 48, 49
Brown (ST; SS) 119
Brown (WF; 2B) 49
Brown (WF; RF) 185, 191
Brown, Jimmy 165, 197
Brown, Wade (ST; RF) 139, 141, 144, 145, 150
Browne, Melissa 116, 117
Broyhill, Fred 139, 141, 144
Bruner, Mrs. T.K. 32
Bryan, R.C. 156, 157, 158
Bryant (ST; 3B) 187, 193
Bunting (WF; 2B) 121
Burkewitz (WF; P) 162
Burrill (Syracuse; 3B) 19, 21
Burrus, Dick 73, 75, 77, 198
Busch (Raleigh Capitals; SS) 66
Butler (Umpire) 195
Butler, Sam 165

Byrd (WF; P) 130, 131, 133
Byrne, Tommy 139, 140, 143, 144, 205

Caddell, John 16, 56, 87, 107, 109, 132, 139, 140, 142
Calfree (Bingham; 3B) 12
Carlyle (WF; 2B) 69, 73
Carney, Jim 147, 154
Carpenter, E.J. 32
Carr, Claiborne 30
Carr, William 30
Carson (Raleigh Capitals; C) 66
Carter (WF; P) 40, 42, 43
Carter, Cutie 147, 149, 150, 151
Carter, P.L. 54
Caserly, William W. 11, 12, 15, 17
Casteen (ST; RF) 195
Castelloe (ST; CF) 68, 80, 85, 92, 93
Castlow (WF; CF) 40, 42, 43
Cates (WF; P) 50, 51, 52
Chappell, Preston 125, 129, 130, 131, 133
Cheek, Don 176, 177, 180, 183, 187
Cheshire (UNC; 1905) 25, 26
Chicago Cubs 42
Chicago White Sox 42, 93
Cincinnati Reds 120
Clark (ST; 1B) 162
Clark (WF; LF) 93, 94, 108, 109, 124
Clark, John A. 53
Clayton (WF; SS) 101, 102, 103, 105, 106
Clement (Trinity; 1906) 28, 29
Cobb (WF; CF) 115
Cochran, Red 153, 154, 163, 165, 167, 173, 175
Cocke (Bingham; 2B) 12
Colby College of Maine 139
Cole (WF; RF) 191, 195
Cole, J.N. Jr. 30
Coleman, Walter 206
Coluni, Bob 185
Cone Family 9
Conlin (Pre-Fllight; 3B) 157, 158
Connelly (WF; C) 154
Conrad, Steve 165
Constant, Leonard 143, 144, 147, 153, 154
Coombs, Jack 119, 128
Cooper, George B. 3
Corbitt, Bill 165, 169
Cornell University 139
Correll (WF; CF) 47, 48, 49, 51, 52, 55, 56, 57, 58, 59, 60, 61, 65, 66, 92, 93, 96, 97, 98

222

Index

Council (ST; 1909) 35, 36, 37, 38, 41
Council (ST; 1B) 177, 181, 183
Council (ST; C) 154, 155
Courts, Bobby 163, 167
Coward (WF; C) 92, 93, 94
Cox (WF; 1B) 67, 68, 69, 71, 72
Cox, General Albert 117
Cox, C.C. 124
Craig (ST; LF) 147, 150
Cramer, Harry 165
Cramer, Louis 165
Crampsey (Pre-Flight; RF) 161
Crockett, David 18
Cross (WF; C) 150
Crozier, Richard 21, 34, 43, 114
Curtis (Syracuse; C) 19, 21
Curtis, D. 93, 94
Curtis, Harry 83, 84, 86, 88, 89, 90, 91, 92, 93, 94
Cuthrell, H.H. 54

Dalrymple (ST; 3B) 129, 130
Dalton (ST; RF) 16
Daniel (WF; 2B) 40, 43, 59, 60, 61
Danning, Jake 134
Darden (Bingham; RF) 12
Davidson, Jerry 129, 130, 131
Davidson College 107
Davis (ST; PH) 68, 71, 72, 73
Davis, Lowell "Lefty" 190, 191, 192, 193, 195
Dawson (WF; 1909) 35, 36, 37, 38
Dayvault (ST; RF) 157, 158
DeBerry, Joe 70, 71, 72, 73, 78, 79, 80, 198
Dee (Umpire) 195
Denning, Jim 135, 140, 143, 144
Dennis (WF; C) 89, 91
Detroit Tigers 165
Devereaux Meadows (Park) 146, 147, 148, 149, 153, 156, 163, 171, 184, 188, 189
Dickens, Irvin 132, 133, 134, 135, 139
Dickman (ST; P) 195
Dinan (ST; 2B) 183
Dixie Baseball Classic 196
Dixon, Fred 126, 128, 131, 132, 156
Doak, C. 151, 154
Doak, Chick 83, 87, 94, 96, 103, 104, 107, 109, 114, 135, 142, 143, 144, 196
Doak, Renfro 144, 145, 147, 149, 150
Doak Field 159
Dorsett (WF; RF) 106, 109
Dorsette, Henry G. 11, 12, 15, 17

Doster, Eleanor 126
Dowtin, Al 102, 103, 106, 107, 108, 109, 110
Drake (ST; 1905) 26
Duke, A.B. 30, 39
Duke, Mary 30
Duke, Willie 116, 119, 121, 122
Duke University 27, 134, 157, 196
Dula, Bebra 3
Duncan (Raleigh Capitals; RF) 66, 68, 69
Dunn, Jack 65
Dunn, John 110
Dunn, Marion 116
Dunon, Duke 94
Dupree, Tallie 134, 135, 140

Earp (WF; SS) 115, 119, 121
Eason, Fred 139, 140, 144 147, 149, 150
Eastman (Pre-Flight; C) 158
Eatman (ST; C) 105, 106, 108, 109, 110
Ebey (ST; SS) 116, 119
Edwards (WF; 1B) 37, 38, 54, 56, 57, 58
Edwards (WF; RF) 115
Edwards, Buck 88, 89, 90, 95, 96
Edwards, F. 175
Edwards, George 149, 150, 163, 167, 169, 173, 175
Edwards, Jimmy 162, 165, 173, 175
Ellis (WF; RF) 63, 68, 69, 70, 71, 72, 73, 74, 75, 77, 80, 83, 84, 85, 86, 89
Ellis, Paul 185
Emmerson (UNC; 1905) 25, 26
English, Bill 165
Eskridge (ST; 1905) 24, 25, 27, 28
Eure (WF; 2B) 59, 60
Eutsler, Bill 135, 140, 143, 144
Evans, Bill 65, 66, 199
Evans, Bill, Jr. 65
Evans, John 161, 162, 175
Evans, Willie 171, 175, 177, 180
Everitt (Horner; 1905) 18
Everly (WF; C) 150

Faircloth (Umpire) 192
Faison, Paul F. 11, 12
Falk (Pre-Flight; 3B) 161
Farley (Pre-Flight; P) 159, 162
Farmer (ST; RF) 27, 28, 29, 35, 36, 46, 47, 48, 50, 51, 52, 55, 57, 58, 60
Farrar, Vince 128, 129, 130, 131
Farrell, Reid 161, 162, 165, 169
Farris (ST; C) 119, 121, 122, 124
Farris, C.H. 165

Index

Faucette (WF; CF) 49, 50, 51, 52, 54, 55, 56, 57, 58, 80, 85, 86, 87
Faulkner (ST; C) 93, 101
Fehley, Pat 143, 144, 145, 147, 150, 151
Fencer (Horner; 1903) 18
Fenner, Bill 11, 14, 15, 17
Ferree (WF; RF) 59, 60
Fetzer (WF; Coach) 77
Fichter (WF; P) 193, 195
Fields (Umpire) 176
Fieser (Pre-Flight; P) 158, 159
Fleet (WF; SS) 167
Fleming (ST; C) 154
Fletcher, John "Rabbit" 142, 143, 144, 145, 149, 150, 154, 155
Fletcher, Stewart 123
Flora (Umpire) 135
Flowers (Trinity; 1906) 29
Floyd (ST; RF) 72, 73, 79, 80, 86
Floyd, Junie 185, 189, 191
Flynn, Lucille 116
Flythe, Stu 123, 124, 199
Foust (WF; RF) 106, 107, 109, 110
Fowler, Billy 171, 173, 175, 177, 178, 180, 181, 183
Fox (ST; 1B) 27, 28, 29, 35, 36
Frank Thompson Gymnasium 111, 117, 126, 128, 136, 137, 152
Franklin (ST; P) 195
Franks (WF; P) 67, 68, 69
Frasier, Julian 53
Freeman (ST; 3B) 107, 109, 110
Freeman (WF; SS) 15, 16, 17, 35, 38, 40, 41, 42, 43, 44
Freeman, Don 165
Fulghum (WF; RF) 173, 175, 175, 180
Fuller (ST; C) 114, 116, 119, 122
Fuller, Caroline 30
Fuller, Dave "Slick" 135, 140, 143, 144, 145
Furtado (ST; SS) 107, 108, 109, 111, 116
Fuscoe (ST; CF) 187, 189, 191
Futrell (WF; CF) 40, 43

Gadd (ST; CF) 129, 130, 131, 133
Gaddy, John 128, 130, 131, 207
Gallovich, Tony 140, 149, 150
Gammon (ST; 3B) 59, 60, 63
Gardner, O. Max 7, 17, 20, 117
Gardner, Pinky 163, 167
Garrity, Coach 95, 97
Gaulin (Pre-Flight; 2B) 161
Gayle, W.W. 165

Gerock (ST; 1B) 119
Gibson, Hoot 154
Gilbert (ST; SS) 96, 97, 101
Gilbert (ST; 3B) 150
Gillespie (WF; C) 108, 109, 111
Gladstone (ST; 2B) 93, 94, 95, 96, 97, 98
Glass (ST; PH) 147, 150
Glass, Forest 132, 133
Gnox, Mrs. A.W. 32
Godwin, Charlie 157, 158
Gold, Milky 124, 126
Gooch, Lee 54, 55, 56, 57, 58, 180, 182, 207
Goodman (ST; CF-1B) 116
Grandy (ST; 1B) 162
Greason, Murray 93, 94, 96, 97, 98, 101, 142, 143, 150, 154, 165, 167, 171, 173
Green, Allen 133, 134, 135, 136, 139, 141
Greene (ST; RF) 192
Griffin (ST; P) 133
Griffin (ST; PH) 119, 122
Griffin (WF; RF) 15, 17
Griffith, Andy 169
Gross, Lester 165
Gudger (UNC; 1905) 25, 26
Guilford College 9, 11, 38
Gurley (ST; SS) 71, 72, 73, 80
Gwynn (WF; CF) 77

Hadley (ST; 1904) 19, 20, 21, 25
Hagstrom (Pre-Flight; 2B) 157, 158
Hall (ST; 1B) 16, 17
Hall (Umpire) 192
Hammond (WF; 1908) 35, 36, 37, 38
Hamrick (WF; 1906) 31, 34, 35, 36
Hardee, Ray 146, 149, 150, 151, 152, 153, 154
Hardison (ST; P) 192
Hargrove (ST; LF) 108, 109, 110, 111, 116
Hargrove, Tommy 190, 192, 195
Harrill (ST; 1B) 101, 102, 104
Harris (ST; 1906) 25, 26, 28, 29, 35, 36, 37, 38, 69
Harris (ST; PH) 109
Harris, C. 16
Harris, Cedar 136, 143, 144
Harris, Dickie 190, 191
Harris, Paul 182
Harriss, Ella 53
Hartness, James A. 117
Hartsell (ST; SS) 37, 38, 40, 41, 42, 43, 44, 48, 49, 50, 51, 52, 66, 87
Harvard University 27
Hawkins (WF; C) 154

Index

Heat (ST; P) 101
Heath (ST; 1905) 16, 25, 26
Heck, C.M. 61
Hefferman (Syracuse; P) 21
Helms, Bobby 165
Henderson (ST; PH) 144
Henderson (Umpire) 96, 97
Henderson, Margaret 116
Hendron (WF; PH) 139, 141
Hensley (WF; 1B) 60, 61
Herbert, Dick 188, 189
Herndon (WF; LF) 68, 69, 71, 72, 73
Herring, Bill 123
Hicks (Umpire) 162
Hicks (WF; C) 115, 119, 121
Hicks, Bob 165, 169
Higgs, Mrs. Jas. A. 32
Higgs, Mrs. Sherwood 32
Hill, Mrs. D.H. 32
Hill, D.H. Jr. 32
Hill, D.M. 53
Hillenbrand, Bruce 190, 192
Hines (ST; RF) 133
Hinton, A.C. 53
Hobgood (WF; P) 15, 16, 17
Hoch, Art 169, 171, 173, 175, 177, 180
Hodgin (ST; 2B) 59, 60, 61, 66, 68, 69
Holaday, Chris 127
Holding (WF; CF) 71, 72, 73, 77
Holland, John 177
Holland, Robert "Dutch" 87, 90, 91, 93, 94, 96, 97, 98, 99, 200
Holloman, Perton 165
Hollowell (WF; C) 86
Holt (ST; P) 18, 19
Holt (WF; LF) 101, 103
Holt, G.A. 126
Holt, Lynwood 190, 191, 193, 195
Honeycutt, Adolph 141
Honzagni (WF; 1B) 192, 193
Hood (WF; C) 96, 97
Hooks, Gene 171, 173, 175, 177, 178, 180, 182
Hoover, Cora "Babe" 151, 152
Horbelt, Ed 187, 188, 191
Horchak (WF; 3B) 154
Hord, Runt 107, 108, 109, 110
Horn (WF; 1955) 193
Horner Military Academy 17, 18
Horning, Dan 165
Hovis (ST; RF) 104
Howe, Betty 68
Howell (ST; LF) 19, 20, 21

Hoyle, B. 141, 144
Hoyle, Dick 139, 140, 146, 149
Hoyle, F. 135
Hoyle, W. 136
Hudson (ST; RF) 77
Humphrey (ST; P) 162
Hunsucker (ST; P) 100, 101
Hunter, Willard 208
Hunting (WF; 2B) 119
Hutchison (Trinity; 1906) 28

Ivey, Ben 165

James (ST; 1905) 25, 26, 36
James, Ralph 102, 103, 106
Jaynes (ST; RF) 51, 52, 56, 57, 58, 63
Jeffrey (ST; RF) 116, 119, 122
Jennette (WF; CF) 80, 85, 86
Jennette, Sid 165
Johnson (ST; LF) 157, 158
Johnson, Doug 119, 121, 124, 125
Johnson, Ernest 173, 175, 177, 178, 179, 180, 181
Johnson, J.I. 53
Johnson, Jim 165
Johnson, P. 12, 69, 71, 72, 73, 75, 76, 77, 80
Johnson, R. 91, 93
Johnson, Stan 184, 185, 187
Johnson, Stanley 80, 83, 84, 85, 86, 88, 91, 92, 94, 96
Johnson, W. 76, 77
Johnston, Al 85, 95, 96, 98
Jones (ST; PH) 144
Jones, Jimmie 165
Jones, Johnny 165
Jones, Sam 83, 85, 93, 94, 95, 96, 97
Jones, "Zeb" 165
Josey (WF; 1908) 35, 36
Joyner, Key 100, 101, 105, 106
Joyner, P. 101, 103, 105, 106, 114, 115, 119, 121
Justus (Trinity; 1906) 28

Katkaveck, Leo 157, 158, 171, 175
Kaufman (Umpire) 61, 73
Kaufman, Sammy 143, 144, 145
Kearney (Umpire) 108, 110, 155, 159
Kearns (ST; SS) 136
Keenan (Syracuse; LF) 19, 21
Keith (Bingham; P) 12
Kelly, Bill 165, 169
Kelly, Pete 165

225

Kendall, Billy 102, 104
Kersh (WF; CF) 180, 182
Kesler (WF; 3B) 70, 71, 72, 75, 77, 85, 86
Kettle (Pre-Flight; C) 158
Kidd (ST; C) 101, 102, 103, 104, 106
Kirkland (ST; PH) 124
Kirkman (ST; PH) 114, 116
Kirkpatrick (ST; RF) 80, 85, 86
Kitchin, Walter 125
Knox (ST; 2B) 20, 25, 26, 27, 28, 29
Knox, A.W. 53
Kolbacher (ST; 2B) 187
Kollnige (Pre-Flight; 1B) 161, 162
Koontz (WF; 1955) 193
Kosler (WF; 3B) 80
Krupa, Gene 152
Kuykendall (WF; C) 106

Lachiotte, N.S. 58
Lamb (ST; SS) 162
Lambeth (ST; 1B) 122, 124, 125
Lampke, Donald 161, 165
Lane, Dane 163, 165, 167
Lanning, John 108, 109, 110, 114, 116, 118, 200
Lanning, Tom 208
Lassiter (ST; 1B) 93, 94, 96, 98, 103, 106, 107, 108, 109, 110
Latta, C.G. 53
Latta, Mrs. C.G. 32
Lattimore (ST; 1905) 25, 26
Laughridge, Hugh 188, 189
Lea, Gordon 171, 173
Lee (ST; LF) 177, 178
Lee (WF; SS) 40, 42, 43, 60, 63
Lee, Clee 53
Lee, Harry 116
Lee, Mrs. Paul 32
Lefelar, George 188
Lefever (WF; RF) 189
Leggett (WF; 3B) 69
LeGrand (Bingham; C) 12
Lehigh University 10, 16
Lew (ST; LF) 175
Lewis (ST; C) 68, 69, 71, 72, 73
Lewis, Buddy 209
Lewis, Lunsford 183, 187, 188, 189
Liptak (WF; 3B) 188, 189, 191
Livengood (WF; LF) 192
Liverman(ST; CF) 59, 60, 61
Livick, Paul 178, 180
Livingston, B. 181

Livingston, H. 181
Long, Johnny 136
Loray Mill Strike of 1929 81
Lougee, Hank 163, 167
Lougett (WF; RF) 150
Love, Colon R. 11, 12
Lovin, "Rusty" 165
Lowe, J.R. 54, 56, 57, 58
Lowremore, J.T. 171
Lyles, Billy 190, 191
Lynn, Bill 121, 122, 165
Lyon, E.B. 30
Lyon, George 30

Mack, Earl 149
Mahoney, Jake 129, 130, 131
Mangum (Bingham; LF) 12
Mann (ST; 1B) 133
Marchand (Pre-Flight; CF) 157, 158
Marousek (Pre-Flight; 1B) 158
Marr (Umpire) 100
Marshall, W.R. 32
Marshall, Willard 209
Martin (ST; PH) 183
Martin (WF; 1B) 95, 96, 97, 101
Martin (WF; PH) 167
Matheson (ST; SS) 104
Matney, Vic 177, 178
Matthews (ST; PH) 102, 103, 104
Matthews (Umpire) 169
Mauney (WF; 1B) 133
Mayfield (ST; PH) 102, 104, 106
Maynard's Southland Serenaders 110
McAdams, T.A. 165
McAfee (Umpire) 195
McAuley (ST; LF) 144
McCall (WF; RF) 144, 165, 167
McCathran (ST; 1907) 27, 28, 29
McColtran (ST; 1907) 28
McComas (ST; SS) 180
McCord (Raleigh Capitals; 2B) 66
McDonald, John 53
McDowell (ST; CF) 104, 105, 106
McDowell, Pete 165, 169
McDuffie, Mac 190
McEachern, D. Ray 151
McGeachy (Agromeck Bus. Manager) 68
McGee, Mrs. W.T. 32
McGee, W.T. 53
McGillis (ST; C) 187
McGinley (WF; 1955) 193
McGraw, John 42

Index

McIntire (ST; 1904) 19
McKeel, Luther 190, 191, 193
McKevlin, A.J. 102, 103, 104, 105, 107, 110, 111, 114, 119, 122, 125, 134
McKevlin, Betsy 126
McKimmon, James 53
McKimmon, Mrs. Jas. 32
McLaughlin (ST; SS) 157, 158
McLaughlin, John 177, 178
McLaurin (ST; P) 20, 21
McLawhorn (ST; PH) 116, 119
McLeod, Louise 126
McNeil, Franklin 53
McNeil, Mrs. Franklin 32
McQuage (ST; RF) 119, 122, 124
McRae, Frank 192, 193, 195
Meadlock (ST; PH) 195
Meador, Joe 115
Mebane Bingham Military School 11, 12
Melton (ST; RF) 109
Melver (ST; P) 99
Meredith College 9, 45, 55, 74, 156
Merritt, "Duby" 165
Meyer, Jack 210
Milaker (Umpire) 169
Miller (ST; P) 16, 19, 20
Miller (ST; RF) 67, 68, 69
Miller (WF; RF) 193, 195
Miller, J.F. 99
Miller, Oscar 161, 165
Milligan, "Hank" 165
Mills (Pre-Flight; C) 161
Mills (WF; LF) 49
Mills (WF; 2B) 111, 114, 115
Mitchell (Umpire) 145
Mitchell (WF; SS) 124
Moffitt, Bonnie 165
Moore (WF; P; 1900) 14, 15, 17, 21
Moore (WF; P; 1914) 60, 61
Moore (WF; SS) 193
Moore, Coach 96
Moore, Johnny 165
Moore, Sam 165
Moran, Ed 165
Morris (ST; 1B) 189
Morris, Dallas 125, 130, 131, 132, 133
Morris, Doyt 129, 130, 132, 133, 211
Morris, Ed 188, 189, 191
Morris, Joel 116, 119, 121, 122
Morrison (ST; 3B) 144, 145, 147, 150
Morrison, Jonah 100, 101
Morson (ST; CF) 15, 17

Motsinger (WF; 1925) 98, 99
Mulhern (WF; LF) 119, 121, 124
Mull (WF; RF) 16
Munoz (Raleigh Capitals; P) 65
Murphrey (WF; 3B) 185
Murray, George 70, 71, 72, 73, 74, 75, 76, 77, 78, 80, 83, 85, 201
Muse (WF; 1955) 193
Mussack (ST; PH) 175, 181
Myers (WF; C) 124

Navy Pre-Flight 156, 159
Neal, Bynum 165
Nelms (ST; LF) 116, 119, 122
Nelson, Paul 140
Neverdausky (Pre-Flight; LF) 158
New York Giants 42
Newborn (ST; SS) 154, 163, 167, 169
Newton, Doc 142, 152, 153
Nicholas, Harry 179, 180, 185
Nixon (ST; RF) 143, 144
Noble, Dr. R.P. 133
Noell, "Speed" 165
Norman, Leslie 11
Norrell (ST; 2B) 177, 181, 182, 183
Norris, Herbert B. 53
Norris, M.T. 53
Norris, Norman 192
Northington (Pre-Flight; LF) 158
Norwood (ST; CF) 80, 85, 86, 90, 91
Norwood, Uriah 125, 132, 133
Novosel, Frank 176

Oakden (ST; PH) 122
Ohio Cotton Pickers 111
Osteen (Horner; 1903) 18
Outen, Chink 102, 103, 104, 105, 106, 201

Pace (WF; 3B) 16
Page (ST; 1B) 50, 51, 52, 56, 58
Page (ST; P) 162
Page, Irv 181, 182, 183
Pan Am Games 187
Parham (Raleigh Capitals; PH) 66
Park (ST; CF) 75, 76, 77
Park, John 141
Parker (WF; 2B) 50, 51, 52, 54, 55, 56, 57, 58
Parsons (ST; C) 80, 85, 86, 90, 91
Pate (ST; 2B) 16
Patton (ST; 2B) 48, 49, 50, 51, 52, 56, 57, 58, 59, 60

Index

Patton (WF; 1B) 124, 129
Payne (WF; 2B) 130, 131
Peace, W.G. 53
Peace Institute 16, 22, 45, 74, 156
Pearce, Jakie 153, 154, 155, 167
Peatross, O.F. "Pig" 136, 139, 141
Peed (ST; 1B) 192, 195
Perry, Lewis 161, 165, 169
Person, Ed 11, 12, 14, 15, 17
Person, Ott 105, 106
Person, W.C. 15, 17
Person, W.H. 11, 12, 14, 15, 17
Phelps (WF; C) 103, 106
Philadelphia Athletics 123, 149
Philadelphia Phillies 118
Pi Kappa Alpha 6, 32, 36, 37, 52, 58, 110, 111, 116, 117, 126, 137, 151
Pierozzi (Pre-Flight; CF) 161
Pittman (WF; 2B) 70, 72, 73, 75, 77
Pittsburgh Pirates 42, 65
Plonk (ST; 1930) 111
Polanski (WF; 3B) 143, 144, 150
Pool (Horner; 1903) 18
Poole (WF; CF) 89, 90, 92, 93, 96
Pope (WF; P) 38
Porter (Umpire) 151, 162
Pou, James H. 53
Pou, Mrs. Jas. H. 32
Powell (Umpire) 145
Powers (WF; 1B) 16
Pressly (ST; LF) 71, 72, 73, 76, 77
Preston, Pat 193
Primm (WF; CF) 150, 154
Pullen Hall 36, 37, 52, 58
Purvis (ST; CF) 162

Rabb, Walter 128, 130, 131, 133, 134
Ragsdale (WF; RF) 80, 85, 86
Ramsey, Curtis 143, 144, 145, 163, 165, 167, 169, 171, 173, 175
Randall, Jimmie 165
Ration League 157, 159, 160
Ravashiere (Pre-Flight; RF) 157, 158
Ray, Carl Grady 147, 149
Red Springs 18
Redfearn, Buck 84, 85, 86, 87, 89, 90, 91, 92, 93, 94, 97, 202
Reid (WF; 3B) 144, 145, 154
Rex (ST; LF) 124
Reynolds (WF; 1B) 105, 106, 108, 109
Rhodes, Braxton 125
Richardson (WF; 1B) 92, 93

Richardson, Julian 132, 133, 134
Richmond University 46
Richtus, Charlie 163, 165, 167, 169, 173, 175
Riddick (ST; 1910) 40, 41, 42, 43, 44
Riddick, W.C. 53
Riddick, Mrs. W.C. 32
Riddick, Wallace 11
Riddick Field 39, 53, 67, 91, 94, 100, 105, 115
Ridge (WF; SS) 71, 72
Riley (WF; 1B) 98, 100, 101, 103
Ripple, Charlie "Lefty" 154, 155, 212
Ritter, Bill 139, 141, 144, 145
Roach (ST; 3B) 121, 122, 124
Roberts (Raleigh Capitals; LF) 66
Roberts (ST; PH) 141
Robertson, Dave 40, 41, 42, 43, 44, 46, 48, 49, 51, 52, 202
Rodgers (WF; LF) 15, 17
Rogers, Kent 176, 177, 185
Ross (ST; 1910) 40, 41, 42, 43, 44, 48, 49
Ross, Beverly 165, 171
Ross, F.D. 11, 12, 15, 16, 17

St. Mary's School 16, 22, 24, 45, 74, 156
Sanford, Taylor 185, 193
Santoli (ST; CF) 191, 192, 193
Saunders, Bob 165
Scales, Fairley 125, 128, 130, 131
Scales, J.F. 126
Scarborough (WF; CF) 106, 108, 109, 110
Scarborough, Rae 5, 137, 138, 139, 140, 212
Schneider (Pre-Flight; CF) 161
Scott, Jean Gray 126
Seal (ST; 3B) 105, 106
Seifert (ST; C) 36, 37, 38, 41, 42, 43, 44, 47, 48, 49, 51, 52
Seitz, Rudy 114, 115, 116, 121
Sexauer, Elmer 213
Sexton (ST; P) 33, 34, 35, 36, 38, 40, 41, 42, 44
Shannonhouse (ST; P) 21
Sharpe (ST; PH) 187
Shelton (ST; P) 100
Sheppard, Porter 125, 129, 130, 132, 133
Shore, J.W. 11, 12
Shore, Sandy 107, 108, 109, 110
Short (Trinity; 1906) 29
Shuford (ST; CF) 27, 28, 29
Shuford, Charlie 95, 96, 97, 101
Shuford, W. 101
Signore (WF; 2B) 191

Index

Simmons (WF; 1925) 97, 98, 99
Simpson, Bill 165
Sims (Pre-Flight; P) 157, 158
Singer, Jack 147, 149, 150, 153, 154
Sipe (ST; SS) 77, 80
Sitton (UNC; P) 24, 26
Skankwilder (Pre-Flight; PH) 162
Skinner, A. 165
Skinner, Atwood 161
Skinner, Mrs. B.F. 32
Slayton (WF; RF) 124
Small (WF; RF) 90, 91, 93, 94, 96, 98
Smart, Joe 165
Smith (ST; LF) 122
Smith (WF; P) 49, 50, 51, 52, 54, 56, 58
Smith, Bob 182
Smith, Gilbert 165, 169
Smith, Larry 134, 136
Smith, R. 183, 187, 189, 191, 192
Smith, W. 183
Smith, W.G. 169
Snipes (ST; LF) 106, 109
Somerville (Pre-Flight; P) 162
Sorrell, Vic 5, 76, 97, 99, 156, 165, 175, 181, 185, 188, 190, 196, 213
Sparrow (WF; RF) 150
Speer (ST; 2B) 41, 42, 43, 48, 49, 50, 51, 52
Spencer, Don 165
Springfield College 139
Springs (ST; C) 20, 21
Springs, J.L. 41
Springs, J.T. 32
Springs, St. Julian 141
Stadler, Don 165
Stafford (ST; 1911) 41, 44, 46, 50, 51, 52
Stafford, Freddie 165
Stallings, Jack 185, 188, 189
Standfoss, Albert 132
Staney (WF; P) 95, 96, 97
Stanton, Bill 163, 165, 167, 169, 175
Staples (Trinity; 1906) 2, 27, 28, 29
Steadman, C.A. 52
Stedman, Clarence 141
Steele (ST; 1906) 27
Steen, "Burt" 165, 169
Steer (ST; 1911) 44
Stem (UNC; 1905) 25, 26
Stephenson (Umpire) 134
Stern, Jack 126
Stevens, Mrs. F.L. 32
Stewart, Earl 153, 154
Stocksdale, O.H. 28

Stokoe (WF; 1955) 193
Stringfield (WF; SS) 48, 49, 50, 51, 52, 54, 56, 57, 58, 59, 60, 61, 80, 84, 85, 86, 90, 93, 94
Styron, Elizabeth 116
Sullivan (ST; 3B) 66
Sutton, H.F. 165
Sweel, Bill 139, 143
Sweet (WF; C) 135
Swell (WF; C) 144, 145
Syracuse University 19, 21

Tarlham (WF; 1B) 15, 17
Tate, Jack 165, 169
Tatum (WF; 3B) 189, 192
Teague, Charley 171, 175, 176, 177, 178, 180, 182, 196
Temple (WF; P) 31, 33, 34
Terry (ST; 1B) 55, 56, 57, 58
Thompson, Frank 5, 6, 25, 27, 28, 30, 31, 35, 41, 44, 54, 55, 65
Thompson, George 187, 188, 189
Thompson, J.W. 34
Thrash (ST; LF) 66, 68, 69
Timberlake (WF; CF) 98, 101
Timberlake, Mrs. Julian 32
Tolar (ST; 2B) 85
Tomlinson, L.A. 30
Trinity College 27, 28, 65
Trust (WF; CF) 60, 61
Tucker (ST; 3B) 49
Turner (ST; C; 1903) 18, 49, 50, 51, 52
Turner (ST; C; 1930) 111, 116
Turner, J. 31
Turner, Tom 153, 154
Turney, Jack 188, 189, 191, 192, 195

Underwood (WF; P) 47, 48, 49
Underwood, Dick 165
University of North Carolina 9, 10, 22, 25, 26, 65, 69, 93, 100, 103, 107, 196
Upchurch (Umpire) 43
Utley, Jean Ritchie 155, 159
Utley, Phil 40, 42, 43, 48, 49, 51, 52, 54, 55, 56, 57, 58, 87, 91
Utley, R.G. "Hank" 1, 2, 10, 11, 20, 39, 44, 62, 64, 138, 145, 151, 155, 161, 165, 167, 169, 175, 176, 177, 180, 181
Uzzle (ST; SS) 187

Vanstory, Bob 165
Vassey (WF; C) 69

Index

Vernon, Herman 157, 158, 159
Vick (ST; SS) 101, 104
Vivian, Art 149, 150, 153, 154, 155

Wade (ST; RF) 100, 101
Waggoner (WF; 1B) 191, 193, 195
Wake Forest Howler 13, 14, 115, 142
Walker (Umpire) 69, 110
Wall, Dwight 124, 125, 129, 130, 131
Walsh (WF; P) 191, 192
Walters, Rasty 134
Ward (Syracuse; 1904) 19, 20, 21
Warren (WF; 1B) 180, 182, 183, 185, 191, 193
Warren, Hal 132, 133
Warren, J.A. 157, 158, 159
Watson (ST; SS) 158
Watts, Lawrence 165
Waywald (Pre-Flight; P) 162
Weathers (ST; LF) 85, 86
Weathers, Billy 140
Weaver (WF; 2B) 15, 16, 17
Webb (Trinity; 1906) 29
Welch (ST; C) 16
Welch (ST; RF) 183
West (ST; C) 195
Westbrook, Charlie 182, 183
Wharton (ST; RF) 66, 69
Wheeler (ST; SS) 59, 60, 61, 66, 67, 68, 69
Wheeler, Grady 150, 153, 154, 155
White (WF; RF) 119, 121
White (WF; 3B) 35, 36, 37, 40, 42, 43, 71, 72, 73, 76, 77
White, "Bo" 165
White, George Henry 9
White, Park 165
Whitehurst (WF; RF) 74, 77
Whitener, Clyde 163, 167, 169, 171, 173, 175
Whitley (ST; 3B) 191, 195
Whitley (WF; 2B) 60
Whitley, Lamont 161, 165, 169, 171, 173, 194, 195
Whitner (WF; RF) 154, 155
Wicker, Bob 133, 134, 136, 139, 141
Wiggins, Ella Mae 81
Wiggs (ST; LF) 162
Wilbur (Syracuse; 1B) 21

Wilhelm (ST; C) 183
Wilkie (ST; SS) 116
Wilkins, Dick 165, 171
Williams (ST; 1B) 42, 48
Williams (WF; P) 189
Williams, Art 163, 165, 167
Williams, Dorous 128, 130
Williams, Jack 129, 131, 139, 140, 143, 144, 145
Williams, Rudy 188
Wilmington Race Riot 9
Wilson, Jimmy 161, 162, 163, 167, 169
Winbourne (UNC; 1905) 26
Wingfield, Hall 165
Winn, W.C. 165
Winstead (ST; CF) 141
Winston, H.E. 25, 26, 56, 57, 58, 59, 60, 61, 62, 63, 66
Winston, Ken 165
Winston, Tom 165
Winthrop, Guy L. 30
Witherspoon, H.K. 165, 169
Wivers, Paul 140
Wolhar, Charles 165
Wood (ST; PH) 154, 158, 162
Wood (ST; 2B) 80
Wood, Ned 11
Woodall, Larry 71, 72, 73, 214
Woodruff (Horner; 1903) 18
Woods (ST; 2B) 116, 119, 122
Woodworth (ST; SS) 105, 106, 108, 109
Wooten, Bob 165
Worth (UNC; 1905) 25, 26
Wrenn (Trinity; 1906) 28, 29
Wrenn (WF; C) 182, 183, 185
Wright, C.C. 53
Wright, Orville 13
Wright, Wilbur 13
Wyles (ST; C) 191, 192
Wynn (ST; C) 130

Yaeger, Dorothy 116
Yount, Eddie 127, 129, 130, 131, 215
Yvars, Jack 190, 192
Yvars, Johnny 188, 189, 190, 191

Zackary (ST; RF) 80

www.ingramcontent.com/pod-product-compliance
Ingram Content Group UK Ltd.
Pitfield, Milton Keynes, MK11 3LW, UK
UKHW041947140426
5217IPUK00014B/689